DATE DUE			

From the Small Town to the Great Community

From the Small Town
to the Great Community

The Social Thought of Progressive Intellectuals

By JEAN B. QUANDT

Rutgers University Press, New Brunswick, New Jersey

For Dick and Stephen

Contents

Preface

Although the idea of community is recognized as an important part of the intellectual history of nineteenth-century Europe, it has not received much attention from students of American history. The neglect stems in part from the assumption that, except for anomalies like Brook Farm or specialized academic pursuits like urban sociology, a native individualism has precluded the emergence of communitarian thought in this country. I do not share this assumption, and in this book I attempt to analyze the theory of community worked out by a particular group of Progressive intellectuals whom I call communitarians—not because they were members of a community which put socialistic theories into practice, as in the standard definition, but because they were committed to a certain vision of a cooperative social order. All the members of the group were products of the small town, and their response to social problems reflected in important ways the values of the small community. In choosing this approach, I have disregarded other important ideas of community which appeared during the period, such as those of the utopian novelists and those of the socialists. In addition, little attention has been paid to men like Herbert Croly whose central vision excluded the small community as an anachronism. Although I think it important to show where the ideas of the communitarians were part of a general pattern of thought, my main concern has been to examine a particular set of ideas and its relation to other aspects of the period.

The major argument of the book is that the Progressive intellectuals considered here relied mainly on communication, moral suasion, and intimate local communities to bring about a sense of national community and its embodiment in institutions. In my view, this position did not come to grips with the issue of basic structural change in American society. It was therefore inadequate to the problems which the communitarians set out to deal with. Insofar as these problems remain unsolved at the beginning of the 1970's, the social philosophy of the group remains an inadequate legacy. Of course many of the issues which concerned Progressive thinkers are no longer alive, but for those that are the terms of the argument have changed very little. The communitarians' emphasis on local community, for example, is strikingly similar to the contemporary call for decentralization and community control. I would hope that an historical analysis of the idea of community might enlarge our understanding of some of these issues.

My debts are many and begin with my teachers. F. Edward Cranz has had a lasting influence on my view of history. Throughout my graduate work, Warren Susman has shown me what it means to keep one's scholarly activity in touch with one's other intellectual concerns. For this, as well as for his critical judgment and understanding during the writing of this book, I am greatly in his debt. I also wish to thank John W. Ward, Richard Schlatter, and E. Lawrence Keyes for reading the entire manuscript and giving me valuable advice. Finally, I wish to thank my husband, Richard E. Quandt, whose encouragement made it possible for me to finish my work.

Jean B. Quandt

Princeton, New Jersey
May, 1970

1

From the Small Town to the Great Society

The idea of community in the nineteenth century is usually associated with European social thought; it is generally assumed that the American mind was too individualistic, too devoted to the legacy of a natural rights philosophy to produce a serious theory of community.[1] Nevertheless, such a theory did play a part in our intellectual history, and this study will explore the idea through the writings of nine intellectuals and reformers of the Progressive period who came out of small-town America. Born between 1855 and 1868, raised in small towns from Vermont to California, they came of age in an increasingly urban and industrial society. Their response to the social landscape was shaped by the religious and intellectual traditions, old and new, which they appropriated; but it was also formed by the values of the face-to-face communities from which they came. Their formulation of the problem of community in the years after 1890 clearly reflected their social origins.[2]

The nine figures include William Allen White, a journalist and influential spokesman for Progressive reform; Frederic Howe, a writer and urban reformer; Jane Addams, the founder of the Hull House settlement; Mary Parker Follett, a political theorist and Boston civic reformer; the two philosophers, John Dewey and Josiah Royce, and three of the founding fathers of modern American sociology, Franklin Giddings, Charles Horton Cooley and Robert Park.[3] Because their central ideas about community were advanced during the years from 1890 through World War I, the writings of that period will receive the most attention.

Although the communitarians pursued careers in different parts of the country, they were loosely linked by personal and intellectual ties. In Chicago, several paths crossed during the years 1889 to 1915. William Allen White, editor of the Emporia *Gazette,* visited Addams' settlement house several times after it opened in 1889. While Dewey was teaching at the University of Chicago, he found Hull House a stimulus for his own social thought. In turn his experimental Laboratory School influenced Miss Addams' views on the relations between education and community. And when Robert Park joined the department of sociology at Chicago in 1915, he found that Addams' diagnosis of the urban malaise agreed with his own.[4]

Another link between members of the circle dated back to college and graduate school days. As a graduate student at the University of Michigan, Cooley attended the lectures which Dewey gave in the fall of 1893 on political philosophy. He was so impressed by those lectures that he planned to incorporate their leading ideas into his own sociological theory.[5] According to Cooley's notes, Dewey dealt with a notion that was to become a major theme in the younger man's work: the bearing of the modern means of communication upon community.[6] Park, an undergraduate at Michigan in the 1880's, also studied with Dewey and through him met the journalist Franklin Ford. Ford's vision of a revolutionized newspaper as an instrument of social solidarity made a lasting impact on both teacher and student.[7]

The remaining thinkers had at least some knowledge of the work of others in the group. In *The New State,* Mary Follett used Royce's concept of the Beloved Community to advance her own theory of social unity.[8] Frederic Howe drew upon the ideas of neighborhood and culture which appeared in Addams' *Spirit of Youth and the City Streets.*[9] Among the three sociologists, arguments took place concerning the relative importance of like-mindedness and interdependence as sources of solidarity in modern society.[10]

But what made these men and women a group was not mutual acquaintance or intellectual exchange but rather a common origin and a common response to social change. Bred in small-town America, moving on to New York, Chicago, Boston, and Cleveland carrying the intellectual baggage acquired abroad and in American universities, they wanted to perpetuate the qualities of intimate community in the new environment in which they found themselves.

The Small-Town Background

From the old Puritan settlement of Quincy, Massachusetts, to the midwestern country town of Red Wing, Minnesota, to the California mining camp of Grass Valley, small towns shaped the early experience of the group. Dewey's home town of Burlington, Vermont, with a population of 11,365 in 1880, was the largest. At that time, the other towns ranged in size from 300 to 10,000 inhabitants.[11]

In such settlements, nearly everyone knew everyone else, and if this was not literally true in the larger ones, it is a shorthand way of saying that those who lived there knew their town and its people in a general way.[12] The network of personal acquaintance was extensive enough in Meadville, for example, to make young Howe's escape from the watchful eyes of the neighbors difficult.[13] Such intimacy, while sometimes resented, produced a sense of belonging to a community, or to what Howe later called the "small-town herd."[14] William Allen White observed—though no doubt he also exaggerated—the extent and significance of face-to-face relations in a town like Emporia. Reading of a wedding or the birth of a child, he noted, "we have that neighborly feeling that breeds the real democracy."[15] Neighborliness was, in fact, often translated into an informal network of mutual aid. With everyone minding everyone else's business, illness or distress was quickly known and called forth a quick response.[16] Jane Addams remembered the uses of village gossip: it kept men informed about who needed help and enabled them to do "the good lying next at hand."[17] In the city informal channels of communication disappeared, and with it went the easy neighborliness of Main Street.

If intimacy led to mutual aid it also led to restrictions on personal freedom. Howe's account of the espionage of conduct in Meadville bears out what Atherton claims in *Main Street on the Middle Border:* in small-town America the price of belonging was conformity. The desire for a close-knit community, bred in the small town, would appear in the mature vision of all these figures, but along with it would appear the demand for a greater degree of freedom than small communities ever permitted.[18]

In the small community, class distinctions existed, but they were typically underplayed by the townspeople. The ethos of most towns was relentlessly egalitarian; the inhabitants liked to think they were too democratic to practice social exclusiveness and too friendly not to mingle freely with those above and below them on the occupational ladder.[19] Several factors accounted for the absence of a strong class consciousness: considerable social mobility, widespread participation in the political affairs of the town, and informal participation by all the inhabitants in the social and ritual activities of the community—holidays, school events, country fairs, and revival meetings.[20]

Similarity of experience and casual intermingling carried over into the world of the child. In his *Autobiography,* White admitted the existence of class lines in the boyhood gangs of El Dorado, but he also remembered that these lines did not prevent his club from rejecting the daughter of a rich lumberman and accepting the son of a saloonkeeper.[21] "There was no line of marked wealth or parental distinction," he recalled. "It was not the rich little boys and the rich little girls in a community where we had few riches, who set the social pattern."[22] In contrast to El Dorado, the larger and partly industrialized town of Burlington exhibited a greater disparity between rich and poor, but here too the social life of the young knew few boundaries. Nearly everyone attended the public school and those few who did not were considered snobbish. Dewey mixed freely with the Irish and Canadians whose neighborhood adjoined his own, as well as with the children of the social elite on whose coattails his parents rode.[23] In this kind of environment, people were held together, in Louis Hartz's phrase, "not by the knowledge that they were different parts of a corporate whole, but by the knowledge that they were similar participants in a uniform way of life."[24]

Along with a feeling of intimacy and a sense of classlessness, the small-town ethos which shaped the values of these intellectuals emphasized widespread participation in the public affairs of the community. In a suggestive article which bears on their experience, Elkins and McKitrick argue that the task of building towns in colonial New England and later, in the Old Northwest, diffused political participation. The vigor of the New England town meeting in comparison with its old-world prototype was but one example of such participation. Another was the availability of township offices in the Old Northwest to all comers. In the absence of an established leadership and in the face of the many problems pressing on a new community, the ordinary citizen was called upon to contribute to the process of decision-making. The result was a political democracy based on an egalitarian rather than a paternalistic sense of community. The significance of Frederick Jackson Turner's frontier, as these authors saw it, did not lie in the empty wilderness but in the collective experience of town building which marked two centuries of American development.[25]

In connection with the set of writers considered here, the making of community can be looked at as a spatial example of the historical process described by Elkins and McKitrick. The ideal of participation which accompanied community building shaped the attitudes of these men and women, beginning with the New Englanders, continuing with those from the more recently settled towns of the Midwest, and culminating in the response of Josiah Royce to life on the California frontier.

For those from New England towns the idea of participation was related to the memory of the town meeting.[26] Giddings and Follett invoked its traditions in their attack on machine politics and on the apathy of the average citizen. The town meeting, embodying the values of common action and rational discussion, was the model for political reform.

The New England town meeting [was] the greatest school of political science and art that has existed among men. Through experiments in

direct democracy, . . . entire peoples are learning now in a large way
as the New England folk generations ago in a small way learned to
think about things as well as to care about candidates.[27]

The town meeting was also the symbol of a once vital neighborhood life which, if it were to be reborn, required new but com-
parable institutions.[28]

A similar stress on participation as a permanent legacy of the
small-town experience characterized the views of those from the
Midwest such as Addams and White, whose childhood years overlapped the years of settlement. In an account of community
building in Stephenson County, Illinois, Addams connected the
process with the development of her own social attitudes. Explaining her eventual rejection of the paternalism which guided the
English settlement movement, she noted that noblesse oblige
"could not but seem artificial to a western American who had
been born in a rural community where the early pioneer life had
made social distinctions impossible."[29] Social distinctions did, in
fact, exist in Cedarville. Moreover, Jane Addams' father was one
of the richest and most influential men in the county. But the task
of settling an Illinois community in the 1850's and 1860's had
engaged the energies of all newcomers, and common experience
had created a strong sense of equality. The significance of cooperative effort, where the "butter and egg money" of the poorest
pioneer had helped build a railroad, came home to her at an Old
Settler's meeting which she attended as a girl. At that point she
put away Carlyle's *Heroes and Hero Worship* and put her faith
in the people.[30] In El Dorado, Kansas, where White lived until he
was eighteen, the story was much the same. Young White watched
the settlers turn a village of one hundred persons into a town of
1,411. He saw "the free school and the free library appear; the city
building rise up, representing municipal solidarity; churches come
to symbolize law and order."[31] For White the greatest achievement
of the West was always the collective creation of the country
town.[32]

By far the most fascinating and self-conscious approach to community building was made by Josiah Royce in reference to the

California frontier of his youth. In his autobiographical statements, in his essays, and in his history of California, Royce laid
bare the roots of his interest in community. Speaking to a gather-
ing of friends in 1915, he reminisced about his early life.

> I was born in 1855 in California. My native town was a mining town
> in the Sierra Nevada,—a place five or six years older than myself. My
> earliest recollections include a very frequent wonder as to what my
> elders meant when they said that this was a new community. . . .
> Plainly men had lived and died thereabouts. . . . What was there then
> in this place that ought to be called new, or for that matter, crude?
> I wondered, and gradually came to feel that part of my life's business
> was to find out what all this wonder meant.[33]

The growth of communal sentiment was an important event in
his life. In a little known essay in *Putnam's Magazine,* Royce
spelled out its significance for him. Growing up in a mining town
when the forty-niners were putting down roots, he watched them
build a community.

> It occurred to people that they might wisely make the best of life by
> having a province, and loving it. In my childhood, this was what the
> better people were doing. They were building homes, and thinking of
> orchards and of gardens and of vineyards, and not merely of gold nor
> yet of further wandering.[34]

This cooperative venture, Royce remembered, "taught to me
personally something of the true value of provincialism."[35]

The special predicament of California continued to interest
Royce after he moved to the East. His history of the state, written
after he came to Harvard, was an attempt to show how wanderlust
and the gold rush had intensified the proverbial rootlessness of the
American pioneer. Neglect of public duty in the mining camps
and in San Francisco produced disorder, lynching, and corruption.
But as Royce told the story, the growth of civic consciousness
gradually triumphed over lawlessness; Californians set to work
to build a community, a task which culminated in the work of
the San Francisco Vigilance Committee of 1856.

What had made it [the popular movement for order] inevitable was a long-continued career of social apathy, of treasonable public careless-ness. What it represented was not so much the dignity of a sovereign people, as the depth and bitterness of popular repentance for the past. What it accomplished was . . . the conversion of honest men to a sensible and devout local patriotism.[36]

Moving to San Francisco in the wake of this movement, young Royce had experienced the force and significance of social loyalty.[37] His *California* was the story of its growth. Later, he saw the California story as the tale of the American frontier—"the tale of the rise of local traditions and of local loyalty."[38] Years after his historical writing was completed, Royce came to grips with the problem of community in twentieth-century America. Finally he constructed an elaborate theory of community, one with social, religious and metaphysical dimensions. By 1915 he could make the following comment on the drift of his intellectual pursuits: "I strongly feel that my deepest motives and problems have centred about the Idea of the Community, although this idea has only come gradually to my clear consciousness."[39]

For Royce, as for the others, early experience of the small town guided the later search for new and wider forms of community. The easy sense of belonging, the similarity of experience, and the ethic of participation might be more easily maintained in the small locality than anywhere else, but this did not preclude their cultivation in different soil.

Protestantism on Main Street

In addition to the small town, Protestant Christianity was also an important influence on the upbringing of the communitarians, and ultimately, on the way in which they formulated the ideal of community.

The Protestantism which shaped their religious experience emphasized both faith and works, conversion and moral duty. The evangelical impulse, based on the conviction that personal regener-ation by faith was a necessary prelude to a moral life, characterized the revival meetings which Howe, White, and Jane Addams attended.[40] It also appeared in the demand for conversion which Cooley, Dewey, and Giddings encountered in the Congregational Church of their youth.[41] Finally, it emerged in the mysticism of Sarah Royce, whose journey to California in 1849, later recorded in *A Frontier Lady,* intensified her faith in God. In moments of crisis, she recollected, "He came so near that I no longer simply *believed* in Him, but *knew* His presence there."[42] The ethical impulse of small-town Protestantism also made itself felt in the early lives of these figures. Howe remembered it as "a morality of duty, of careful respectability. It was the code of a small-town, of the Sunday-school, of my church. . . . One could not forget that life was a serious business, that duty should be always before one's eyes."[43] Perhaps life in the small community intensified the Protestant emphasis on personal responsibility for the fortunes and the morals of others.[44] Certainly Cooley, Howe, White, and Jane Addams testified to the strong sense of personal responsibility which flourished in small-town piety.[45] Every man could be his brother's keeper where his brother was quite literally his neighbor. Evangelistic morality, which Howe equated with the code of the small town, became for him the distinguishing mark of his generation; it explained "the nature of our reforms, the regulatory legislation in morals and economics. . . . Missionaries and battleships, anti-saloon leagues and Ku Klux Klans . . . are all a part of that evangelistic psychology that makes America what she is,"[46] Howe asserted.

Of the two traditions, moralism clearly had a greater impact than evangelicalism on the early religious experience of the communitarians. Their personal history suggests that the Protestant code of duty left a permanent imprint on their thinking, but that the conversion experience either eluded them or was rejected in favor of a purely ethical Christianity. That they thus tilted the scales of piety is not surprising given the direction in which Protestantism was moving in the second half of the nineteenth century. Not only was the conversion experience less cataclysmic and more mechanical than it had been in the heyday of revivalism, but its primary meaning came from its use as a tool for enforcing morality.[47] Moreover, the theology of liberal Protestantism, which gained ground after 1865, was approaching the position, soon to be advanced by the New Theology, that faith was a moral and rational act of obedience to God's will rather than a sudden response to the miracle of God's grace. The rejection of divine transcendence implicit in such moralism also found expression in the idea that God was immanent in society and in its gradually improving institutions. Expectations about the coming kingdom were not new to American Protestantism; what was new, however, was the attribution of self-sufficiency and benevolence to the historical process.[48] Not a change of heart among individuals but the working out of the "redemptive forces, wrought into the soul and into the divine institutions of the family and the nation,"[49] would usher in the kingdom of God. These developments in the practice and theology of Protestantism paved the way for the social religion of the communitarians, who regarded the "triumph of righteousness in human relations"[50] as the essence of Christianity.

Accounts of their early religious experiences indicate a falling away from evangelical Protestantism. Giddings was depressed by the orthodoxy of his father, a Congregational minister, and by the strict Puritan atmosphere of his home.[51] Dewey, though entering the First Congregational Church of Burlington at the age of eleven, could not feel that love of Christ which he formally confessed.[52] Others in the group have left firsthand accounts of their indifference to the profession of faith. Fortifying himself with Emerson's opposition to formal creeds, White refused to attend the revival meetings at Emporia College.[53] Howe suffered through two winters of revivals at Allegheny College before he rebelled. "I had no conviction of sin, no sense of guilt, or of being abandoned. And nothing happened."[54] One of the few unconverted girls at Rockford Seminary, Jane Addams attributed her stance to her Quaker father, who had taught her that morality was more important than dogma.[55] Royce's early rebellion against his mother's Biblical faith was reinforced by the study of science and by the impact of historical criticism.[56]

Darwinian science and historical criticism helped push some away from a religion of dogma, miracle, and conversion by grace toward one in which God did not break into the natural order but was immanent in nature, history, and the ethical aims of human beings. The new scholarship led Dewey and Royce down this road. Dewey's revolt against dualism, the first stage of which included a Hegelian version of Christianity, was stimulated by the doctrine of evolution.[57] And Royce met the challenge of materialism first with philosophical Idealism and then with a modernized Christian theism.[58] The impact which the new sciences had on the religious development of the others is not as clear. Giddings' early reading of Darwin, Spencer, and Huxley may have helped him break away from the dogma of his father's church.[59] White's encounter with biblical criticism during his college days probably made religious dogma even less important then it had already become. What Giddings, Addams, White, and Cooley did share was a reliance on Emerson as an alternative to both orthodoxy and materialism. In their hands, Emerson became the prophet of love over doctrine or the formal profession of faith, as well as the philosophical spokesman for the idea of the spiritual nature of the universe.[60]

Although these intellectuals rejected the Protestant orthodoxy of their parents, its ethical impulse remained and entered into their mature vision of community. The concepts which they used to elaborate the moral basis of community—love, communion, and loyalty—had a religious as well as an ethical dimension in their thought. The coming community which they hoped for resembled the coming kingdom of God, but except for Royce, its success did not depend on the regenerating power of grace. Like many of their contemporaries in the Social Gospel movement, they put their faith not in a radical change of heart but in gradual evolution toward a just society.

A Generation Comes of Age

As the members of the circle came to maturity, they underwent certain kinds of experience which formed the groundwork for their elaboration of the problem of community in American society. Graduate study, travel, involvement with national political issues and with the problems of the city shaped the ways in which they thought about social questions.

The new currents of thought which they encountered at American and European universities represented a break with the academic orthodoxy and its political corollaries which had dominated their undergraduate education. The graduate schools were knocking down the intellectual pillars of laissez faire, economic individualism, and the belief that social order emerged from the self-interested actions of individuals. When Dewey went to Johns Hopkins in 1882 he found Hegel's organic social philosophy a welcome alternative to the individualism of New England culture.[61] Howe's work with Richard T. Ely, Woodrow Wilson, and James Bryce opened his eyes to the evils of the industrial system and party politics. From these teachers at Johns Hopkins, Howe accepted the creed of "responsibility and service."[62] Royce's visit to Germany in 1875 brought him into contact with the kind of thinking which Dewey and Howe had met at home; he returned to America steeped in the Idealist philosophy of Schelling, Schopenhauer, and Fichte, whose idea of the unity of nature and of society he found congenial.[63] Finally, Robert Park went to Germany in 1899 and took up the study of sociology with Georg Simmel; Simmel's interpretation of the city and his theory of interaction as the essence of society were the main influences on Park's own sociological theory.[64]

Travel abroad brought Mary Follett and Jane Addams into contact with some of the English reform movements of the later nineteenth century. Follett's stay at Cambridge University in 1890-1891 probably stimulated her interest in the liberalism of T. H. Green and his followers and in the varieties of English socialism which figured so importantly in her own work.[65] Jane Addams' visit to the London settlement, Toynbee Hall, gave direction to her work when she returned to America in 1888 to found Hull House.[66]

The influence of national political problems also played a part in forming attitudes toward society. After Cooley's graduation from the University of Michigan in 1887, he worked for the Interstate Commerce Commission in Washington. His father, a constitutional lawyer and advocate of greater federal regulation of transportation and business, was then chairman of the Commission. Thomas Cooley believed that the recent ascendance of the federal government stemmed from the interdependence created by the telegraph and the railroad. When his son returned to Michigan to get his Ph.D. in economics and sociology, he wrote a thesis on the unifying role of transportation in an industrial society.[67] William Allen White was also influenced by the national political scene. He began to reject the individualistic ideology of conservative Republicanism when he met the Assistant Secretary of the Navy, Theodore Roosevelt, in 1897. A zealous disciple of Roosevelt and a convert to his notion of stewardship, he soon used his newspaper to advance the cause of Progressive reform.[68]

In the years following those spent in study, travel, and the start of a career, the encounter with the industrial city sharpened the problem of community for these intellectuals. While they were growing up in the small-town milieu, technology and urbanization were transforming the society which they would enter as adults. The rise of industry and the spread of a network of transportation and communication were turning a society of independent producers into one of large organizations whose scope and influence undermined the economic autonomy of the small town and its hinterland. The railroad, rural free delivery, the mail-order house, and after 1900, the interurban trolley and the automobile, meant the decline of local independence.[69] Moreover, the city was rapidly overtaking the small town in total population. Attracting industry and immigrants from Southern and Eastern Europe but ill-prepared to cope with the problems which ensued, the large cities of the 1880's and 1890's were well down the road to communal disintegration. Class conflict, residential segregation, and the lack of communication between different segments of the population created a world which differed sharply from that of small-town America.[70] Chicago was the catalyst for Dewey, Park, and Jane Addams. With a population of over one million in 1890, the city was plagued by industrial unrest, neighborhood disintegration, and lack of understanding between immigrant and native.[71] Newly come to Chicago, Dewey and Jane Addams sought an answer to these problems. "The social organism has broken down in large districts of our great cities,"[72] Miss Addams noted in 1892. The residents of Hull House, she continued, "are bound to regard the entire life of their city as organic, to make an effort to unify it, and to protest against its over-differentiation."[73] Dewey's educational philosophy represented a similar effort to create communication and common purposes in an urban environment. Comparing the ideal school to Hull House, he pictured it as "a social clearing house" where the barriers to "real communion" might be removed.[74] And Robert Park, who came to Chicago a decade after Dewey left, began his academic career with an essay on the decline of intimate community in the city.[75]

By 1900 Boston was the fragmented city of half a million which Warner's *Streetcar Suburbs* has described;[76] and there Mary Follett began her career as a civic leader and a writer. Raised in the nearby town of Quincy, educated at Radcliffe and abroad, she started work at the Neighborhood House in Roxbury, one of the old suburbs then enlarged by the streetcar.[77] There her goal was to stimulate communication and civic consciousness within the neighborhood.[78] When she wrote *The New State* (1918), which began as a study of Boston community centers, the neighborhood had become the key to the larger problem of community.[79] "The acute problem of municipal life is how to make us men and women of Boston feel that we *are* the city, directly responsible for everything concerning it. Neighborhood organization . . . increases and focuses this sense of responsibility,"[80] she concluded.

Although Frederic Howe found inspiration in Albert Shaw's lectures on municipal administration at Johns Hopkins, it was not until he became Tom Johnson's political lieutenant in Cleveland at the turn of the century that "the possibility of a free, orderly, and beautiful city became . . . an absorbing passion."[81] Confronted with the problems of an industrial city, his "herd instinct," which had once attached him to the small town, expressed itself in the dream of an urban community.[82]

In Emporia, Kansas, White felt the shadow of the city fall on the country town when the mail-order house began to cut into local trade; this threat to the small town provoked one of his first editorial attacks upon the city in the name of the face-to-face community.

The mail order house unrestricted will kill our smaller towns, creating great cities with their . . . inevitable caste feeling that comes from the presence of strangers who are rich and poor living side by side. Friendship, neighborliness, fraternity or whatever you may call that spirit of comradry that comes when men know one another well, is the cement that holds together this union of states.[83]

That spirit, he insisted, did not exist in great cities.

Aware of the threat to community in modern America, the members of this group turned to the task of diagnosing the malady and prescribing the remedy.

The Problem of Community

What the communitarians claimed to see when they looked about them was the breakdown of the small, close-knit group under the impact of urbanization and industrialization. A social organization based on family, neighborhood, and small-town solidarity was being replaced by one based on the more impersonal and tenuous ties of the market place. The division of labor, together with modern methods of communication and transportation, had created a physical unity based on the interdependence of parts, but a moral unity corresponding to this economic web had not yet emerged.[84] Cooley defined the challenge when he said: "There is union on a low plane but isolation on a higher. The progress of communication has supplied the mechanical basis for a spiritual organization far beyond anything in the past—but this remains unachieved."[85] So far technological changes had produced what Park and Dewey, borrowing a phrase from the English writer Graham Wallas, called the Great Society—an urban, industrial order whose size and complexity precluded a sense of belonging.[86]

In their interpretation of social change, the three sociologists, Cooley, Giddings, and Park, drew on a wide range of thinkers, most of them European. From 1861, When Sir Henry Maine's *Ancient Law* appeared, to 1902 when Simmel published "The Metropolis and Mental Life," European social scientists were developing typologies to indicate the contrast between a rural, homogeneous, and group-oriented society and an urban, differentiated, and individualistic one.[87] Beneath differences in terminology lay a common content. Maine's status versus contract, Spencer's militant versus industrial society, Tönnies' community (Gemeinschaft) versus society (Gesellschaft), Durkheim's mechanical versus organic society, and Simmel's comparison of town and metropolis described a contrast between two types of social organization.[88] The first type, often centered on small units such as family, village, and tribe, was characterized by a high degree of like-mindedness, with common ends taking precedence over individual ends. In such a society, solidarity was based on the similarity of its members. Social roles, moreover, covered nearly all aspects of behavior and implied a wide range of obligation to others. The second type, usually associated with large units like the city, as well as with the forces of industrialization, was marked by a lesser degree of like-mindedness. As the division of labor increased, the area of common values contracted and the area of individual autonomy expanded. Social roles covered a limited aspect of behavior and involved limited obligations.

This type of analysis by major European thinkers was part of the professional reading of Cooley, Giddings, and Park, first as students and, later, as academics. The theory was not swallowed whole; indeed it did not even appear to be a body of theory at that time. The Americans simply read the important works in their field and appropriated the ideas relevant to the social changes which interested them.[89]

Rarely using the exact typologies of their European counterparts, but often drawing on the ideas behind them, the three sociologists worked out their own version of the transition from a society of small-scale and intimate relations to one of large-scale and impersonal contacts. Their starting point, however, was not the ancient tribe or the medieval village but the American country town. Although they saw more room for individualism in the nineteenth-century American town than in the European peasant community, they regarded this milieu as the fairly confining one of neighborhood and small community. There face-to-face contact controlled behavior. Primary groups produced the "sort of sympathy and mutual identification for which 'we' is the natural expression." But the intimacy of the small local community had "been broken up by the growth of an intricate mesh of wider contacts."[90] What resulted was a weakening of the older forms of social control; individuals were prey to vagrant impulses. Moreover, they were detached from "intimate, direct, and spontaneous contacts with social reality."[91]

The diagnosis offered by the others reflected the same viewpoint without the sociological trappings or the detailed analysis.[92] As Howe argued in 1905, transportation, communication, and "the genii of industrialism" had already enveloped much of town and country in a large semiurban landscape and would continue to do so at an increased rate. In such a social order, they observed, relationships tended to be superficial, the restraints imposed by public opinion weak, and common cause with one's neighbor lacking.[93] Technological advances not only destroyed older forms of community but also impeded the growth of new forms on a larger scale. Royce's lament for the decline of the province—any city, county, state, or region with "a true consciousness of its own unity"[94]—was matched by his pessimism about the possibility of a national community. On so great a scale, the forces shaping men's lives were too complex and impersonal to create a sense of identification on the part of the individual. Analyzing the city, Park concluded that it could function without a conscious sense of participation on the part of the city-dweller. Indeed, its bureaucratic complexities discouraged a feeling of belonging.[95] The others agreed with Park that the values of the face-to-face community were difficult to recreate in an urban environment. Class conflict, the complexity of a large community, and the physical isolation of social classes in city and suburb impeded mutual understanding. "American conceptions of patriotism have moved, so to speak, from the New England village into huge cosmopolitan cities,"[96] Addams wrote, and they had not fared well in transit.

A greater psychic and moral integration to match the increasing physical integration of society was essential to the realization of their notion of community. As they saw it, the growing unity of the social organism only laid the groundwork for that interpenetration of minds, that consciousness of and identification with the whole which characterized a sense of community. With all interests now intertwined, modern communications could create greater mutual understanding and common purpose. Thus the Great Society provided the material basis for its moral equivalent, the Great Community.[97]

In this vision, the small community became the scale model for the larger one. Its values of intimacy, mutual identification, and face-to-face communication appeared in the blueprint for the city, the province, and the nation. At the same time, the small local community became the training ground for a larger loyalty, a link in the chain that would lead from neighborhood to nation. But the optimism of the circle was tempered by the suspicion, if not the clear recognition, that the forces of modern society were working against as well as for them. In their view, the growing complexity of social organization was obstructing the re-creation of mutual sympathy and full communication on a large scale. Furthermore, the trend toward economic integration was weakening local loyalties.[98] But they did not consider these dangers as seriously as they should have. Otherwise they would not have believed so readily that modern communications produced communion or that twentieth-century Americans could find "God in their own village."[99]

Part I The Uses of Communication

2

Patterns of Thought

In their search for a large-scale version of small-town solidarity, the communitarians made use of certain assumptions which not only guided their thinking on the uses of communication but also contributed to the optimism with which they pursued their goal. First, they believed in the power of communication to turn spatial or physical coordination into a community characterized by a high degree of mutual identification and shared values.[1] Noting that the physical integration of modern society had outrun its moral unity, they nonetheless believed that the sharing of ideas and sentiments, the exchange of opinion, and the transmission of knowledge could correct this imbalance. Communication carried such weight because of their second assumption, which centered on the notion that society was not a loose collection of self-sufficient individuals but an organic whole made up of interrelated parts. According to this view, "society not only continues to exist *by* transmission, *by* communication, but it may fairly be said to exist in transmission, in communication."[2] The common values which unified the social organism were created by the mutual exchange of ideas and attitudes. Finally, the communitarian thinkers hoped that greater social unity would result from recent improvements in technology. Given their faith in the efficacy of communication and their tendency to describe society in terms of wholeness and interaction, it was quite logical to rely on the telegraph, the telephone, and the high-speed press to foster the desired unity.

These ideas shaped the approach to the problem of community and often suggested certain kinds of answers.

For these intellectuals, coordination without the shared ends produced by communication ran counter to their ideal of the good society. In their eyes, modern America exhibited just this combination of interdependence and lack of common purpose. "Mankind has become bound together by millions of Lilliputian bands drawing . . . [it] into an intimate relationship, a common dependency, from which there is no escape,"[3] Howe observed. But physical integration did not mean unity of purpose. "The mere mechanical fact of interdependence amounts to nothing,"[4] Jane Addams contended. The benchmark of community was not coordination of function but consciousness of common ends. Royce explained the importance of the latter element.

Men do not form a community . . . merely insofar as the men coöperate. They form a community . . . when they not only coöperate, but accompany this coöperation with that ideal extension of the lives of individuals whereby each coöperating member says: "This activity which we perform together, this work of ours, its past, its future, its sequence, its order, its sense—all these enter into my life, and are the life of my own self writ large."[5]

Where Royce contrasted cooperation and community, others spoke of cooperation versus communion, society versus community, or aggregation versus association.[6] But the distinctions were similar. Only when cooperation was accompanied by identification with a common cause would they speak of community.

Many areas of American life lacked the requisite fusion of physical and psychic solidarity. Writing from Cleveland where he was an aide to the reform mayor, Howe described the contemporary city as an organism with an imperfectly developed nervous system.[7] "When . . . there arises a city-consciousness, that instinct which is willingness to struggle for the common weal, and suffer for the common woe—then, and not until then, does the city spring into life,"[8] he asserted. Royce argued that the corporations and other giant organizations of modern society "excite our loyalty as little as do the trade-winds or the blizzard."[9] Noting the dangers of size, these thinkers compared modern America to the ancient Roman Empire; like the Romans, Americans were creating an organizational network "so vast that the individuals concerned no longer recognize their social unity in ways which seem to them homelike."[10] By the time that Dewey wrote *The Public and Its Problems* in 1927, the danger of organization outrunning intelligence seemed closer than ever. "The Great Society created by steam and electricity may be a society," he acknowledged, "but it is no community."[11] For the activities of the machine age transcended not only the boundaries of local communities but also the interest and intelligence of its members.[12]

Nevertheless, the solution to the problems of the Great Society did not lie in the direction of radical social change. Graham Wallas, the English social scientist who coined the term, saw in socialism the answer to both the problems of organization and of the "balked" human impulse for loyalty and fellowship.[13] But the American social thinkers depended instead on better communication among all groups in the society and on greater use of the new technology of communication which had already tightened "the web of life" in the modern world.[14] Dewey explained the role of communication in these terms:

There is more than a verbal tie between the words common, community, and communication. Men live in a community in virtue of the things which they have in common; and communication is the way in which they come to possess things in common. What they must have in common . . . are aims, beliefs, aspirations, knowledge—a common understanding—like-mindedness the sociologists say. Such things cannot be passed physically from one to another, like bricks; they cannot be shared as persons would share a pie by dividing it into physical pieces. . . . Consensus demands communication.[15]

Communication, they contended, would strengthen the psychic sources of unity: mutual sympathy, consensus, or common values, and the sense of one's special function in the whole which a complex social organism required.[16] Dewey spoke for all except Howe —whose enthusiasm for the single tax and municipal socialism gave his thought a more radical cast—when he called for a "socialism of the intelligence and of the spirit." And he further indicated the direction of their thought by adding, "To extend the range and fullness of sharing in the intellectual and spiritual resources of the community is the very meaning of the community."[17]

Following the lead of the new psychology, these intellectuals embraced the idea, pioneered at the turn of the century by Cooley, James Mark Baldwin, and George Herbert Mead, that the nature of the self is social; they then used this idea to show how communication might expand mutual identification beyond the bounds of family, town, class, or section.[18] Because the personality supposedly developed through sympathetic identification with others, men had, in Cooley's words, "a natural allegiance to the community ideal."[19] The older faculty psychology, they argued, sundered self and society, then glued them back together with social sentiments like benevolence; it described moral development in terms of innate faculties; it ignored the social medium which shaped personality and explained social cooperation by recourse to the self-interest or benevolence of the individual.[20] In contrast, the new psychology thought that "self and society are twin-born . . . and the notion of a separate and independent ego is an illusion."[21] The bonds of sympathy and identification which held society together were forged on the bedrock of that psychic interaction which turned every infant into a social self. As the personality developed, the individual tended to extend his sympathy to ever-wider circles.

The process of communication, according to these writers, built on this propensity to make others "a part of ourselves and identify our self-feeling with them."[22] Through communication, sympathy would have a wider field of operation. Men would apply their altruism to a society newly unified by steam and electricity.[23] Greater like-mindedness would result from "comprehension by each mind of some portion of the thought and feeling of all other minds."[24] For given an initial "consciousness of kind" or sense of likeness, communication enabled people to "think, feel, and will alike, and each consciousness becomes a microcosm of the social system."[25] Moreover, communication would break down the barriers of ignorance which made one indifferent to the fate of others.[26] The new media showed men the far reaching consequences of their acts; perceiving these consequences, they would be less likely to sacrifice the welfare of others to their own narrowly conceived interests—whether these be profits or power. They would be more likely to have what Dewey called intelligent sympathy, "a cultivated imagination for what men have in common and a rebellion at what unnecessarily divides them."[27] Finally, as Royce argued in his theory of "interpretation," communication mediated between conflicting wills to create a common will. An interdependent society required mediators between its parts; the methods of science and of insurance suggested the ways in which this mediation might operate to create the Great Community.[28]

Behind their belief in an elastic sense of mutual identification, behind the optimism about the ease with which sympathy springs up between men, lay the organic bias with its assumption of social unity and its readiness to see the individual as a microcosm of the whole. This way of thinking, which stressed the concept of the interdependence of functions and the influence of society on personality, dominated much of late nineteenth-century thought.[29] "Not merely in sociology, but in every department of knowledge, the organic concept is the most distinctive modern note,"[30] Albion Small observed at the turn of the century. In the area of social theory, the organic concept represented an effort to come to grips with the changes brought about by industrialization and urbanization. Society was analyzed in terms of the interrelatedness of all its elements; it was seen, to use Cooley's words, as "a complex of forms or processes each of which is living . . . by interaction with the others, the whole being so unified that what takes place in one part affects all the rest."[31]

In America, Herbert Spencer's version of organic theory did much to stimulate this way of thinking about society. In his evolutionary philosophy, matter in motion produced progressive differentiation and integration; applied to society, this theory posited increasing division of labor and interdependence of parts. As industrialization proceeded, a growing coordination of society occurred which he likened to that of cells in a living body.[32] It was this evolutionary organicism which enabled American social scientists to explain the drift of economic and social change at the end of the century.[33] Both William Graham Sumner and

Lester Frank Ward, though poles apart on most issues, described
society as a system of increasingly interrelated parts.[34] And this
Spencerian theme soon became the property of other sociologists
and economists, including Giddings, Cooley, and Park, who used
Spencer's formula to explain the direction of change in industrial
society without subscribing to his economic individualism or his
metaphysical materialism.[35]

The organic concept appealed to the communitarians on both
intellectual and moral grounds. Much of nineteenth-century
social thought had assumed that harmony resulted from the actions
of individuals separately pursuing an enlightened self-interest.
But by this time, the idea of society as an aggregate of individuals
seemed increasingly fallacious. During a period of growing economic concentration, the belief in the self-sufficient individual
was regarded in many quarters as a source of intellectual confusion
and social injustice. So when it came to formulating a social
theory of their own, these thinkers turned to intellectual traditions which stressed concepts of interaction and process.

From Darwin and Spencer they took the notion that reality
was a seamless web in which all parts were interrelated. From
them too came the idea of evolution as progressive differentiation
and integration. Although the academic members of this group
used Spencer to attack atomistic patterns of thought, they soon
moved beyond him for a more consistent and satisfactory social
philosophy. There were several reasons for finding his system
inadequate: Spencer clung to a laissez faire economics and an
individualistic psychology which conflicted with his own organic
framework; more important, his explanation of social solidarity
was wholly mechanistic. In his system society was held together
by physical and economic ties but not by ideas and sentiments.[36]
Thus Spencer sanctioned what they criticized—coordination without community.

The Idealistic tradition in philosophy and in European social
science supplied a corrective to Spencer by describing society as a
mental as well as a physical organism, a whole whose unity
depended upon common values and sentiments. Emerson, Kant,
and Hegel proved useful to both the sociologists and the philos-

ophers in the group as a counterweight to the materialist explanation of social processes. So did those European thinkers, like Durkheim, Comte, and Schäffle, who took from Idealism the notion that society was unified by collective norms and ideas. These men helped Giddings, Cooley, and Park explain the importance of shared values in social life.[37] Meanwhile the neo-Hegelian Wilhelm Wundt and his American student, James Mark Baldwin, were among those who provided the psychological ingredients for an organic social theory.[38] Like George Herbert Mead, whose important work was quite inaccessible at that time, they showed how personality emerged through the interaction of self and others in such a way that the individual himself became "a special phase of society."[39]

Among the communitarians, the organic bias and its interactionist psychology fostered an optimistic attitude toward the expansion of community. If society were thought to be a physical organism whose unity, as Giddings described it, lay in the mutual sympathy of its members, then one might presume that growing social sympathy would accompany growing economic integration.[40] Then too, if each person expressed the unity of the whole in microcosm, the increasing integration of society would manifest itself in one's greater sense of identification with others. As Mary Follett explained it: the individual "is in himself the whole of society. It is not that the whole is divided up into pieces; the individual is the whole at one point. This is the incarnation."[41] Then she added, "As our lives become more and more intricately interwoven, more and more I come to desire not only when I am feeling personal desires. . . . Every day the 'claims' of others are becoming My desires."[42] The whole concept of the social nature of the self and the plasticity of human nature that was part of the organic philosophy made these thinkers enthusiastic about the extent to which men could merge their self-interest with those of others in a constantly enlarging circle.[43]

Drawn to an organic theory of society, these intellectuals turned to various instruments of communication to foster a wider sense of community in modern America. The industrial revolution had extended and tightened the web of interdependence among men. By making the fate of one the fate of all, it had encouraged the growth of a wider consensus. But better channels of communication had to be found if a greater sense of common purpose were to materialize. Such channels would include more contact between immigrant and native, between people of different classes and different neighborhoods; they would involve the "miniature community" of the school and the settlement, the telegraph, the newspaper and the municipal research bureau—all these would "make social intercourse express the growing sense of [the] economic unity of society."[44]

If there was novelty in their scheme, it lay in the role assigned to the communications revolution.[45] The technological advances of which they took note were indeed impressive: the telegraph of the 1840's which speeded up newspaper reporting; the rotary press of the 1870's which accelerated the printing of newspapers; the improvements in papermaking and bookbinding which made possible the production of inexpensive books in the 1840's; the telephone, patented in 1876; and finally, the motion picture, launched as a commercial enterprise in 1906, and the radio, given its first commercial station in 1920.[46] For the communitarians, these inventions contained the unprecedented promise of making "the nation a neighborhood."[47] Mutual sympathy would flourish on a larger scale than ever before. What firsthand acquaintance provided on Main Street, the communications media could create for the whole society.

This was not the first generation of intellectuals to ponder the significance of "steam and . . . magnetic wires."[48] In the mid-nineteenth century, books and sermons already pointed to the unifying effects of the canal, the railroad, and the telegraph. The poet James Russell Lowell remarked on the unity of sentiment produced by the modern means of communication.[49] The one-time nationalist turned Southern apologist, John C. Calhoun, referred to the new technology as if the sectionalism which he defended were in some sense outmoded. "Magic wires are stretching themselves in all directions over the earth, and when their mystic meshes shall have been united and perfected, our globe itself will become endowed with sensitiveness, so that whatever touches on any one point will be instantly felt on every other."[50] Midcentury revivalists and theologians also looked favorably on such worldly developments, viewing the new media as agents of a nationwide spiritual awakening.[51]

After the Civil War, the utopian writings which represented one wing of social protest during the Gilded Age often touched on the promise of mechanical inventions for the ideal society. Sometimes new uses were found for existing organs of communication. In Edward Bellamy's *Looking Backward* (1887), the capitalist-dominated press of 1870 had been replaced by a system of publishing which, because it was controlled by subscribers, better expressed public opinion in the year 2000 than had the old-time newspaper.[52] The nationalist clubs inspired by Bellamy's novel included in their reform program a plan to nationalize the telephone, the telegraph, and the other means of communication.[53] A lesser-known novel, *The Crystal Button* (1891), by Chauncy Thomas, predicted a new kind of printing which compressed complex ideas into single symbols; this enabled students to learn faster, to go beyond their narrow specialties, and to arrive at a point where their interests were "identical and mutual."[54]

In a different vein, Morrison Swift's utopian novel, *A League of Justice* (1893), described a press which had been taken from the control of private entrepreneurs by a group of enlightened men and was consecrated thereafter to the cause of truth and "the church of science." This newspaper centralized publishing and reporting throughout the country, with branch papers set up in outlying areas.[55] Except for the method of financing, Swift's scheme had much in common with Franklin Ford's plan for a revolutionary newspaper, outlined in his "Draft of Action" (1892), which aroused the interest of Dewey and Park at the University of Michigan. Ford began from the premise that "the means of communication are in place but these could not be brought to the highest use until the realities flowing out from the locomotive and the telegraph, their spiritual meaning, should be wrought out"[56] in a special system of newspaper publishing. Such a system would deal with the news "in the light of the whole" because it would be free from local prejudice and capitalist distortion.[57]

Less visionary thinkers like the economist David Wells, who later impressed his ideas on Giddings, noted the importance of the new forms of communication and transportation in a book called *Recent Economic Changes* (1899). Wells maintained that the "intercommunication of ideas" and the easy interchange of products, although temporarily disruptive of the economy, would eventually assure progress.[58] Younger economists like Richard T. Ely carried on this line of thought by emphasizing the way in which communication and commerce created economic interdependence and moral solidarity in modern society.[59]

Beginning in the 1890's, social science and utopianism quickened an interest in the communications revolution among the seekers of community. In a series of lectures delivered at Bryn Mawr in 1891, Giddings cited Wells on the significance of transportation and communication for recent economic progress.[60] And Giddings' later discussions of communication, like those of many of his contemporaries, were presented in the biological terminology of Herbert Spencer's *Principles of Sociology*. Spencer had argued that advances in modes of transportation and communication affected the "sensorium" or nervous system of society, which transmitted ideas, and the circulatory system, which moved goods, so that the social organism was unified as never before.[61] Giddings continued to employ this organic analogy in his own treatment of social evolution.[62]

In the same year as Giddings' lectures, Dewey wrote to William James about the remarkable ideas of Franklin Ford: the intellectual forces of the modern world, Dewey believed with Ford, would get their "physical leverage" in the telegraph and the printing press and would thereby possess the social authority which their modernity and utility entitled them to.[63] Both Ford's pamphlet of 1892 and Dewey's lectures on political philosophy, which followed a year later, bore the unmistakable imprint of Spencer's philosophy. Spencerian language wound its way through their description of communication in society. Ford's "Draft of Action" spoke of the newspaper as "the arterial system" and the "Distributive University"; the university appeared as the "ganglion in the nervous system of the state."[64] Dewey's lectures referred to language as "the nervous system" of society. New mechanisms of communication enabled the social nervous system to function more intelligently; if knowledge were organized along scientific lines and distributed by the "social sensorium" or press, a more unified and intelligent society might develop.[65] Dewey was no Spencerian, but as he remarked a few years later, Spencer "has so thoroughly imposed his idea that even non-Spencerians must talk in his terms."[66]

When Robert Park visited Ann Arbor shortly after his graduation in 1887, Dewey introduced him to Ford. In an autobiographical essay, Park remembered that Ford came to believe, "and I did too, that with more accurate and adequate reporting of current events the historical process would be appreciably stepped up, and progress would go forward steadily, without the interruption and disorder of depression or violence."[67] Park's fascination with the newspaper took him into journalism for eleven years, and then brought him to Harvard where he studied philosophy with James and Royce because he "hoped to gain insight into the nature and function of the kind of knowledge we call news."[68] His doctoral thesis, written in Germany under the philosopher Wilhelm Windelband, represented a continuing interest in the nature of communication. Here he explored the difference between "the public" and "the crowd," a theme he returned to when his interest in American politics matured.[69]

Cooley was the last to move into the orbit of the Ann Arbor group. In 1893, he recalled in his Journal, two influences converged to fix his attention on the communications media. One was the work of Albert Schäffle, the German sociologist, who combined Spencer's evolutionary organicism with an Idealist emphasis on the spiritual and cultural bonds which unify society. The other influence was Dewey's lectures on political philosophy, which suggested that modern communications enabled society to move simultaneously toward greater specialization and greater unity.[70] Like Park's first work, Cooley's earliest sociological writings, "The Theory of Transportation" (1894) and "The Process of Social Change" (1897), revealed his interest in the process of communication.[71]

But the notion of a new era in communications was not confined to intellectuals at the University of Michigan. In the 1890's and thereafter, it appeared in the work of the sociologist Albion Small, who later brought Park to the University of Chicago; it also pervaded the evolutionary economics of Richard T. Ely, the social prophecy of the Social Gospeler, Josiah Strong, and the work of Progressive intellectuals such as Herbert Croly and Walter Lippmann.[72] As a concept that was fast becoming the common currency of reformers and intellectuals in this period, the communications revolution entered the thinking of Royce, Addams, Howe, White, and Follett after the turn of the century.[73]

All the communitarians saw the new machinery as a means to scale the obstacles to moral unity—ignorance, parochialism, and antagonism between classes. They believed that the new technology would encourage the growth of a mutual sympathy and a rational public opinion that transcended the boundaries of class and locality. Although Willian Allen White outdid the rest in his millenial expectations, he spoke for the others when he concluded *The Old Order Changeth* on this note:

> Our children grow up with the feeling of community strongly upon them. The "we" feeling is pressed upon them in the common schools, in the common playgrounds and in homes, linked to humanity as no other homes have ever been joined. The electric wire, the iron pipe, the street railroad, the daily newspaper, the telephone, . . . have made us all of one body. . . . There are no outlanders. It is possible for all men to understand one another. . . . Indeed it is but the dawn of a spiritual awakening.[74]

Thus modern machinery might even transfer the values of the intimate community to the larger society.

The assumptions made by these intellectuals concerning the social process of communication, the organic nature of society and the uses of the new technology entered into their search for greater community at the level of face-to-face relations and beyond.

As we shall see in the following chapters, these assumptions contributed to the belief in an ever-expanding process of mutual identification and in the reproduction on an ever-larger scale of the virtues of the small community.

3

Mary Parker Follett and Face-to-Face Communication

For the seekers of community, direct, personal communication had special qualities which set it apart from other ways of transmitting experience and information—qualities which were of crucial importance to their ideal of social life.[1] An inquiry into the thought of Mary Parker Follett, political philosopher, leader of the Boston community center movement, and spokesman for the values of face-to-face communication, will clarify the significance which these qualities had for the communitarians. For her ideas about the importance of this kind of communication, together with the views of those who shared her enthusiasm, were part of a larger philosophy of society and were related to a particular vision of social organization.

In their account of America's past, these intellectuals gave a prominent place to the face-to-face relations of the small community. Tracing the tradition back to the Anglo-Saxon town, to the Teutonic village assembly, and more recently, to the New England settlement, the midwestern town, and the frontier outpost, the communitarians agreed with Park that "historically, the background of American life has been the village community"[2] with its network of intimate acquaintance. Moreover, they used the personal relationships of the small community as the yardstick for measuring the deficiencies of contemporary life. The informal give-and-take in the settlements of an earlier day was regarded as the source of a fast-vanishing mutual sympathy.[3] As Jane Addams observed, present conditions discouraged its cultivation.

We have all seen the breakdown of village standards of morality when the conditions of a great city are encountered. . . . The spirit of village gossip . . . may be depended upon to bring to the notice of the kind-hearted villager all cases of suffering . . . but in a city divided so curiously into the regions of the well-to-do and the congested quarters of the immigrant, the conscientious person can no longer rely upon gossip.[4]

Personal communication with one's neighbor was still of vital importance, she maintained, but one's neighbor was no longer just the person next door and old channels of communication were no longer sufficient.[5] In a society where both large cities and small cities grew spectacularly, where city neighborhoods contained a greater diversity of ethnic groups than ever before, and where compact urban neighborhoods turned into larger suburbs—as was the case in Roxbury, Massachusetts, where Follett began her work—new channels of communication were needed.[6]

Although they often overlapped, personal communication and the face-to-face relations of the local community were not synonymous for these thinkers. "A postage stamp may be a more efficient instrument of participation than a village meeting,"[7] Park readily admitted. The conquest of distance had increased the number and variety of contacts which transcended geographical boundaries altogether. In their view such contacts, like all communication, contributed to "the loyalties and understandings that make concerted and consistent collective action possible"[8] in many areas of society. But central to their ideal of community was the communication that took place in the neighborhood and the small locality. Consequently, the inquiry into the question of direct communication often merged with the discussion of primary group association.[9]

Explaining the need for cohesive local communities within an urban society, Dewey maintained that the "words of conversation in immediate intercourse have a vital import lacking in the fixed and frozen words of written speech."[10] Along with Dewey, the rest of these intellectuals put great store by the new media but did not see them as replacements for verbal exchange. For in the modern media, Cooley, noted, "the 'we' does not live in face-to-face contact, and though photo-engravings and stereopticons and exhibitions and vivid writing are a marvelous substitute, they are often inadequate, so that we do not feel the cogency of the common interest [as] immediately"[11] as did men whose lives were circumscribed by the local communities of the past.[12] But the local communities of the present were not what they had once been. Urban neighborhoods were segregated along class and ethnic lines more than ever before; improvements in transportation had dispersed the population into suburbs which had as loose a hold on their residents as cities did.[13] In Follett's view, Bostonians identified neither with their neighborhood nor with their city.[14] And Robert Park observed that most Chicagoans were "either physically or in imagination, abroad most of the time," their suburbs assuming the character of mere "dormitories."[15] What Follett, as well as the others, wanted was the kind of neighborhood where interaction was frequent and informal; where the reasons for coming together were social and civic. In short, they wished to unite the virtues of direct communication with those of local solidarity.

Follett's Philosophy of Communication

At the turn of the century, Mary Parker Follett began the work of neighborhood organization which shaped her philosophy of communication when she joined the staff of the community center in Roxbury, an old Boston suburb three miles from the city.[16] By 1900, as Sam Warner indicates in *Streetcar Suburbs,* the street railway had increased Roxbury's commuting population as it had those of other suburbs. Roxbury had become "a zone of emergence" for lower middle-class immigrants escaping the working-class districts of Boston. Irish, Canadians, and Jews lived beside older residents—the Irish poor and the native middle class. According to Warner, Roxbury resembled other suburbs in its lack of community consciousness and organization. The physical arrangement of the town—the grid pattern of rectangular blocks seized upon by real estate developers—prevented the growth of a geographical or social center. Without a strong central focus, the town split into numerous voluntary groups which had little to do with each other. Nor did the residents have much to do with the city of Boston either; unattached to their own neighborhood, they were even less attached to the city as a whole. On the contrary, they were eager to leave its problems behind.[17]

It was the absence of community which Follett found in Roxbury and set about to remedy. To her way of thinking, the place already had the makings of a more genuine community than did the more homogeneous suburbs of the well-to-do on the fringes of greater Boston. For mixed neighborhoods discouraged the narrow sympathies and exclusiveness which came from mingling only with one's own kind.[18] But fragmentation existed here, as elsewhere, due to increasing size, scattering of population, and group conflict. "A free, full community life lived within the sustaining and nourishing power of the community bond . . . is almost unknown now,"[19] she argued. Americans had been strengthening national ties and the federal government, but "meanwhile much of the significance and richness of the local life has been lost."[20]

Taking up the problem of local community, Follett turned to the task of stimulating face-to-face communication in Roxbury and in nearby Boston neighborhoods, where she led the movement to establish community centers in the public schools. In the decade before World War I, when the school center idea was taken up in many cities, she sought to make the centers into institutions for overcoming civic apathy, furthering mutual understanding among groups, and creating a local framework for the integration of churches, trade associations, lodges, and youth groups.[21] Later these goals became part of the social philosophy of *The New State* (1918) and *Creative Experience* (1924).[22]

Follett's writing reflected her belief that more contact among members of a neighborhood would overcome indifference and complacency. "The first object of getting people together is to make them respond somehow, to overcome inertia. To disagree, as well as to agree, with people brings you closer to them. I always feel intimate with my enemies. It is not opposition but indifference which separates men."[23] To be sure, one could fight apathy through mass meetings and the deliberate arousal of political passions, but these methods submerged the rational individual in a travesty of the deliberative group—the crowd. To link the individual to his neighborhood, city, state, and nation through discussion and cooperative work was a better cure. And this process began at the grass roots.[24]

Starting with the conquest of indifference, direct exchange would encourage the growth of other social virtues. Mutual sympathy, she agreed with the others, stemmed from face-to-face communication. It did not spring from an instinct of altruism as particularistic psychology had supposed. Instead sympathy "is born within the group—it springs forever from interrelation. The emotions I feel when apart belong to the phantom ego; only from the group comes the genuine feeling *with*—the true sympathy."[25] And nothing taught this sympathy better than small, intimate groups. Here that process of intense mutual identification which Follett desired, that "enlargement of each by the inflowing of every other one,"[26] could most easily begin. Then it could spread until no one in the society, nor, she suggested sometimes, even on the planet, would be left out.[27] Curiously, she did not wonder whether this expansion of solidarity would diminish the individual's attachment to the face-to-face group. Fervent loyalty was not scarce currency to be spent in one place at the expense of another. For Follett, whose sentimental psychology and optimistic temperament converged at this point, there was more than enough loyalty to go around.

Like sympathy, common purpose, or what she called the collective idea, depended upon personal communication. An idea was collective if everyone involved had contributed a share—not by the ballot box or by the consent of the majority but by an exchange of individual opinions. Compromise was a fake reconciliation to be avoided in favor of the integration of formerly conflicting desires.[28]

For a genuine group idea to appear, no individual could be passive; each had to add his thoughts. Not only that, he had to add "a share which is related to and bound up with every other share."[29] Dismissing what was idiosyncratic, Follett insisted that "the only use for my difference is to join it with other differences."[30] Only then did the common idea prevail; only then did the true group supersede the "mere kaleidoscope of community."[31]

Follett's idea of genuine democracy required all residents of the neighborhood to contribute to common purposes through direct and regular interchange. To encourage frequent communication and overcome the fragmentation of social life into unrelated groups, a school center or neighborhood house was needed. Here residents could meet to discuss common problems. What was more important, they could rise above the temptation to mix only in voluntary associations and then, only with people like themselves. For acquiring a new playground or any other material thing was subordinate to the less utilitarian task of acquiring a deeper sense of the common life.[32] And the goal applied to young people as well as adults. The community center should offer them classes and recreation, but its overriding goal should be to prepare the young for their participation in the neighborhood, and beyond that, for their contribution to the "social organism."[33] Team games, orchestras, civic groups and debating societies—all should be directed toward the individual's identification with the whole.[34]

In Follett's view, the community center would also be the cornerstone for a new kind of nonpartisan politics. As neighborhoods joined together outside the framework of political parties to modify existing political institutions, the face-to-face communication which started at the level of the community center would remain the surest means of creating solidarity. For solidarity did not come from calls to conscience or dissemination of information; it came from linking one small group to another, thereby involving the individual fully and vividly in the fate of others. Moreover, unlike political parties whose main concern was getting out the vote, the small group was more likely to aim beyond such perfunctory involvement as casting a ballot; it could engage its members in working out an integration of all interests. For these reasons, Follett urged that neighborhood groups become the basis of the new politics. To do this, neighborhoods should be connected to all the higher levels of government. She thought, for example, that they might send representatives to the city council and the state legislature. She also suggested that the national government maintain close contact with neighborhood organizations such as community centers and their wartime offshoots, the community councils for national defense, through a system of state bodies. In this way, the more remote levels of government would be leavened with the sense of fellowship which started at the grass roots.[35]

In Follett's political philosophy, institutions were modified to accord with the values of such fellowship. For it was that value above all others which she treasured. Follett was deeply convinced that "we are lost, exiled, imprisoned until we feel the joy of union."[36] Moreover, she believed that the comradeship of wartime, which aroused her unqualified enthusiasm, and the interdependence of modern society were awakening the people to a similar awareness.[37] Central to her ideal of the Beloved Community was the individual's total, ceaseless involvement in the common life.

Despite her insistence that an intense degree of involvement would not subvert the freedom and separateness of the individual, Follett constantly returned to two ideas which did much to undercut her argument. First, as others in the circle did, she talked of the true individual as one who lived the life of the whole; to express oneself through manifold relationships was the meaning of individuality and the fulfillment of human nature.[38] Since she equated freedom with the "harmonious, unimpeded working of the law of one's own nature" a man was free "only so far as he is interpermeated by every other human being."[39] This way of thinking left little room for the concept of the individual's rights against society; hence her lack of interest in the legal protection of individual rights or civil liberties.[40]

Her definitions of liberty and individuality in part stemmed from her psychological theories about the influence of society on personality and the false dichotomy of self and society. She typically asserted that "what we think we possess as individuals is what is stored up from society, is the subsoil of social life."[41] But she usually went beyond psychology because her notion of true selfhood required the capacity for greater union with others than the socialization of personality ordinarily produced. She described her ideal thus: "The measure of individuality is the depth and breadth of true relation. I am an individual not as far as I am apart from, but as far as I am a part of other men. Evil is non-relation."[42] Thus Follett tended to judge the worth of the individual and of his experience in terms of his connection with society. "The fulness, bigness of my life is . . . measured by . . . how far the whole is expressed through me."[43] No place existed in her philosophy for a strictly private vocation, one in which relations with others and society rightfully took a back seat.

Her second attack on individualism took a similar direction. To have worth, she maintained, an experience must have a public aspect; not in the sense in which all private acts may be said to have social consequences, but in the sense that we should deliberately make our private experiences serve public ends. In a manner similar to Jane Addams', she contended that the more the family merged with the extended home of the neighborhood, the better the members of the family and the larger society would be.[44] For personal relations are just "a frittering away of energy . . . [unless] all our private life is to be public life."[45] What she meant comes across more clearly in asides like the following:

This does not mean that we cannot sit with a friend by our fireside; it does not mean that, private and gay as that hour may be, at the same time that very intimacy and lightness must in its way be serving the common cause not in any fanciful sense, but because there is always the consciousness of my most private concerns as tributary to the larger life of men.[46]

A parallel existed in the insistence of Royce and others that "lonely enterprises"—Royce mentioned those of the mystic and the scientist—"have moral value only when they are indeed a part of one's service of the cause of humanity."[47] In Follett's thought, where social harmony and individuality coexisted so easily, the public self merged completely with the private self.

Several factors contributed to her assumption that the intense solidarity she prized was easily achieved. A psychology that stressed what she termed the interpermeation of persons supported the notion of harmony between self and others. As the entire group tended to do, Follett attacked the whole notion of the separate ego. She typically described the person in Jamesian terms as "a complex of radiating and converging, crossing and recrossing energies."[48] "When I realize fully that there are no things-in-themselves," she wrote, conflict between myself and others disappears, and I know us as "two flowing streams of activity which must meet for larger ends than either could pursue alone."[49] After disposing of the dichotomy between the self and others, Follett could shift over to saying that "our interests are inextricably interwoven. The question is not what is best for me or for you, but for all of us. . . . I vote for prohibition, even although it does not in the least touch me, because it does touch very closely the Me of which I am now coming into realization."[50] The utility of the new psychology lay in the factual basis which it gave to her social ethic. In the neighborhood movement, in Progressive reform, in the spirit of wartime America she thought she saw the fruits of this ethic.[51]

Follett's psychology also posited an urge to unity on the part of human nature. Speaking variously of this tendency as an instinct or as a product of social life, she noted that "we are always reaching forth for union; most, perhaps all, our desires have this motive. The spirit craves totality, this is the motor of social progress."[52] Biology, psychology, and evolutionary theory testified to nature's tendency to wholeness, and a metaphysics derived from empirical data in these fields enabled her to generalize about a universal movement toward unity.[53]

Although Follett relied on psychology and other fields of study to support her ideal of the fusion of self with others, she relied on the actuality of face-to-face communication to achieve it.

Real solidarity will never be accomplished except by beginning somewhere the joining of one small group with another. . . . We are capable of being faithful to large groups as well as small, . . . but this can be effected only by . . . actual experience. Only by actual union, not by appeals to the imagination, can the . . . varied neighborhood groups be made the constituents of a sound, normal, unpartisan city life. Then being a member of a neighborhood group will mean at the same time being a member and a responsible member of the state.[54]

Exhortation and enlightenment were no substitutes for first-hand experience; communication had to begin in the neighborhood and grow via intermediary groups for a comprehensive sense of community to prevail.[55] A vigorous local life would also prevent the national government from becoming too bureaucratic. "Our political forms will have no vitality unless our political life is so organized that it shall be based primarily and fundamentally on spontaneous association,"[56] she contended. Without such association, she argued, further reforms meant to foster a cooperative social spirit would be ineffectual.[57]

In Follett's thought, the emphasis on intimate local community was a protest against a narrow individualism, but it was not meant to preclude mobility and freedom for the individual. She insisted that she did not want "to shut . . . [people] up tight in their neighborhoods and seal them hermetically."[58] Neighborhood organizations, for example, were not intended to substitute for voluntary groups which represented a variety of interests. But she did object to people escaping their neighborhood in order to associate solely with others like themselves. This search for sameness struck her as the sign of a meagre personality; it was also at odds with her ideal of a vital local life. Therefore, she favored the kind of neighborhood which was cogent enough to capture the allegiance of its residents and to unify the activities of its special-interest groups.[59] What Follett stood for was the cohesiveness of the face-to-face community without the curtailment of individual choice. "The unified . . . community is the bored community,"[60] a social scientist wrote recently. Mary Follett would not have agreed.

• • •

The preference for face-to-face communication which characterized Follett's social philosophy also appeared in the work of the other communitarians, who saw there qualities of vivacity and immediacy which alternative forms of communication did not have. These qualities compelled involvement where other methods failed. Fellowship, loyalty, and devotion to common ends, they believed, flourished best in intimate association. The large, formal institution "does not enlist and discipline the soul of the individual, but takes hold of him by the outside, his personality being left to torpor or to irreverent and riotous activity,"[61] Cooley argued. Direct communication, on the other hand, encouraged the growth of social sentiments. In William Allen White's country town, it supposedly fostered the spirit of neighborliness.

Men come to know one another and when any two human beings become known [to] each other, in the one who is intelligent and wise, respect always arises for the other. To know one's fellow's ways is to sympathize with them. Neighborliness spells fraternity.[62]

If the new media were to contribute to an enlarged social conscience, they reasoned, the means of communication must draw strength from intimate community life.

In this scheme of things, the primary relations of the community would be the seedbed in which a larger sense of solidarity might take root and grow. Without tight communities to catch the interest and compel the attention of the individual, he was apt to escape into privatism or "the romantic temper"—a restless search for novelty and excitement outside the normal round of communal obligations.[63] The discussion of leisure and recreation revealed the nature of their concern. According to Park, commercial forms of recreation in the city capitalized on the unrest caused by the loosened bonds of primary association and in turn created an escape from whatever bonds remained. Howe and Addams shared his dislike of commercial entertainment—dance halls and saloons were favorite targets—and his preference for types of recreation which were not only wholesome but which strengthened communal ties. Jane Addams, for instance, approved of neighborhood bands and festivals because they produced "companionship and solidarity.'"[64] And they believed that solidarity on a small scale contributed to a larger social loyalty.[65]

Despite their preference for close-knit neighborhood, most of the communitarians sought to combine it, as Follett did, with a greater degree of personal choice than the small town allowed. "We have tasted the wine of many wants,"[66] Howe noted, and the freedom of the city could satisfy what more circumscribed communities never could. If some people chose the saloon or the cheap theatre over the family, the church, and the opportunity for culture, that was the price paid for a more varied environment.[67] Robert Park revealed a similar attachment to intimate community at the same time that he applauded the release from its constraints that the city offered. In an urban environment, vice, loneliness, and instability increased, but so did the opportunity to work out a plan of life suited to one's own nature. "Neither the criminal, the defective, nor the genius has the same opportunity to develop his innate disposition in a small town that he invariably finds in a great city,"[68] Park wrote; the same was true for the ordinary man. Park could therefore argue the case for stronger neighborhood to satisfy the need for belonging, but he could also sympathize with those who did not want to be confined by it.[69] Likewise, Cooley put a high value on primary group relations, but he too welcomed the new freedom which modern society offered. The small, isolated localities of an earlier day severely restricted the individual's alternatives; but now "through the arts of intercourse association [was] throwing off the gross and oppressive bonds of time and place, and substituting congenial relations of sympathy and choice."[70] Communication and transportation were liberating the individual from dependence on any one group, including the local community. Cooley, like the others, wanted the face-to-face community to flourish but not at the expense of freedoms newly gained.[71]

The commitment of these intellectuals to face-to-face communication led them to support those institutions which could further the process. Among those institutions were the settlement, the school, and the community center. Addams' trust in personal contact for building social loyalty clearly shaped her attitude toward Hull House. Her settlement in South Chicago not only sought to bring Irish, German, Russian, Italian, and Greek neighbors together but also sought to bring slum dwellers into direct communication with members of the privileged classes. For "certain social sentiments . . . live only by communion and fellowship, [and] are cultivated most easily in the fostering soil of a community life."[72] Belief in the efficacy of personal acquaintance made her see the clubs and discussion groups at Hull House as potent agents of social change. It also accounted for her attitude toward surveys and investigations to cure abuses on ward, city, or state levels. She considered these campaigns to be more effective, the more the middle-class audience had had direct contact with the poor before reading the statistics. Class antagonism, she believed, was best modified by "the kindly attrition of a personal acquaintance."[73]

Addams thought that urban political organization should also rest on primary relations. The folk-motes and mirs idealized in the course of the nineteenth century's discovery of folk society were her favorite models.[74] In these early European assemblies and village communities, the people met to discuss public questions and to govern themselves. The model of informal and local self-government appealed to Addams as the antithesis of all she disliked about contemporary city government: the rigid organization, the inflexible bureaucracy, and the lack of local autonomy. If city government were less mechanical and more responsive to the wishes of the people, the need for the boss and his machine would vanish. The boss was preferable to administrative officials, she sometimes thought, because he was a "stalking survival of village kindness."[75] But a better, more inclusive kind of face-to-face organization than the ward gang could arise through neighborhood cooperation and self-help. If welfare measures replaced the alderman's handout and local autonomy replaced centralization, city dwellers could create a political milieu which satisfied man's need for participation and fellowship.[76]

Dewey's idea of the school as "an embryonic community" put a similar premium on personal contact and exchange within a setting of cooperative work and inquiry. Group work involved the give-and-take of ideas in the service of a common end. Unlike formal learning about the right, and duties of a democratic society, it taught the meaning of community. In Dewey's mind, firsthand knowledge had an urgency and moral force which knowledge of the written word did not have. Learning at second hand about society was too remote and detached from experience.[77] "Social perceptions and interests can be developed only in a genuinely social medium—one where there is give and take in the building up of a common experience. . . . Playgrounds, shops, workrooms, laboratories not only direct the natural active tendencies of youth, but they involve intercourse, communication, and cooperation,—all extending the perception of connections."[78] Only knowledge rooted in direct experience molded the habits which community required.[79]

Besides being a little community for the young, the school would be an ideal social center for the neighborhood. Here Howe, Dewey, and White joined Mary Follett in relying on the school to unify the local community. Pointing to the achievements of Rochester, New York—the city which gave the initial push to the school center movement—Howe proclaimed that each school could be "a university centre, . . . a people's club-house, . . . a democratic town meeting,"[80] According to Dewey, the school of the future should promote recreational, educational, and civic activities with a view to breaking down the barriers which separated men. The school as a social center would be "a place where ideas and beliefs may be exchanged, not merely in the arena of formal discussion—for argument alone breeds misunderstanding and fixes prejudice—but in ways where ideas are incarnated in human form and clothed with the winning grace of personal life."[81] By fostering personal communication, the community center would bridge the barriers of class and race, creating sympathy among men who might otherwise segregate themselves into mutually exclusive groups. In Dewey's view, only the proper cultivation of face-to-face communication would prepare the ground for other forms of communication to do their good work.[82]

Dewey's later writing on public opinion revealed his continuing concern with the importance of verbal communication in creating community. "Signs and symbols, language, are the means of communication by which a fraternally shared experience is ushered in and sustained,"[83] he wrote in the 1920's. But "vision is a spectator; hearing is a participator. Publication is partial and the public which results partially informed and formed until the meanings it purveys pass from mouth to mouth."[34] Without the vitality of close, direct interaction, he reasoned, the formal transmission of information could not carry the burden of creating mutual sympathy. For Dewey, as well as for the remaining figures, the communications revolution required intact and intimate communities to do its own work well. The mutual understanding and sympathy that "radiate from the attachments of a near-by union"[85] were the building blocks of a larger sense of common purpose.

In the end, the direction of social change did not match their hopes. The movement for local community represented by the social settlement and the community center reached its height during World War I, when, according to a popular slogan, "every school house [was to be] a community capital and every community a little democracy."[86] But after the war, the movement lost momentum. The 1920's saw the failure of the settlement and the community center to create the kind of local solidarity which these intellectuals thought desirable. As social work became more specialized and centralized, the ideal of primary group life in the neighborhood became less important to its practitioners.[87] It remained an important but by then nearly lost cause for the communitarians. As Cooley remarked in his last book, "We splice the broken strands [of neighborhood] with such makeshifts as we find and trust that time will knit them up."[88]

4

Charles Horton Cooley and the Communications Revolution

The face-to-face relationships celebrated by the communitarians in connection with the small town, the urban neighborhood, the settlement, and the community center represented but one side of their notion of communication.[1] Of equal importance was the technology of communication—a phenomenon which overcame the limits of geography, multiplied the frequency and variety of contacts, and gave access to a nearly endless supply of information and opinion. But an increase in the amount of words in circulation was hardly sufficient for "a life of free and enriching communion."[2] What these intellectuals wanted were certain special kinds of communication. The new agencies were not only expected to extend the range of information and sympathy but were also expected to convey the vivacity and immediacy of more personal contact.[3] By enlarging the boundaries of communication, the new machinery would reproduce on a larger scale the virtues of primary group association. For these writers—and Cooley will receive special attention here—belonging to the larger community often took on some of the qualities associated with smaller and more intimate groups.

For the seekers of community, modern means of communication contained the promise of wider solidarity. But new inventions did not simply create opportunities for greater social unity while leaving older institutions untouched. Rather, they loosened the hold on the individual which face-to-face communities once had at the same time that they laid the foundation for new forms of social control. In his essay on the city, written on his arrival in Chicago in 1915, Park observed that "the easy means of communication and transportation, which enable individuals to distribute their attention and to live at the same time in several different worlds, tend to destroy the permanency and intimacy of the neighborhood."[4] The decline of informal social controls, like those exerted by the neighborhood and small town, was set in motion by precisely those forces which he hoped would forge new bonds between men in an impersonal and urban environment.[5]

Similarly, Giddings saw the new technology in the dual role of wrecker and builder. Before the coming of the railroad, the telephone, and the telegraph, each isolated locality had its own habits and customs. But now the stability which isolation entailed was threatened by these new inventions. As the ties of family and locality weakened, divorce, crime, and mental illness increased. Others joined Giddings in cataloging the social ills which ostensibly stemmed from the decline of older institutions.[6]

While Dewey saw the new agencies of transportation and communication bringing classes, races, and ethnic groups into closer contact, he too thought that they created a temporary vacuum in the organization of social life. By massing a heterogeneous population in the cities and by circulating news and new ideas through the population, they undermined the authority of family, church, and neighborhood. Men were pried loose from older customs and from moral dogmatism but were left momentarily adrift. Cooley's concern over the decline of the neighborhood as a form of social control revealed the same ambivalence toward the results of technological innovation. On the one hand, he celebrated its potential for wider forms of association; on the other hand, he wondered if better communications and transportation would make up for what was lost: "It is not at all certain that we shall form new relations equally intimate and cogent with the old,"[7] he confessed at one point.

But if the communications revolution unsettled the older face-to-face communities, it did not spell their end. And meanwhile technology moved into the breach with the promise of newer means of social control. Standardized consumption, the rapid imitation of styles and ideas through the quick distribution of goods and the dispersion of information, were already creating greater homogeneity, Giddings asserted in an early version of Riesman's description of the consumer-oriented, other-directed society.[8] In Dewey's view, modern communications were so enlarging the minds of men that an intelligent altruism was becoming the natural response to the misfortunes of others.[9]

For these intellectuals, the technology of communication had the advantages of speed and geographical scope. At the same time the new media were thought to be perfect vehicles for transmitting the values of face-to-face relations to a society characterized by large and impersonal communities. For the spoken word no longer set the boundaries of community. The medieval village, the colonial town of New England, and the American country town of the nineteenth century had required direct intercourse and personal acquaintance with the whole round of life for a sense of belonging to flourish.[10] Dewey continued the argument with reference to ancient Greece and its political theory: the size of the city-state which Aristotle prescribed did not exceed the range of the human voice, for the good state was one in which the citizen identified with the whole and dealt knowledgeably with all aspects of public affairs. But small size was no longer a requirement for community. "Our political problem," Dewey asserted, "is how to reach a free common intelligence like the Greeks, and yet make it cover a much wider territory."[11] The answer lay in exploiting the "physical annihilation of space."[12] In the modern world, the printed word replaced speech as the architect of the common will and an enlightened public opinion. Along these lines, Frederic Howe suggested that the press might convert the American city into a larger version of those ancient and medieval cities which evoked such loyalty from their citizens.[13]

Cooley's Sociology of Communication

Of all the men who explored the importance of the new communications, none devoted more attention to their social consequences than the sociologist Charles Horton Cooley.[14] His introduction to the field came early and in practical form; after graduating from the University of Michigan, he took a job with the Interstate Commerce Commission. By 1892 he was back in Ann Arbor writing a doctoral dissertation on transportation.[15] "The Theory of Transportation" discussed modern transportation as a means to division of labor, specialization of function, and economic interdependence. The conquest of distance through the telegraph and telephone also received some attention as Cooley attempted to deal with what he called physical communication. The transportation of both commodities and ideas, he asserted, held together the increasingly specialized parts of modern society.[16]

The work of Herbert Spencer had first convinced Cooley that the progressive integration of society was a historical law, but Spencer's system was too mechanical and biological for Cooley's Emersonian mind. Criticizing Spencer for his physical analogies, he maintained that "you can never compress reason and beauty and hope and fellowship and the organic being of communities and nations into differentiations, coherences, and heterogeneities."[17] Not Spencer but Schäffle, who fused biological analogies with an Idealist stress on the role of culture in shaping society, provided Cooley with the framework for his study of transportation.[18] Following Schäffle's *Bau und Leben,* he argued that modern communications not only created economic unity but also cultural, scientific, and artistic unity. Science in particular represented the peak of civilization because of the perfect communication which characterized its world-wide organization. Underscoring the need for greater understanding of the social meaning of communication, Cooley indicated before the end of his essay on transportation the direction which his own sociological thinking would soon take.[19] Meanwhile, he heard Dewey lecture on the communications revolution, and, his graduate work finished, he decided to start a new project combining the approaches of Schäffle and Dewey with the insights of psychology.[20] His major works: *Human Nature and the Social Order* (1902), *Social Organization* (1909) and *Social Process* (1918) attempted such a synthesis.

These three books, along with some of his essays, dealt with communication as the central process of social organization. "The history [of communication]... is the foundation of all history,"[21] he announced in an essay of 1897 on social change, written shortly after he began teaching at Michigan. In preliterate times, he continued, social groups were necessarily small. The invention of writing gave birth to wider political organizations like the Roman Empire, but communications had not advanced to the point where the people could experience a sense of identification with the whole.[22] Hence coercive social relations and military despotisms prevailed. Describing these early types of social organization, Cooley wrote: "Since communication is the precise measure of the possibility of social organization, of good understanding among men, relations that are beyond this range are not truly social, but mechanical."[23] Until the circulation of knowledge and sympathy increased, these wider relations were destined to remain mechanical.

The invention of printing in the fifteenth century enabled the populations of large states to enjoy a more conscious relation to the social whole.[24] The possibility arose of organizing society on the basis of sympathy and intelligence, rather than on the basis of caste and routine. The result of free communication, he implied, was a democratic form of government. Until the nineteenth century, however, the immaturity of communications spelled the immaturity of democracy, for the quick exchange of views on the issues of the day was confined to the local area.

In the United States ... at the close of the eighteenth century, public consciousness of any active kind was confined to small localities. Travel was slow. ... The newspapers, appearing weekly in the larger towns, were entirely lacking in what we should call news. ... The isolation

of even large towns from the rest of the world, and the consequent
introversion of men's minds upon local concerns, was something we
can hardly conceive.[25]

The price of a vital local life was the weak organization of public
sentiment on a national scale.

The developments of the nineteenth century—fast mails,
cheaper printing, photography, telephone, and telegraph—
brought a new epoch in communication and in social organization. The new era produced several important changes. One was
the enlargement of the meaning of democracy. The founding
fathers had intended the burden of political debate to fall on the
men of quality who held national office. But now that all citizens
could promptly inform themselves and exchange views, the center
of political gravity was shifting. Through the quick give-and-take
of opinion, the public could control ever larger areas of the
common life. The swift exchange of ideas which up to now made
democracy a reality only on the town-meeting level could now
exert an influence on national affairs.[26]

Another change involved the invasion of self-contained communities by the liberating forces of communication. Cooley welcomed the fact that technology was destroying the homogeneity
of an older America where rural isolation bred a narrow conformity. With no barriers to the circulation of ideas, "one lively mental
whole"[27] could now replace the enforced parochialism of the past.
Cooley, like Giddings, refused to worry about social leveling or
the debasement of culture. He denied "the dead level" theory of
de Tocqueville, which maintained that a stultifying sameness and
absence of individuality followed the diffusion of culture. For
Cooley, the free dissemination of ideas and tastes carried no such
penalties. Instead it had the double advantage of enabling men to
achieve greater individuality through the selection of congenial
ideas and influences, while creating a sense of sharing in a common whole. By extending the range of knowledge and sympathy,
communications made wider relations as potentially social as
local relations had always been.[28]

When Cooley's *Social Organization* appeared in 1909, the accent was still on the word "potentially." "The spiritual identification of the member with the whole . . . is the ideal of organization,"[29] he remarked, but it was still largely unfulfilled. Instead "our life is full of a confusion which often leaves the individual conscious only of his separateness, engaged in a struggle which, so far as he sees, has no more relation to justice and the common good than a dog-fight."[30] A lower individualism prevailed, one in which men failed to harmonize personal ambition with devotion to the common good.

For Cooley the root of the trouble lay in social disorganization —the breakdown of one set of social institutions before another set was ready to replace it. The isolation of the city dweller, the selfish ambition of the businessman, and the practice of conspicuous consumption convinced him that older institutions had lost their authority.[31] Changes in transportation, communication, and industry had undermined the power of the family, the church, and the local community to control "native impulse" and "private reason." Moreover, the gap between these institutions and the larger society left the individual adrift. Now that the family was no longer a producing unit, for example, it could not connect the young with the larger world of work and social cooperation. And other institutions were disappearing altogether. The system of apprenticeship, resembling "those snug nests of special tradition"[32] in which Europe abounded, had vanished, taking with it an important source of group loyalty. Cooley surely magnified a lost *Gemeinschaft* in his analysis of social disorganization; he never spoke, as Park occasionally did, of the individualistic pioneer, farmer, or preindustrial entrepreneur.[33] And one would infer from reading Cooley that mobility was a recent phenomenon and apprenticeship a central fact of economic organization until the twentieth century. But he did put his finger on the shift from small-scale to large-scale organization and its consequences for older loyalties.

While the institutions of a preindustrial era decayed, Cooley reasoned, the network of interdependence spread over the face of America. But as a means to solidarity, the organization born of this economic nexus was inadequate. "The vast structure of industry and commerce remains . . . unhumanized, and whether it proves a real good or not depends upon our success or failure in making it vital, conscious, moral,"[34] he argued. To close the gap between the external organization of modern life and the moral commitment of the individual was one of the crucial tasks of the communications revolution. Other changes were required: the strengthening of labor unions to create esprit de corps as well as to redress economic grievances; a shift in emphasis from private profit to social efficiency on the part of business. But the climate favorable to such social and economic changes depended on the ability of the new communications to create a unity of interest among all segments of the society. Cooley hoped that modern technology might foster a "sense of community, or of sharing in a common social or spiritual whole, membership in which gives to all a kind of inner equality, no matter what their special parts may be."[35] From this sense of community would flow the concrete social and economic measures necessary for a just society.

The new communications assumed enormous importance in Cooley's mind because they were the means by which the ideals of the primary group—family, neighborhood, and play group— could be extended to the whole society. The primary group, which figured so prominently in his sociology and psychology, created the capacity for communion among human beings.

By primary group I mean those characterized by intimate face-to-face association and coöperation. They are primary in several senses, but chiefly in that they are fundamental in forming the social nature and ideals of the individual. The result of intimate association, psychologically, is a certain fusion of individualities in a common whole, so that one's very self . . . is the common life and purpose of the group. . . . One lives in the feeling of the whole and finds the chief aims of his will in that feeling.[36]

Because the primary group was the nursery of human nature, one which tamed egotism to the point where a common spirit absorbed disruptive impulses, men had a built-in propensity for identifying with others. The machinery of communication could turn this tendency into actuality on a scale never before dreamed of. The telephone, telegraph, newspaper, and photograph enabled previously invisible persons to live in our imagination. And Cooley concluded optimistically, "one who entertains the thought and feeling of others can hardly refuse them justice; he has made them a part of himself."[37]

Although Cooley admitted that universal sympathy was an impossible achievement for mortal man, whose time and energy was limited, he tended to lose sight of so sobering a thought. Euphoric about man's capacity for response and sympathy, he often ended up talking as if universal communion were possible after all. With all groups becoming imaginable through communications, they had by virtue of that fact become lovable too. At first, Cooley had distinguished between simply entering into and sharing another's state of mind, which he called communion, and feeling sympathetic identification with the other person. But then he telescoped these two processes by arguing that love was the normal accompaniment of communion.[38] What started out in his theory as selective communion became universal fellowship through the union of his belief in man's infinite capacity for brotherhood with his faith in the power of the new communications. He once expressed this alchemy as follows: "Assuming that the human heart and conscience, restricted only by the difficulties of organization, is the arbiter of what institutions are to become, we may expect the facility of intercourse to be the starting-point of an era of moral progress."[39] Thus Cooley's ideas about human nature and technology served to reinforce each other.

The expansion of sympathy laid the foundation for a sense of solidarity appropriate to the complex, interdependent society which Cooley saw emerging. In such a society, solidarity would depend on the ability of the individual to engage in highly specialized tasks and at the same time to see these tasks as parts of an interdependent whole. Far from isolating men in separate worlds, specialization and the division of labor could make them conscious of their inextricable involvement in the larger network of events. And nothing offset the centrifugal force of the division

of labor more effectively than an extensive network of communications. Such a network could bring the burgeoning diversity
of function and different styles of life within the compass of our
imaginations. Even where the press degenerated into "organized
gossip," as Cooley admitted it did, the newspaper still promoted
a sense of community among people unknown to one another.
And the prospects were bright for an even fuller organization of
public consciousness in literature, politics, and science.[40]

Cooley's enthusiasm for the new means of communications
owed much to his sociological theory, a theory which his contemporary, George Herbert Mead, described as an account of the
face-to-face relationships of the small community to which he
belonged.[41] Indeed, his ideal of community required the kind of
intimacy which he associated with rural and small-town America.
Although he defined the primary group in terms of the type of
relationship which existed among its members rather than in
terms of spatial relationships such as the neighborhood—insisting
that personal intimacy rather than physical proximity was the
determining factor—he nonetheless turned for his models to the
family and the neighborhood. And the kind of family unity and
neighborliness which met his standards of primary group fellowship
flourished best, he thought, in the smaller communities of the past.[42]

Cooley's notion of the primary group laid the foundation for
a theory of society as an organism unified by the identification of
self with others. In the primary group, the egotism of the individual was transformed into the drive to win a favored place in
the minds of others by abiding by the rules of fair play and
kindness. The idea which arose in such a group was "that of
a moral whole or community wherein individual minds are
merged"[43] so that each person included the ends of all others in
his own. Cooley insisted that a better society called for no change
in human nature, just a wider theater of operation for the impulse
to fellowship which the socialization of the personality produced.
Just as in the primary group the person enlarged his self through
identification with others and with ideal ends, so in the greater
world he naturally sought his private good in the service of the

whole, provided the environment contained incentives and opportunities for the higher self to develop.[44] As William Allen White
counted on men becoming "greedy for the common good,"
Cooley counted on the emergence of a "higher greed" or a desire
to assert oneself through passionate service to others.[45]

Running through his analysis of the primary group and the
society beyond it was a bias toward harmony which stemmed from
his organic social theory. In this theory, which owed much to the
psychology of James and Baldwin, society was not an aggregate
of individuals but an interacting whole. Only an outdated atom-
ism insisted that "there are persons as there are bricks and
societies as there are walls.... Living wholes have aspects,"
Cooley maintained, "but not elements."[46] As an aspect of society,
the individual was "the looking-glass self," a self comprising the
ideas which he had of others mingled with the ideas which others
had of him.[47]

Extending his theory to emphasize the psychic nature of the
social organism, he argued that "the imaginations which people
have of one another are the *solid facts* of society."[48] Cooley's emphasis on the "psychical fact" of society expressed more than a
leaning toward Idealism; it represented an attack on an atomistic
social philosophy whose practical consequences and theoretical
assumptions he rejected. The imaginative as opposed to the material way of viewing society led one to see men not as separate atoms
best let alone—as one side of Spencer's thought would have it
—but as parts of a mental whole who depended for right development on the workings of a healthy social order.[49] From this position Cooley argued that the social process "absorbs individuals
into its life, conforming them to its requirements and at the same
time developing their individuality. There is no general opposition between the individual and the social whole."[50]

The bias toward social harmony was linked, then, to Cooley's
notion of a psychic whole of which each person was an expression.
He merely extended the argument when he maintained that the
nonmaterial forces of sympathy and communication could bring
the theoretical harmony of all men into actual existence:

He whom I imagine without antipathy becomes my brother. If we feel that we must give aid to another, it is because that other lives and strives in our imaginations, and so is a part of ourselves. The shallow separation of self and other in common speech obscures the extreme simplicity and naturalness of such feelings. If I come to imagine a person suffering wrong it is not "altruism" that makes me wish to right that wrong, but simple human impulse. He is my life, as really and immediately as anything else.[51]

In Cooley's thought, modern communications drew much of their importance from this organic bias. Add to this bias the belief, which he shared with the other intellectuals, that the social organism was evolving toward greater physical and spiritual unity, and he had the ingredients of a utopia whose advent was only delayed by the temporary gap between association and feeling.[52]

With this vision before him, Cooley overlooked those barriers to sympathy which any theory of social solidarity should reckon with: the social distance between groups, the segregation of people in a narrow milieu in the city or the economic system, and the barriers to communion in an impersonal society. Cooley did not completely ignore these factors; he simply gave them much less weight than he gave the unifying power of communication. His casual remarks on the deficiencies of new forms of communication revealed the way in which he started a line of thought inimical to his main argument and then pulled back. He mentioned the mental strain and consequent inattention produced by the quickened tempo of communications. He spoke of the "superficiality of imagination" which occurred when the individual was too heavily bombarded with information to sort out his responses. Both the new media and the din of urban life made people put up barriers to others, that reserve which Robert Park associated with superficial human relationships and a reliance on "fashion" and "front." All this would suggest that Cooley sensed the limits of attention and sympathy or agreed that technology might play a less grandiose role than anticipated. But he failed to pursue such a sobering line of thought. Instead he suggested that the problems were temporary, the result of a period of rapid innovation. When the transition period was over, and men had become accustomed to the new technological messages, the problem of overloaded human circuits would disappear.[53] Noting that much current writing is done for those who read on the run, he expected people to slow down and stop scattering their attention. He failed to admit that the radio and the motion picture might possibly speed everyone up even more.

•   •   •

Cooley's enthusiasm for the possibilities offered by the communications revolution was shared by the other communitarians. Concerned with the conflict between immigrant and native cultures in this period, Giddings saw the new technology as the means to a broad like-mindedness which transcended differences in ethnic background and religion. "Communication and travel," be observed in 1911, "have left few spots within our national domain in practical isolation. Ideas, fashions, fads, 'crazes' of every description, are carried by imitation from east to west and from north to south . . . with unfailing certainty and astonishing rapidity."[54] From this process grew "a national sympathy, a national sense of kinship, and of things mental and moral in common."[55]

Giddings argued his point without any of the reservations about leveling or loss of individuality which disturbed Royce or Park when they considered the effects of the new agencies. For Royce, the spread of sympathy was offset by the dangers of cultural uniformity and the emotionalism of the mob mind.[56] For Park, modern communications stimulated a crowd mentality already encouraged by the decline of older social controls.[57] Not so for Giddings, who predicted the emergence of a "rational like-mindedness" untainted by the sentiments of the crowd. Moreover, it was a like-mindedness which did not dampen individuality. Here he met the European conservative argument head on. The conservative maintained that similarity and equality were inimical to individual liberty. Giddings turned conservatism on its head; he insisted that only homogeneity fostered liberty, for only where men shared common attitudes could they cooperate without authoritarian control from above.[58]

When circulating ideas came into conflict, Giddings relied on man's "passion for homogeneity" to invent new ideas for reconciling conflict. In accordance with Spencerian ideas of adaptation, these ideas would win acceptance because of the satisfactions which cooperation in an industrial society produces. He even envisaged a world-wide culture which, because of the relentless movement of ideas, enveloped historically isolated civilizations like China.[59]

For William Allen White, who saw history as the interaction of material environment and moral law, the technology of communication served mainly to instruct the American conscience about the disparity between our industrial organization and our moral ideas of justice and fraternity. The nation would tame the world of steam and corporate power, he thought,

[by] the basic unselfishness of man widened and applied to men, in their new relations. Only as man's range of unselfishness has extended from the family to humanity has he grown useful . . . upon this globe. So in the conquest of steam will he win by no new set of morals, but by awakening to the widening life that steam has brought, and applying to that greater life his divinely given kindness.[60]

Communications would recreate the moral obligations and emotional intensity of the family and the neighborhood on a national scale. In White's view, the environment of the home and the local community, when combined with the effect of the electric wire, "burns the spirit of human brotherhood" upon the child. No mere lip service to the democratic dogma but a highly charged "charity" was in the offing.[61]

Our national character, White insisted, had always been Puritan and moralistic. Americans had pursued righteousness from the start and only ignorance had held back the victory of social justice. Social evil thus became a defect of the mind which in White's optimistic philosophy could be wiped out by instruction and enlightenment. Here he joined the others, Park and Royce excepted, who regarded selfishness as an intellectual vice fed by a circumscribed milieu. When isolation gave way to contact and knowledge, the argument ran, a universal sympathy would flourish.[62]

Jane Addams expressed the same view in assuming that the painstaking collection and dissemination of the seamy facts of American life would cause "altruistic feeling" to spread to ever larger groups. Her confidence in human nature was supported at this point by the belief that the expansion of altruism was the central drama of evolution. Emphasizing the importance of intellectual awareness for progress, she thought "that much of the insensibility and hardness of the world is due to the lack of imagination which prevents a realization of the experiences of other people."[63] She liked to quote Dewey in this connection: he told them at Hull House "that the general intelligence is dormant, with its communications broken and faint, until it possesses the public as its medium."[64] In her most optimistic moments, Addams thought that the public was on the verge of expanding indefinitely until sympathetic understanding of social problems was "stretched to world dimensions."[65]

Dewey also advanced an intellectualist account of growing social solidarity. He argued that a public commensurate with the dimensions of the larger society, one in which communion was wedded to socially useful knowledge, grew from the human impulse of sympathy nourished by intelligence. Travel, commercial intercourse, and communication tapped a large reservoir of good will while showing men the rational basis for the morality of universal brotherhood. Through these agencies, "sympathetic ideas" and "reasonable emotions" had circulated more widely than ever before. No sentient human being could fail to see that society was an organic union of individuals where the good of one was intimately connected with the good of all.[66] A morality appropriate for such a society, Dewey thought, would spring from a combination of the adult's intellectual grasp of the world and the child's "sympathetic curiosity, unbiased responsiveness, and openness of mind"[67]—qualities which, if properly nurtured, would carry over into adulthood.

For Dewey, too, selfishness was essentially a mental defect which free communication would cure. Once aware that social evils were not facts of nature, but problems with intelligible causes and solutions, we would have to do justice to the needs of all men. As Dewey summarized his views on the relation of knowledge and morality, "The number of persons who after facing the entire situation would still be anti-social enough deliberately to sacrifice the welfare of others is probably small."[68] Here Dewey's ideas paralleled Cooley's belief that he who became vividly aware of misfortune through the new communications media would wish passionately to alleviate it.[69]

A technological solution to the problem of community put these writers squarely in the tradition of Edward Bellamy, Andrew Carnegie, and Henry Ford, the tradition in American thought which attributed progress to invention, mechanization, and efficiency.[70] The technological bias also gave them common cause with later representatives of this tradition, men like Herbert Croly, Josiah Strong, Thorstein Veblen, Albion Small, Brooks Adams, and Walter Lippmann, for whom science, efficiency, and technology gave the best answers to social problems. They often included the means of communication among the tools of progress. In Croly's *Progressive Democracy,* for example, newspapers and magazines ostensibly reproduced the New England town meeting on a national scale. And a new concern for community was rising as "the active citizenship of the country meets every morning and evening and discusses the affairs of the nation with the newspaper as an impersonal interlocutor."[71] For the Social Gospel minister, Josiah Strong, steam and electricity ushered in a new era in which diversity and unity, liberty and organization could grow simultaneously. Now formerly antithetical elements of the good society could flourish together in harmony.[72] The marriage of communitarian sentiment and technological optimism was similarly complete for Cooley and the other seekers of community.

5

The Promise of
Technology

In the social thought of the communitarians, the new means
of communication were powerful instruments for solving the
problems that obstructed the emergence of the Great Community.
Indeed, technology sometimes took first place in their reform
thought. Not that communication was the whole answer; problems of exploitation, inequality, poverty, and health required
their own separate, practical solutions. But the promise of technology was the wave which carried specific reforms in its wake
and made it seem unnecessary to consider questions of basic
social and economic structure. Their attitude toward the uses
of technology brought together the impulse toward reform, the
faith in a scientific approach to social ills, and the belief in the
coming of that universal fellowship which was at once the ideal
community and the true religion.

The communitarian thinkers put great store by the quick
exchange and the systematization of information which the communications revolution had made possible. "Knowledge is no
longer an immobile solid; it has been liquefied. It is actively
moving in all the currents of society itself,"[1] Dewey noted. But
ease of communication had to contribute to the rational, methodical organization of knowledge if the mission of technology was
fully to succeed. The new media would not only be sources of
extended perception but also agents of publicity and social control. Through surveys like *Hull-House Maps and Papers;* through

reports like those of the Industrial Relations Commission, the National Child Labor Committee and the Russell Sage Foundation; through the work of the many municipal research bureaus, new kinds of information were appearing.[2] Such information might then find its way into the columns of the daily press, the weekly and the monthly magazines. High expectations were based on the belief that "large questions [were] driving out trivial interests"[3] from the public mind.

With information organized and transmitted in a systematic way—a way superior to that of muckraking and yellow journalism —the scientific method would become the "social motor" of progress.[4] For only when "free social inquiry . . . [was] indissolubly wedded to the art of full and moving communication,"[5] said Dewey, would democracy fulfill its promise. Such communication would publicize the enlightened solutions to social problems. At the same time, it would convey the information with so much of the vivacity of person-to-person communication that the public would be roused to action.

Following this line of thought, Robert Park visualized a press bureau for the newspaper which advertised the work of social agencies in the city as the Creel Committee on Public Information advertised the war effort after 1917.[6] Whereas Cooley welcomed the human interest story, Park viewed it as a throwback to the "evangelical tradition" in reform thought which put sentiment before utility. He preferred to see the press as a source of scientific knowledge about social problems. From this position, muckraking stood halfway between the sensationalism of yellow journalism and Park's own scientific ideal of social advertising. He noted that William Randolph Hearst of *The New York Journal,* one of the pioneer muckrakers, had found that the way to fight popular causes was not to write editorials but to advertise them through the news section of the paper.[7] Park's own version of social advertising ran as follows:

The social agencies are every day experimenting with the principles of a slowly growing science of social life. The social agencies, moreover, give us most of our social legislation. To make this legislation effective, it must have the support of the community. One way to educate the community is through the press.[8]

The social sciences would team up with the newspaper to create a new "community of purpose."[9]

For Park, the press was a potent form of "secondary" or indirect control in an urban society where the primary controls of family and neighborhood were weaker than they had been in small-town America. "In secondary groups and in the city . . . public opinion, rather than the mores, becomes the dominant force in social control."[10] And the newspaper was the most important agency for the control of public opinion. Moreover, the press publicized and thereby strengthened other agencies of secondary control: the research bureau, the government commission, the settlement, the school, and the juvenile court. These institutions did not envelop the individual as completely as the primary group did; in fact, they touched only a segment of his life and relied more on scientific technique than on intimate contact between persons to establish norms of collective behavior. Hence secondary controls, Park concluded, often remained "crude and inefficient."[11] But despite their deficiencies they helped heterogeneous but interdependent groups in the city to cooperate in a minimal way. In the absence of homogeneity, a sense of interdependence, Park had learned from Durkheim, was an essential source of solidarity in modern society. What was true of society in general applied with special force to the metropolis. Chicago's gold coast, bohemia, slums, and ethnic enclaves did not share a common way of life; the city was "a mosaic of little worlds which touch but do not interpenetrate."[12] In such an environment, secondary agencies could not substitute for intimate community, but they could establish the rules by which interdependent but dissimilar groups played the game of urban life.

Park's attitude toward secondary controls was not entirely consistent, however. He recognized the forces undermining primary communities in the city and sought a replacement for neighborhood solidarity in the realm of impersonal controls. At the same time he would not give up hope of reviving intimate local communities in an urban environment.[13] A similar impulse characterized his view of the press. Though the newspaper might be impersonal when compared to small-town gossip, Park nonetheless sought to model it after the face-to-face communication of the small locality.

If we propose to maintain a democracy as Jefferson conceived it, the newspaper must continue to tell us about ourselves. We must somehow learn to know our community and its affairs in the same intimate way in which we knew them in the country villages. The newspaper must continue to be the printed diary of the home community.[14]

The newspaper would be an extension of conversation which would involve the reader as immediately as personal contact did.[15] For Park, the new media were impersonal controls; yet he wished to put them in the service of intimate community.

John Dewey joined Park in a plea to organize knowledge and communication so that the social benefits of the annihilation of distance might be won. Dewey's belief in science as the historically ordained social motor of modern life was crucial to his argument. Science, with its empirical method of inquiry, its elimination of intuitive or private avenues to truth, its stance toward the environment as an object to be mastered, formed the core of a new world view to be promulgated by the schools of tomorrow and the communications media.[16]

But Dewey's assumption of science as a source of solidarity depended on the direction which science, and indeed, modern knowledge as a whole, was going to take. For Dewey had a deep distrust of the specialization of knowledge which he thought endemic to the modern mind. This wariness, emerging in the 1890's, continued to characterize his later work. The following remarks from his *Ethics* of 1908 defined a fairly consistent attitude on his part:

Knowledge in its ideas, language, and appeals is forced into corners; it is overspecialized, technical and esoteric because of its isolation. Its lack of intimate connection with social practice leads to an intense and elaborate over-training which increases its own remoteness.[17]

Dewey wanted to see science wedded to literature and vivid intercourse on the one hand, and to its practical bearings for society,
on the other hand. Only then could it act as a normative force in
modern society as well as a source of technological innovation.[18]

The dissemination of organized information presented a further problem for Dewey. Echoes of Franklin Ford's "Intelligence
Trust" sounded in his description of the proper distribution of
knowledge: "A genuine social science would manifest its reality
in the daily press, while learned books and articles supply and
polish tools of inquiry."[19] Dewey deplored the crisis mentality
of the modern press, its habit of reporting events which briefly
caught public attention while ignoring the social substratum
below the news. In Dewey's view news should be synonymous
with the continuous and systematic coverage of social problems.
In fact, his ideal newspaper sounded much like a daily install-
ment of an encyclopedia of the social sciences.[20]

But Dewey's approach to the news, while satisfying his urge
for a comprehensive and publicized science of society, raised
difficulties which had engaged his attention since his early work
on the social role of science. The denotative and factual language
of social science, he concluded, failed to involve the lay audience
or the average citizen in a manner sufficiently compelling to rouse
his emotions or stir him to action. The task ahead was to marry
science and art, fact and imagination. If the public were to be
mobilized "the highest and most difficult kind of inquiry and a
subtle, delicate, vivid and responsive art of communication must
take possession of the physical machinery of communication and
breathe life into it."[21] The evocative and connotative presentation
of news would enable the impersonal means of communication to
approximate person-to-person communication. By deepening feeling and perception, "artistic" news might come nearly as close
to engaging the whole person as conversation did.[22] Then the
new media might mobilize the larger public as conversation
aroused the members of smaller groups. By grafting onto technology the qualities of personal interchange, Dewey suggested the
central importance of face-to-face communication for his vision
of community.

The communitarians leaned heavily on the technology of communication to create justice and a cooperative social order; the confidence which they had in this lever of social change had important consequences for their political philosophy. The beneficent workings of the new technology, by-passing the issue of group conflict or questions of social structure and private property, became a seductive alternative to fundamental social change. William Allen White, for example, was openly skeptical about any "preconceived social plan of salvation," but he believed "that the people, through the telegrahp [sic], the telephone, the rural free delivery, . . . and all sorts of organs of communication and understanding, are getting ready for another step in . . . evolution."[23] This step toward social justice, which these intellectuals maintained avoided the mechanical collectivism of socialism, would depend on the cooperative spirit fed by the vast network of modern communications.[24] As Lewis Mumford said even then about Dewey: "He has . . . written as if the telephone did away with the necessity for imaginative reverie—as if the imagination itself were just a weak and ineffectual substitute for the more tangible results of invention."[25]

Dewey revealed another facet of his attitude in an essay of 1902 which noted the significance of the communications revolution. Referring to the questions of the immigrant and the labor movement, he said, "We find that most of our pressing political problems cannot be solved by special measures of legislation or executive activity, but only by the promotion of common sympathies and a common understanding."[26] He ended by questioning the validity of "material socialism" but proclaiming the unarguable virtues of a socialism of "art, science, and other modes of social intercourse."[27] Elsewhere Dewey spoke of putting science and the communications media in tandem; interestingly, he suggested that if complete information about society were accessible to everyone, socialism would be superfluous.[28]

Writing in a similar vein, Park argued that the aims of socialism—vaguely described as wider control of the common interests of the community—would prevail if capitalists and reformers united beneath the banner of national efficiency and publicized the scientific solutions to crime, poverty, and other social ills. All that was needed for social harmony was a common purpose and the instruments of enlightenment: the school, the press, the motion picture, and the social survey.[29] When the scientific answer to public problems was spread abroad, Park and the others concluded, the Great Community would materialize.

In the thought of the communitarians, the spiritual freight carried by the means of communication was considerable: indeed a deification of these wonders reminiscent of mid-nineteenth-century revivalism was central to the religion of community which they professed. "Modern communication," Cooley wrote in his Journal, "fulfills one condition of 'the Kingdom' by bringing all mankind into somewhat familiar intercourse." And where it organized fraternity, he added, "we have something in the way of a 'Kingdom of God.' "[30] Dewey, too, regarded communications as an instrument of the coming kingdom because they contributed so importantly to the realization of democracy. And "it is in democracy," he wrote in the 1890's, "the community of ideas and interest through community of action, that the incarnation of God in man . . . becomes a living, present thing."[31] His later, naturalistic form of piety continued to stress the identification of religion with the cause of social unity.[32] A similar alliance between the idea of communications and a social form of religion characterized the views of White; it was the printing press which was instructing the mind and refining the conscience of modern man, thereby ushering in an age of unparalleled righteousness.[33] And for White, it was not the profession of faith but "human service to bring about the coming kingdom of righteousness"[34] which was the essence of religion.

This emphasis on the social factor, expressed in the impulse to sanctify the community, was typical of the communitarians' religious bent. Dismissing conversion, belief in personal immortality, and individual communion with God as of little or no importance, they accorded the highest value to man's communion with man.[35] This kind of communion—sometimes expressed as fellowship, loyalty, or love—was the crucial religious experience as well as the binding force of democracy.[36] Therefore they wanted to see the distinction between the sacred and the secular realms abolished. For Cooley, this meant a common recognition of the fact that the divine was immanent in the spiritual ties which linked men together in society: "An ideal democracy is in its nature religious, and its true sovereign may be said to be the higher nature, or God, which it aspires to incarnate in human institutions."[37] And he entered a plea for the religion of "higher patriotism," a devotion to social wholes like the community, the nation, and the Commonwealth of Man.[38] Others in the group shared Cooley's ideas, inasmuch as they believed that democracy was the incarnation of the divine in the world. White went one step further in secularizing the eternal by proclaiming that Progressivism itself was a manifestation of God on earth.[39]

It was Josiah Royce, however, who worked out the most elaborate version of the religion of community. In his philosophy of the Beloved Community—the community of mankind viewed not as a biological entity but as a spiritual whole[40]—Royce analyzed the way in which the secular and the sacred, society and the Kingdom converged. To begin with, he reinterpreted many Christian doctrines in the light of the idea that "man the community," where Christ's spirit dwelt, won salvation for the individual.[41] Like the rest, Royce played down inner religious experience, but he did not abandon the concepts of grace and conversion; instead he gave them a social meaning. Saving grace enabled men to love and serve the spiritual community of mankind.[42] And spiritual community, though not identical with any worldly society or institution, the church included, becomes partly visible through the worldly triumphs of peace, unity, and brotherhood. These manifestations of the Kingdom of God come to earth Royce called the Great Community.[43] What finally resulted from such an interpretation of Christianity was a notion of immanence in which the lines between sacred and the profane all but disappeared. Everything which served the Beloved Community was religious; and certain special achievements of man, especially those of science, became the means of grace and the "organs of religion" because they represented the unifying spirit of the Beloved Community.[44]

What Royce and the other communitarians exhibited here was the kind of secularism which invested worldly achievements with the attributes of the eternal and the transcendent.[45] In the process, the community and all its instruments were sanctified.[46] Thus the modern means of communication not only became the agents of scientific reform and social harmony, but also the redemptive agents of the kingdom of God in America. The identification of religion and culture was nearly complete.

• • •

In their analysis of the uses of communication, these intellectuals harmonized two quite different kinds of communication which for later generations would not coexist and complement each other so easily. According to their view, face-to-face communication and intimate community, though facing the chill winds of urbanization and functional specialization, would survive intact. Meanwhile, through the new means of communications, the values of intimacy and immediacy would permeate the whole structure of organized society. The frequent reference to society as a large family was no accident but rather an expression of the romantic desire to personalize the entire social order. They were able to yoke together these two aspects of community because they believed that social evolution moved in the direction of greater physical and spiritual unity, a movement which required no loss of personal forms of community as it forged the wider bonds of the Great Community. Moreover, they carried over into their ideal of society the quasi-religious notion of communion, with its qualities of intensity and fellowship. For these intellectuals, the social order aimed beyond justice toward love.

Just as these writers tried to harmonize the small community and the larger society through a theory of communication, so they tried to impose a unified vision on the specialized, segmented aspects of modern culture. The search for wholeness which characterized their approach to communication also shaped their approach to the division of labor and to the specialization of knowledge.

Part II The Problem Of Culture

6

Culture and Community

For Matthew Arnold and the American representatives of "the genteel tradition," culture was primarily a state of mind, and one largely literary at that. Arnold's classic definition of culture found support among "liberal humanists" in American intellectual circles such as Irving Babbitt, Charles Eliot Norton, Andrew West, Bliss Perry, and Meredith Nicholsen.[1] Following Arnold, they thought of culture as "a pursuit of our total perfection by means of getting to know, on all the matters which most concern us, the best which has been thought and said in the world."[2] The humanities were the means for creating not merely groups of cultivated people but "great communities animated by ideals of nobility and beauty,"[3] ideals which could save society from a divisive and vulgar materialism. The office of literature lay in the maintenance of social discipline and high standards for national life.[4] The humanists of the period continued the literary emphasis of the early nineteenth-century proponents of mental and moral discipline, meanwhile shifting attention from classical to modern writers and emphasizing the importance of the humanities for social solidarity.[5]

In contrast to the humanists, the group of intellectuals considered here rejected the idea of community based on the saving remnant's command of the sources of "sweetness and light." Discarding a literary, genteel, and elitist ideal of culture, they came to define culture as a whole way of life, embracing economic, social, and intellectual sides of society[6] But like its counterpart in the humanist camp, their concept of culture had a strong

79

communitarian thrust. As Royce's essay on the "Present Ideals of University Life" put it, individual minds are "the servants of the one great cause"; the real mind to be trained by higher education "is the mind of the nation, that concrete social mind whereof we are all ministers and instruments."[7] The communitarians insisted that culture promote the kind of social unity suited to a scientific, industrial nation.

Disturbed by the fragmenting effects of the division of labor and the specialization of knowledge, these intellectuals elaborated an ideal of culture as a close, harmonious relationship among the spheres of utility and work, liberal studies, and civic life. Cooley suggested something of this amalgam when he censured genteel culture for its aloofness and technical training for its Philistinism.

> Culture is growth to fuller membership in the human organism; not a decoration or a refuge or a mystical superiority, but the very blood of life, so practical that its vigor is quite as good a measure as technical efficiency of the power of the social whole. Indeed the practice of regarding the technical and the cultural as separate and opposite is unintelligent.[8]

So too was the practice of separating the individual from the social aspects of culture. The communitarians deplored the kind of education which Jane Addams disparagingly called "intellectual accumulation," a refined but to her deadly form of egotism which put personal distinction before the development of the social feelings.[9] True culture, she asserted, and here she agreed with Dewey, was inseparable from the social efficiency of the individual—his "capacity to share in a give and take of experience" at work, at play, in the arts and in politics.[10]

To restrict the notion of culture to personal, inner cultivation drew attention away from the cultural possibilities of industrial occupations: the historical story inherent in the evolution of technology and changing modes of work; the scientific and artistic dimensions of production. These aspects of work, if connected with routine tasks, would connect the worker with the broader

stream of culture from which he was separated by narrow vocational training and an equally narrow job.[11] Then, too, culture
conceived as a badge of personal distinction, a superficial refinement announcing one's status, drew energy away from civic life,
leaving the public sphere at the mercy of commercialism, "backward, inferior to countries far less fortunate, in the richness,
beauty, and moral authority of its public life."[12] Learning, taste,
and aesthetic appreciation could be as much a part of the conspicuous display of the acquisitive individual as expensive goods,
and just as inimical to the enrichment of the public realm. The
alternative to conspicuous consumption was the "communal use
of wealth."[13] "Let us have beauty, even luxury," Cooley exhorted,
"but let it be public and communicable."[14]

In their plea for a broader definition of work, a regenerated
civic life, and an education directed to those ends, these intellectuals sought a union of self and society, material and ideal, utility
and culture—those dualisms which had haunted Dewey in the
1880's and which, in different guises, became the target of "the
revolt against formalism" on the part of many thinkers in the
period.[15] They envisaged nation, city, and factory redeemed from
"an unhuman commercialism" by an infusion of the values of
science, craftsmanship, art, and social service.[16] It was this high-
minded idealism, rather than a statist mentality, which lay behind
Cooley's resurrection of Hegel's view that "the state is the march
of God in the world." As he explained:

The idealization of the state, the impressing of a unitary life upon
the hearts of the people by tradition, poetry, music, architecture,
national celebrations and memorials, and by a religion and philosophy
teaching the individual that he is a member of a glorious whole to
which he owes devotion, is in line with the needs of human nature,
however it may be degraded in use by reactionary aims.[17]

Cooley was joined by Royce and Follett, among others, in exalting
the state, yet without suggesting any dramatic changes in its role.

In seeking an approach to the question of culture which might
lead to an enhanced communal life, these writers by-passed the

answers worked out by nineteenth-century European thinkers who also confronted the problem of the division of labor and the specialization of knowledge. Such answers included the paternalistic state of Ruskin, in which the craftsmanship destroyed by the division of labor and the perverted use of the machine would be revived; the rule of Comte's "priests" of science, in which the specialization of work and knowledge would be counteracted by government coordination, moral education, and a reorganization of all learning along hierarchical and monistic lines; the socialism of Marx, in which a man could "hunt in the morning, fish in the afternoon, rear cattle in the evening, criticize after dinner . . . without ever becoming hunter, fisherman, shepherd, or critic";[18] and the corporate state of Durkheim, in which occupational solidarity replaced that of family and locality. The ideas of the American communitarians paralleled those of their European counterparts at several points: in the emphasis on the occupational group as a new form of community, in the use of education to counteract the division of labor, and in the Ruskinesque appeal for self-expression in work. But despite these similarities, the Americans avoided both the statist and the socialist framework which shaped these ideas abroad. Looking elsewhere for sources of integration, they turned to education and the cultivation of a new consciousness to destroy the barriers to cultural unity.

The first of these barriers was the division of labor. Under the present system, Royce wrote in 1913, "most individuals, in most of their work, have to coöperate as the cogs coöperate in the wheels of a mechanism. They work together; but few or none of them know how to coöperate."[19] He went on to explain the difficulty of cultivating loyalty to enterprises which "outstrip, in the complexity of its processes, the power of any individual man's wit to understand its intricacies."[20] Such intricacies had not bedeviled the older kind of workman. And precisely because the artisan allegedly controlled his own product and understood how it fitted into the economic needs of his community, his image exerted a strong pull on the sympathies of these thinkers. Dewey's nostalgia for the "household and neighborhood system"[21] of production, so evident at the beginning of his *School and Society* and so crucial for his notion of the ideal educational environment, typified their attitude. Small-scale production for local needs left room for personal self-expression and, just as important, represented an outward and visible sign of what a community was: "a number of people held together because they are working along common lines, in a common spirit, and with reference to common aims."[22] Although neither Dewey nor his contemporaries wanted to return to local or handicraft production, except as a marginal type of enterprise, they tried to offset the divisive and stultifying aspects of the division of labor by calling for training in the intellectual and social meaning of work, for partial control of the industrial process by the workers, and for the release of "the art impulse"[23] within the machine system.

This emphasis on what they called "the instinct of workmanship," the "power of variation," and "the expressive impulse"[24] signaled a recoil from the impersonality of the industrial process —a reaction which Thorstein Veblen, who supplied much of their vocabulary, would have thought regressive. "No force will be sufficiently powerful and widespread to redeem industry from its mechanism and materialism save the freed power in every single individual,"[25] Jane Addams insisted. But this redemption required nothing less than an overhauling of the educational system and a reorganization of work.

The division of labor had its analogue in the life of the mind, in the growing specialization of knowledge so characteristic of the higher learning in the period.[26] The curriculum offered by American colleges in the earlier part of the century had been hierarchically organized into a neat package consisting of natural philosophy, mental philosophy, moral philosophy and their capstone, natural religion. The man of liberal culture, trained in this body of knowledge, was not subject to the centrifugal force of increasing specialization and vocationalism which was associated in the post-Civil War era with the emphasis on research and with the elective system.[27]

The communitarians were acutely aware of the changes which had occurred. In most cases, their undergraduate education had consisted of the old classical curriculum, but their graduate training had brought them into the orbit of the new learning. They

quickly became champions of the new.[28] The three who attended
the Johns Hopkins graduate school in its pioneering days—Howe,
Dewey, and Royce—experienced a euphoric conversion to the
emerging ideals of scholarship and research.[29]

But this did not mean that this generation of intellectuals
abandoned the notion of a unity of knowledge for a potpourri
of unrelated and competing specialties. Although the older education was too static, too dependent on fixed truths and decidedly
inhospitable to all inquiry not anchored in the certainties of
"Protestant Scholasticism,"[30] it represented something that could
justly be called "a common culture."[31] And only a common culture, they argued, could offset the increasing fragmentation of
knowledge and work so characteristic of modern times. The new
educational system and its ideal of culture must make a home for
scientific inquiry, utility, and research without succumbing to the
dispersive forces of excessive specialization or a narrowly conceived vocationalism.[32]

What gave substance to the belief that a vivid sense of the unity
of culture would march hand in hand with proliferating knowledge and accelerating specialization was the conviction that society was an interrelated whole, not in some occult sense known
only to sociologists or anthropologists, but in the tangible, concrete way described by Cooley:

> In a truly organic life the individual is . . . devoted to his own work,
> but feels himself and that work as part of a large and joyous whole.
> He is self-assertive, just because he is conscious of being a thread in the
> great web of events of serving effectually as a member of a family, a
> state, of humanity.[33]

The individual could experience this unity despite the complexity
of society because inherent in every occupation and special skill
was the power to lead "the mind out to embrace the whole of
which the specialty is a member."[34] From the perspective of an
organic vision of reality, all particulars clearly mirrored the whole:

> Influences . . . are transmitted from one part to any other part, so that
> all parts are bound together into an interdependent whole. . . . The

total life being unified by interaction, each phase of it must be and is, in some degree, an expression of the whole system.[35]

Specialization, therefore, did not compete with breadth of knowledge; on the contrary, it provided a vantage point from which to understand the totality. As Mary Follett remarked in this connection: "Difference is only a part of the life process. . . . It behooves us children of the twentieth century to search diligently after the law of unity that we may effectively marshal and range under its dominating sway all the varying diversities of life."[36]

Drawing on the nineteenth-century legacy of grand but finite syntheses of knowledge, while pushing in the often incompatible direction of an endless and unpredictable inquiry whose outcome might easily defy unification, the communitarians rallied around the cultural ideal of unity in diversity with little discomfort.

7

Jane Addams and the Division of Labor

The concept of the division of labor had occupied a place in political economy at least since Adam Smith celebrated its contribution to productivity in *The Wealth of Nations*. But not until American intellectuals of the post-Civil War period tried to analyze the processes inherent in the industrialization and urbanization of the nation did it become an important idea in American social thought generally. For those seeking a framework for such analysis in the years after 1879, Herbert Spencer proved a useful guide. Many social thinkers found in his writing a theory of social evolution in which the increasing division of labor reflected the general differentiation and complexity of society in the industrial stage of development. Spencer's organic theory, in which greater specialization of function created greater interdependence, provided social scientists with the framework they needed for explaining the characteristics of an industrial society.[1]

The communitarians also found Spencer's theory suggestive on this point. Following his lead, they accepted the notion that the division of labor created the basis for a closer coordination and cooperation among the diverse parts of society than had ever existed before. But here their dependence on his sociological edifice ended. Spencer had assumed that functional interdependence created social unity, and so pursued the question of solidarity no further.[2] His contemporaries in America took up where he left off. In their minds, the division of labor and its relation to social unity was problematical: the greater interdependence which it produced could not obscure another, and countervailing, effect— the shrinking of the area of common experience which the greater complexity of economic and social life entailed. In taking this tack, these intellectuals moved away from Spencer's position at the same time that they moved closer to that of Emile Durkheim.[3] Durkheim, whose classic work on the subject appeared in 1893, made the division of labor the key to what he termed "organic solidarity." Organic solidarity was based on the cooperation of a heterogeneous population with few common values. The division of labor encouraged cooperative behavior among the highly individualized members of modern societies. But it also acted as a disintegrative force, weakening the ties of family, neighborhood, and local community, yet not replacing them with anything to counteract the new "moral isolation" of the individual. The norms or social rules rising out of functional interdependence were too tenuous and abstract to end this isolation. What modern men needed, Durkheim concluded, was membership in newly organized occupational groups which in their inclusiveness would rival the once vital institutions of family and locality.[4]

Although the work of his American counterparts lacked the theoretical elegance which informed Durkheim's discussion of the division of labor, it shared a similar ambivalence toward the consequences. On the one hand, the division of labor meant material progress, wider forms of cooperation, and an outlet for the special talents of the individual.[5] On the other hand, it fragmented one's vision of society, undermined one's attachment to the local community—no longer a relatively self-contained center of production—and weakened common values.[6] Sometimes the division of labor stood as a symbol for the disturbing intricacy of modern social life, as in Dewey's comparison between the factory and society.

Life is getting so specialized, the divisions of labor are carried so far, that nothing explains itself or interprets itself. The worker in a modern factory who is concerned with a fractional piece of a complex activity . . . is typical of much in our entire social life. . . . The whole is so vast,

so complicated, and so technical, that it is next to out of the question
to get any direct acquaintanceship with it.[7]

Similarly, Royce regarded the division of labor as just one instance
of the complexity and outward cooperation which constantly
warred with the spirit of community. "It is the original sin of
any highly developed civilization that it breeds coöperation at the
expense of a loss of interest in the community."[8] And Royce wondered whether the division of labor so circumscribed men's vision
and so obscured the ways in which men now cooperated that the
individual could no longer feel himself to be a part of the whole;
or if he could, whether the feeling was grounded in any rational
"understanding of the coöperative process upon which we all
depend."[9]

At the time these writers were voicing doubts about the social
consequences of the division of labor, important changes in the
organization of work had already occurred. By 1850 the subdivision of work in the clothing and food packing industries was
highly developed. In the second half of the century, specialization
of function enlarged its hold on the factory, the office, and the
department store. There, division of labor, coordination of opera-
tions, and hierarchical organization grew side by side.[10]

The assembly line represented a further refinement of these
tendencies. First, the stationary assembly line appeared in the man-
ufacture of bicycles, carriages, and sewing machines. Then in 1915,
the Ford Motor Company put the first moving assembly line into
operation, advancing the division of labor still further. The final
push in this direction came from the new practice of scientific management, the brainchild of the engineer, Frederick Winslow Taylor. Taylor's time and motion studies at the Bethlehem Steel Works,
widely publicized after the congressional hearings of 1911, pointed
toward further specialization of industrial tasks and greater rationalization by management of the entire work process.[11]

Whereas Taylor believed that these organizational changes
resulted in "the development of each man to his greatest efficiency
and prosperity,"[12] those thinkers who valued things other than
efficiency did not greet these developments with such unequivocal

enthusiasm. Although Cooley sometimes argued that specialized production exercised the freedom and intelligence of the worker, he also feared that the growing division of labor thwarted his self-expression. Jane Addams too had strong reservations about such developments. Judging work on educational grounds, as she invariably did, Addams thought "the subdivided labor" of the modern store and factory dull and narrow in contrast to work in the old-time store or manufacturing establishment.[13] For Robert Park, modern methods of production not only straight-jacketed the individual at work but also isolated him from what was public and common in the life of the community. "Most of us now, during the major portion of our waking hours, are so busy on some minute detail of the common task that we frequently lose sight altogether of the community in which we live."[14]

For someone like Dewey, who had high hopes for the educational function of machine production because of the scientific knowledge which it embodied, scientific management seemed especially offensive. By stressing physical efficiency to the neglect of "social efficiency," Dewey argued, it turned the worker into a mere machine tender. If social efficiency meant an awareness of the social and intellectual meaning of one's work together with the ability to translate one's knowledge and skill into greater control of the work process, then scientific management effectively sabotaged it by ensuring the mindless routinization of labor.[15] Even Mary Follett, whose study of business administration inclined her toward scientific management, deplored the current infatuation with the division of labor on the grounds that it reduced to the vanishing point the worker's control of the industrial process.[16]

What the communitarians wanted, as we shall see more clearly when we consider Jane Addams' position, was a new orientation to work which would arm men with the understanding, skill, and power to counteract the prevailing tendency toward fragmentation. If the "narrow, drudging, meaningless, unhuman"[17] aspects of work were done away with, then the individual, whatever his occupation, would comprehend his contribution to the whole and would serve with the dedication and esprit de corps usually reserved for the professional classes.

Addams' Ideal of Work

The Chicago of the 1890's, where Jane Addams formed her ideas on work and culture, provided an ideal setting for the development of a critique of the industrial system.[18] Chicago, whose growth was faster than that of any other city in the nation, was home to some of the country's worst strikes, slums, and working conditions. The conspicuous wealth of its two hundred millionaires contrasted with the conspicuous poverty of the immigrants in the stockyards and the sweating trades. Private wealth flourished at the expense of public amenities and of civic improvements more substantial than the dazzle of the Columbian Exposition.[19]

By magnifying the deficiencies of the urban industrial order, the "White City in the Muck,"[20] as it has been pungently called, provoked some of its thoughtful citizens, including Addams, Dewey, and Veblen. The thrust of their social criticism was similar, stemming in part from their shared experience. Dewey was involved with Hull House as a trustee, a lecturer, and a sympathetic observer.[21] Both Addams and Dewey were active in the movement to reform Chicago's public schools.[22] Moreover, Dewey and Veblen were colleagues at the University of Chicago.[23] During the 1890's their writings converged on the disasters of the industrial system: the rigid class divisions; the overrefined life style of the leisure class; the separation of manual work from educational, artistic, or scientific content. Addams' "A Function of the Social Settlement," Dewey's *School and Society,* and Veblen's *The Theory of the Leisure Class*—all published in 1899—condemned the hiatus between the leisure and learning on the one hand and work and utility on the other.

Jane Addams saw the problems of work at close range because the Nineteenth Ward, the seat of Hull House, was the center of the sweatshop system in the garment trades. Here the wholesaler's agents parceled out clothing to be finished at piecework rates. In the tenement workrooms of the Nineteenth Ward and in the clothing factories of the First Ward, low wages and poor working conditions were accompanied by considerable division of labor.[24]

Addams was not one to ignore bread-and-butter issues because of her concern with the qualitative defects of work. She devoted much effort to improving the sanitary conditions of the sweatshops, curbing abuses in the factories, and promoting unionization in the clothing industry. But she was also troubled by the fact that the workers had, as she put it, "no real participation in the industrial and social life with which they come in contact."[25] Addams put much of the blame for this state of affairs on the priority assigned to technological mastery: "We are still childishly pleased when we see the further subdivision of labor going on, because the quantity of the output is increased thereby, and we apparently are unable to take our attention away from the product long enough to really focus it upon the producer."[26] If we did, she argued, we would see that the purported unity of purpose created by the division of labor was a myth. A system which obstructed both the interest and comprehension of the workers could hardly be expected to arouse a sense of interdependence among them. To make matters worse, the schools failed to cultivate the social feelings and divorced book learning from all but commercial and professional occupations.[27] Thus many young people lost "the chance to realize within themselves the social relation of that service"[28] which they would perform through their labor.

Addams' criticism of education separated from work and action had its roots in the restless pursuit of culture which marked the years between her graduation from Rockford Seminary in 1881 and her decision to found Hull House in 1888.[29] Looking backward, she found that her education had not prepared her to participate in the larger society beyond the family. Although the woman's college trained the mind for the larger society, it did not nourish the social sympathies and obligations which might later propel the young woman beyond the duties of home and the cultivated embellishment of her social circle. What awaited her upon graduation was only "the shock of inaction"[30] as she found no outlet for her training.

Addams brought the charges of irrelevance, initially developed in response to her own education, to the doorstep of the public school system. In her view, the highest goal of any educational enterprise should be the application of learning to life and on this score the schools, along with the colleges, failed. Neither the three R's nor vocational training approached her ideal of useful learning, for the useful was not what helped one get ahead but what helped one get into right relation with others.[31] In part, this view simply reflected her belief that industrial society would always need a large pool of unskilled labor. She spoke of the "many who are doomed to the unskilled work which the permanent specialization of the division of labor demands."[32] For those marked for manual labor, an education geared to improving one's lot was pointless. But Addams also felt that improving one's lot was itself often pointless.

Quite as the country boy dreams of leaving the farm for life in town and begins early to imitate the travelling salesman . . . so the school boy within the town hopes to be . . . a clerk or salesman, and looks upon work in the factory as the occupation of ignorant and unsuccessful men. The schools do so little really to interest the child in the life of production, or to excite his ambition in the line of industrial occupation, that the ideal of life . . . becomes not an absorbing interest in one's work and a consciousness of its value and social relation, but a desire for money with which unmeaning purchases may be made.[33]

Although Addams believed in equal opportunity, she had reservations about the way the ladder of opportunity was frequently climbed.[34]

Looking askance at orthodox methods of schooling, Jane Addams pressed for an educational scheme less bookish and remote from experience than the current type but also less narrow than ordinary vocational training. Like John Dewey, she thought that all children would benefit from a change in the educational system, but her attention was fastened on the children of the poor. Recent technological developments made their educational needs urgent. As the division of labor and the use of machinery made manual dexterity less important, she reasoned, "it becomes all the more necessary, if the workman is to save his life at all, that he should get a sense of his individual relation to the system."[35] But this was not all. Education should not only counteract the effects of routinized labor; it should also try to change the system by fostering what she called the art impulse and the power of variation in the people headed for industrial occupations.[36] In the workshops and classes at Hull House, as well as in her writings, Addams launched this double and often ambiguous attack on the division of labor.

In her attack, the more modest strategy was to accept the industrial system as it was and try to redeem it by emphasizing the historic connections and social utility of work which she believed to be intrinsically unsatisfying.[37] The Labor Museum, established at Hull House in 1900, was a case in point. Addams hoped that the spinning and weaving of the older immigrants would show the young factory workers of the district how the complicated machinery which they used had evolved from the tools of an earlier generation.[38] If the young came to treasure "the inherited resources of their daily occupation,"[39] they would understand the historic significance of the part they themselves were playing in the life of the community. And this sense of continuity, counterbalancing the subdivision of their everyday tasks, would turn work into a vocation.[40]

The cultivation of historical consciousness represented by the Labor Museum was central to her ideal of education. The worker "needs the conception of historic continuity in order to reveal to him the purpose and utility of his work."[41] But the culture which characterized the public school system and the university extension courses did not make the connections which the residents of her district needed. The public schools, too bookish to be helpful, concentrated on reading and writing.[42] Higher education made the mistake of pursuing knowledge for its own sake.

As the college changed from teaching theology to teaching secular knowledge the test of its success should have shifted from the power to save men's souls to the power to adjust them in healthful relations to nature and their fellow men. But the college failed to do this, and made the test of its success the mere collecting and disseminating of knowledge, elevating the means into an end and falling in love with its own achievement.[43]

The application of knowledge to life was overshadowed by "the idle thirst for knowledge."[44] As a result, a university extension course on astronomy would deal with the spectrum analysis of star dust rather than with the broad relationship of man, the earth, and the solar system. Such instruction neither illuminated the connection between man and nature nor applied the mandates of science to human life.[45] It in no way counteracted the overspecialization that men met at work. "Unfortunately," Addams concluded, "the same tendency to division of labor has also produced over-specialization in scholarship, with the sad result that when the scholar attempts to minister to a worker, he gives him the result of more specialization rather than an offset from it."[46] What Addams judged to be the bankruptcy of higher learning led her to find a solution elsewhere.

The solution lay in an education which counteracted the division of labor by demonstrating the historical, moral, and social dimensions of work. Tending a machine without knowledge of the product or its connection to the community made it impossible for a man to become "a cultivated member of society with a consciousness of his social and industrial value."[47] For this to occur he must experience the connections between his work and the larger society.

To make the moral connection it would be necessary to give him a social consciousness of the value of his work, and at least a sense of participation and a certain joy in its ultimate use; to make the intellectual connection it would be essential to create in him some historic conception of the development of industry.[48]

Addams admitted that this task involved "a difficult idealization . . . but not an impossible one."[49]

In fact, the difficulty of investing drudgery with cultural significance and moral force tended to disappear in the face of Addams' passionate belief in the solidarity of the human race. For example, the history of industrial development, emphasized in Hull House classes and in some experimental schools, was no mere chronicle of past achievements but a kind of hymn to the evolutionary drama of mankind. She spoke of machinery as a treasured inheritance, a gift from one generation to the next.[50] Ignorance of these gifts deadened the minds and hearts of the unwitting beneficiaries; knowledge of them brought salvation in the form of expanded mental and moral perceptions. For Addams, an education which transmitted a sense of orderly industrial evolution was, in Mazzini's words, "a Holy Communion with generations dead and living."[51]

Along with Dewey and Cooley, Jane Addams believed that education could repair most of the losses caused by the division of labor. Monotonous work could be transfigured by understanding the relation of one's circumscribed task to the end product and to the history of the industry.[52] In her reliance on this solution, she asked a great deal of the educational process.

Addams' second approach to the division of labor was more fundamental because it involved an effort to change the industrial system. But her proposals, though more ambitious, were less consistent. She knew that the industrial revolution was here to stay; she also felt that it was inhospitable to the "art instinct" and the "self-expression" of the individual. But it was precisely these values which she wished to inject into the system of production.[53] Drawing on the English arts and crafts movement of Ruskin and Morris, she wanted to unite art and labor. Like her contemporary in Chicago, the architect Louis Sullivan, Addams defended the virtues of craftsmanship.[54] In her scheme, the machine would remain but would not dominate the workman; the division of labor would persist but would be minimized by the prominence given to the individual's creativity and powers of variation.[55]

Although the Hull House shops in pottery, woodcarving, and metalwork were meant to offset the deadening effects of the factory, her interest in palliatives was a limited one. To add a bit of art to a day spent wrapping bars of soap was at best a stopgap.[56] The restorative function of the workshops was important, but even more important was their use as guidelines for the future organization of industry. In an essay on industrial education, she saw them as models for neighborhood centers where businessmen and workers might meet. The businessmen would learn to appreciate the skill of craftsmen; and compelled by the charm which self-expression always conveys, they might begin to accommodate industrial routine to the needs of the individual.[57]

Addams also welcomed pressure from other sources to effect drastic changes in the system. She supported the Chicago garment workers in their protest against the subdivision of work, her enthusiasm quickened by their use of a rhetoric reminiscent of John Ruskin's appeal to the values of craftsmanship.[58] She called on educators "to direct the play impulse into the art impulse"[59] so that the army of youth marching into the factories might somehow stamp the products of their labor with skill, imagination, and artistic merit.[60] It did not matter to her argument whether circumstances in the factories would permit the exercise of these abilities; the mere fact that the new breed of workers would possess them was reason enough for changes to occur.

At this point, her discussion of how to modify the industrial system trailed off into vagueness and wishful thinking. Nowhere in her writing does a picture of the new modes of production even appear. Addams reached this dead end, it seems, because she found it hard to reconcile the factory system with the values of art and workmanship. It has been said of Jane Addams that she did not oppose the machine but that she did oppose its crushing of what Veblen called the "instinct of workmanship."[61] But this statement, rather than describing an unproblematical viewpoint, as it was supposed to do, suggests the essence of her difficulty. Along with Cooley, she often used Veblen's terminology to describe her own attitude to work, but this borrowing is misleading. Addams' "instinct of workmanship" was equivalent to creativity in the use of materials and the fabrication of objects.[62] Veblen, however, used the term to refer to an interest in technological mastery, efficiency, and utility. Unlike Addams, he accepted the logic of the impersonal machine process—"a logic of masses, velocities, strains and thrusts, not of personal dexterity, tact, training, and routine."[63] Whereas she often invoked Ruskin's plea for the union of art and labor, he had the technocrat's contempt for the sentimentality and wastefulness of the English handicraft movement.[64]

Although Addams admitted that the hand-tool method of Ruskin and Morris was impractical, she was unable to deal with the question of alternatives.[65] Clearly she wanted to graft the virtues of craftsmanship onto machine production but could not resolve the conflict between constricting technological imperatives and the art impulse of the individual. Therefore, she tended to retreat from the position she had staked out on the question of less subdivided and confining tasks.

A man who makes, year after year, but one small wheel in a modern watch factory, may, if his education has properly prepared him, have a fuller life than did the old watchmaker who made a watch from beginning to end. . . . In order to make the watch wheel, or the coat collar interesting, they must be connected with the entire product— must include fellowship as well as the pleasures arising from skilled workmanship.[66]

This was a far cry from the kind of personal self-expression which would follow if the machine were "subordinated to the intelligence of the man who manipulates it."[67]

Another form of retreat was to play down the importance of craftsmanship. Addams reminded the reader of *Democracy and Social Ethics* that "even Ruskin's famous dictum, that labor without art brutalizes, has always been interpreted as if art could only be a sense of beauty or joy in one's own work, and not a sense of companionship with all other workers."[68] When Addams suspected that much work would remain routinized and narrow, she fell back on the solace of fellowship. At these times, too, she called upon education to supply the worker with the perception of the artist or the insight of the student.[69] If she occasionally despaired of changing the industrial system, there remained the saving power of education that had always been her alternative line of defense.

·   ·   ·

Jane Addams was not alone in her criticism of the division of labor. Other communitarians agreed with Cooley's indictment of the industrial system. "We do not make it natural," he wrote, "for the individual to identify himself and his task with the whole."[70] Dewey and Cooley took up the question of how education might create solidarity in a world of highly specialized functions.

John Dewey's educational philosophy was in large part governed by the desire to compensate for the loss of community which occurred when the factory system replaced the "neighborhood system" of production.[71] The old worker, he contended,

knew something of his process and business as a whole. If he did not come into personal contact with all of it, the whole was so small and so close to him that he was acquainted with it. . . . He saw and felt it [his work] as a vital part of the whole. . . . The situation is now the opposite. . . . Hence we must rely upon instruction.[72]

Dewey's "miniature community" of the school—at the elementary level centered on practical tasks like weaving, cooking, and carpentry—was a substitute for the old neighborhood where industrial tasks were highly visible and where children learned early to shoulder their share of the work.[73]

The school was to offset the splintering effects of the division of labor and the factory system in several ways. First, by focusing on the occupations whereby men have dealt with their environment through the ages, it would provide a simplified but vivid picture of cooperative social behavior and the chance for children to experience such cooperation directly. Participation in occupational tasks in the little community of the school would teach the student the virtues of common effort, "saturating him with the spirit of service"[74] which the larger society needed so much.

Second, the emphasis on the historical and scientific dimensions of work would form the basis of a world view consistent with the thrust of modern society, a world view embodying the values of utility, cooperation, and the use of intelligence to master nature. The old literary culture did not transmit these values; in fact it turned its back on the realm of material concerns and economic necessities. It thereby forfeited its claim to constitute the core of education. For Dewey, the occupations by which man transacted his business with the environment took priority because they marked the crossroads of utility and culture: occupational tasks, while practical, were also the primary sources of historical understanding and scientific insight.[75] If this educational philosophy required a great deal of educational mileage from making a living, it should be remembered that for Dewey history meant mainly industrial and economic history, for it was these studies that told of man's "progressive adaptation of natural forces to social uses."[76] And science meant the perfecting of knowledge initially gained through man's interaction with nature, thereby putting a premium on the empirical as opposed to the theoretical method in science. And if history taught us that "we are citizens of no mean city,"[77] Dewey in turn defined that city in pragmatic and operational terms: education would unify men by creating an intelligence "pregnant with the belief in the possibility of the direction of human affairs by itself."[78]

Third, the school would counterbalance the tendency of industrialism to turn people into mere auxiliaries of the machine by giving them an insight into the social and scientific meaning of their work. In Dewey's mind, insight invariably led to concern for the enterprise in which one was engaged and thus to a community of purpose which overrode the division of labor.[79] Like Addams, Dewey put great store by the ability of education to undo the damage caused by the machine system. Thus, an education which reconciled liberal and practical interests would "of itself tend to do away with the evils of the existing economic situation. In the degree in which men have an active concern in the ends that control their activity, their activity becomes free or voluntary and loses its externally enforced and servile quality, even though the physical aspect of behavior remain the same."[80] Dewey also hoped that the physical aspect would change as scientific and technical education encouraged greater initiative and control on the part of the worker.[81] But he no more than Addams was able to resolve the conflict between the rationalization of activity inherent in the industrial system and the individual's free selection of the means and ends of work.

Cooley's conception of the school as a model society for the practice of group life and the habits of loyalty, discipline, and service had much in common with Dewey's vision of the school. For Cooley, as for Dewey, the school was to be a microcosm of the ideal cooperative society: "As a good family is an ideal world in miniature, in respect of love and brotherhood, so the school . . . should supply such a world in respect of self-discipline and social organization."[82] Such a miniature community would overcome the moral isolation of the individual by particularizing the abstract ideals which governed the larger society; hence, the emphasis on socialized class work, the teamwork of the athletic field, and the exercise of student self-government.[83]

Cooley's desire to make education serve community also found expression in his views on culture in the schools. Traditional culture was aristocratic in origin and therefore too rarefied to fulfill the needs of an industrial and egalitarian society. Democratic culture, on the other hand, took account of both present needs and the utilitarian side of life.[84] Defining culture as growth to membership in the human organism or "the larger mind that comes from the larger life,"[85] Cooley sought to ally liberal studies with group life and technical training. Professing admiration for the humanistic tradition of literature, philosophy, and history, he nonetheless insisted that it be shaped by the needs of the day. What these needs were was not always clear; at times Cooley viewed the humanities as the means to commerce with great minds; at other times he contended that they belonged in the curriculum in so far as they bore directly on the social and economic questions of the present. In either mood, Cooley saw in the alliance of the liberal and the practical a way for students to visualize society as an organic whole and to see the specialized tasks that awaited them as parts of a larger pattern.[86] When education connected technical training with the larger movements of society; when training in craftsmanship connected work with ideals beyond pecuniary reward, then "the common life [would be] more real and attractive, and the individual more conscious of his part in it."[87]

The themes of wholeness and concreteness were central to Cooley's view of the school as the nursery of community. With the division of labor and the enlargement of the economic system threatening to make the whole invisible to the participants, some way to restore its visibility and hence its ability to evoke loyalty, had to be found.[88] Cooley found it in art. The schools should devote themselves to "a humane enlargement of the thought and spirit of a people, including especially primary social knowledge and ideals; inculcated in no merely abstract form but appealing to the imagination and assimilated with experience."[89] Ideals which might otherwise be remote and uncompelling, such as service, cooperation, and progress, would take on cogency and force if embodied in symbols. America lacked the vivid symbols of the Old World, the church and the state, the dignitaries and the traditions, but she could use art in their place.[90] For art gave life to abstractions and enlarged moral perceptions; it made us "*see* society—see it beautiful and inspiring—as a whole and in its special meaning for us, building up the conception of democracy until it stands before us with the grandeur and detail of great architecture."[91] Through the arts the school could project a vision of the whole more inspiring than the bare liberal credo of the greatest good of the greatest number. Through ideals and symbols the individual would have direct access to the larger life currently denied him.[92]

In pointing to the crucial role that schools might play in combating the division of labor, both Dewey and Cooley were responding to the apparent weakening of the neighborhood, or more precisely, to its increasing inability to connect the individual with the economic, social, and moral forces of the larger society. These forces had burst the bounds of the small community; therefore direct acquaintance with the network of society had to give way to instruction in the nature of the largely unseen environment.[93] Along with Addams, they hoped to approximate through education the direct perception of reality enjoyed by the members of a simpler society. Thus Dewey, with his idea of the school as a miniature community, and Cooley, with his notion of a common culture based on art, technical training, and social ideals, joined Jane Addams in seeking an educational solution to the problem of the division of labor.

8

John Dewey and the Unity of Knowledge

Unity versus Specialization: Old and New Answers

Speaking about the division of labor in modern society, President Eliot of Harvard University noted its importance for learning: the educated man, he argued, "will be sure that the too common belief that a Yankee can turn his hand to anything is a mischievous delusion."[1] But the growth of knowledge and expertise which so enthused Eliot caused concern among many other intellectuals. To Henry Adams the spectacular gains of science brought fragmentation and confusion into the world of thought. Darwinism, with its story of unbroken evolution, had briefly satisfied his admittedly eighteenth-century desire for unity, but soon revealed its inability to guarantee design in the universe. All that science could tell him by the turn of the century was that "Multiplicity, Diversity, Complexity, Anarchy, [and] Chaos"[2] reigned supreme. Accepting reluctantly the notion that science supplied convenient explanations but not absolute truth, Adams pursued the goal of unity with the help of the laws of the accumulation and dissipation of energy—"a spool on which to wind the thread of history"[3] as well as that of nature. Another critical response to the growth of knowledge was represented by Hugo Münsterberg, professor of psychology at Harvard and spokesman for the philosophical Idealists of his day. Münsterberg organized the St. Louis Congress of Arts and Science in 1904 "with the one mission in this time of scattered specializing work, of bringing to the consciousness of the world the too much neglected idea of the unity of truth."[4] Allied with the Idealists in their opposition to overspecialization, the "liberal humanists" of this era found the antidote to the narrowing effect of science and research in the standards of the past. Like Matthew Arnold, who thought logic too technical to claim a place in liberal education and science too specialized to constitute its core, the American humanists saw in literature the embodiment of standards which gave education its wholeness.[5]

The communitarians approached the specialization of knowledge with the same reluctance, if not the same program, that other intellectuals had. The division of intellectual functions aroused the same mixed feelings among them as the division of labor. Just as they were citizens of the machine age but attracted to the values of the artisan, so they were often practitioners of the new scholarship but committed to an older ideal of the unity of knowledge. The persistence of this ideal has been obscured by the attention which historians have given to the dramatic changes which transformed higher learning after the Civil War: the new prestige of science; the devotion to research, the growth of the graduate school, and the acceleration of the free elective system.[6] These developments demolished the traditional college curriculum and the world view which it embodied. Therefore it became deceptively easy to say, as did *The Harvard Report on General Education* (1945), that the intellectual leaders of that generation not only failed to replace the unity which they had destroyed but also failed to see the need for it.[7]

But this judgment does justice neither to the generation in question nor to the group of thinkers which concerns us here. The members of the group, nurtured in the new academic climate which prevailed at Michigan, Johns Hopkins, and Radcliffe, indeed adopted its values. But the commonly accepted distinction between the "conservers" who dominated the early nineteenth-century colleges in the name of piety and cultural unity, and the postwar "seekers" who pursued truth with little regard for the old verities or the old unities, simply does not apply to them. On the

one hand, they were in some sense seekers. As part of a new
generation of research-minded scholars, exemplified by the psy-
chologist G. Stanley Hall and the historian Herbert B. Adams of
Johns Hopkins, they were devoted to the cause of disinterested
inquiry.[8] They opposed all limitations on inquiry based on appeal
to moral absolutes or intuition, devices used by Scottish Realism
to tame the empiricism of the Enlightenment. Moreover, they
rejected Protestant Scholasticism with its reliance on revelation to
preserve the harmony of science and morals.[9] On the other hand,
the group firmly believed that free inquiry would result in the
unity of all knowledge; neither theological directives nor traditional guidelines were necessary to achieve it. Their faith in the
oneness of knowledge rested on the assumption that scholarship
would reveal the harmony of man, nature, and society. Such a
revelation would bring the multiplying but disparate pieces of
modern intellectual life back into one intelligible whole. In
crucial ways these thinkers resembled English Victorians like
Arnold, Mill, Kingsley, Spencer, and Buckle, who were often
overwhelmed by the rising tide of facts and theories but who still
held to one intellectual certitude: belief in the existence of ultimate truths in science, politics, ethics, and religion and in the
capacity of reason to discover them. Historical relativism, the
division between facts and values in the social sciences, and the
results of scientific method had not yet created the "terminal
skepticism" of the twentieth century.[10]

In order to examine the way in which the ideal of unity worked
itself out in the late nineteenth century, we shall look more
closely at Dewey and some of his contemporaries; but first, a glance
at the concept of intellectual unity which the traditional college
had stood for.

The early nineteenth-century college was built upon a prescribed curriculum of natural philosophy (physical and biological
sciences), mental philosophy (epistemology and psychology) and
moral philosophy (ethics, political economy, and history). Unifying the three fields were the philosophical tenets of Scottish
Realism, which reconciled reason and revelation, science and
Christianity, by blending empiricism with self-evident truths about

the existence of the soul, of God and of His design for the universe. Although new subjects entered the curriculum before the Civil War, they were usually fitted into the deductive framework of natural theology. Thus chemistry and geology were trimmed to fit the needs of the conservative college for a science which gave evidence of God's providence.[11]

The faculty psychology which dominated the American college also represented the desire for order and coherence. Each mental faculty could best be developed by a particular subject: demonstrative reasoning by mathematics; inductive power by science; judgment of the excellent and the virtuous by classical literature. The aim of the college was that "expansion and balance of the mental powers, those liberal and comprehensive views"[12] which guaranteed right thinking and right doing. Defending the prescribed curriculum which produced such a balance, the Yale Report of 1828 asked, "What subject which is now studied here, could be set aside, without evidently marring the system?"[13] The answer, of course, was none.

The key term in this line of argument was "the system." The educators of the period assumed that all fields of learning were so intertwined that the disturbance of one part threatened the entire intellectual system. And the coherence of the system was essential to the integrity of their world view; the harmony of the academic edifice mirrored the harmony of God's handiwork—the cosmos. Thus Francis Wayland, a leading spokesman for the orthodox position, could reason as follows: the best scientists were those who saw that the parts of the universe resembled the whole and that the whole resembled its creator.[14] According to this view, all areas of knowledge reflected the coherence of the whole. As one of the clerical economists put it: "That science and religion eventually teach the same lesson, is a necessary consequence of the unity of truth."[15]

Although the curriculum which perpetuated this academic scholasticism was breaking down well before midcentury, most notably at Harvard and Brown, it was not until after the Civil War that the movement toward specialization and elective courses gained real momentum. Pressures against the old system mounted as demands for more practical subjects increased, as institutions appeared which were free of sectarian control, and as a new generation of educators took over the presidencies of colleges and universities. These men moved away from the notion of a fixed curriculum and rejected the idea that revealed religion was the proper cornerstone of the educational system. Presidents Charles W. Eliot of Harvard, Daniel C. Gilman of Johns Hopkins, James B. Angell of Michigan, and Andrew D. White of Cornell supported the ideal of research with its corollary of highly diversified inquiry on the part of the faculty. Moreover, they favored a parallel form of specialization for students in so far as they welcomed some choice of studies. That they sided with the free inquiry of science rather than with the dogmatism of Protestant orthodoxy completed the picture.

Eliot, President of Harvard from 1896 to 1909, started the move away from prescription at the older institutions by gradually abolishing required courses. Michigan, Amherst, Yale, Brown, Dartmouth, and Williams followed suit, though all stopped short of Eliot's free elective system, settling instead for some balance between required and optional courses. In the new universities like Cornell (1868), Johns Hopkins (1878) and Stanford (1885) students had some choice of studies from the start.[16]

The rationale of the elective system was best stated by Eliot, a leading interpreter as well as a leading organizer of the new learning. Eliot contended that the growth of knowledge prevented anyone from mastering all its aspects and so made some selection of studies imperative. The educated man would henceforth be one who had a general knowledge of some things and a special knowledge of some one thing. Moreover, specialization was the only proper solution to the problems posed for the educator by the diversity of mind and character among students.

It is for the happiness of the individual and the benefit of society alike that . . . mental diversities should be cultivated, not suppressed. The individual enjoys most that intellectual labor for which he is most fit; and society is best served when every man's peculiar skill, faculty, or aptitude is developed and utilized to the highest possible degree.[17]

For Eliot, specialization of function and service to the whole were identical.[18]

Opposition to academic specialization came from both traditional and modernist advocates of liberal culture. Noah Porter, President of Yale from 1871 to 1886 and a moral philosopher of the old school, saw no compromise between elective studies and the breadth of mind which was the mark of an educated man. President James McCosh of Princeton (1868-1888) accepted the notion of elective subjects but insisted on a core of required studies in languages, literature, science, and mental and moral philosophy.[19] The relation between the two kinds of courses was hardly a casual one. Using an analogy between nature and education, McCosh summed up his position in these words:

> Nature is a system like the solar, with a sun in the centre and planets and satellites all around, held together by a gravitating power which keeps each in its proper place, and all shining on each other. You cannot study any one part comprehensively without so far knowing the others. In like manner, all the parts of a good college curriculum should be connected in an organic whole.[20]

It is not surprising then that McCosh acknowledged the need for specialists on the faculty but insisted that there was no room for those who were "narrow" or "one-sided."[21]

The ideal of breadth was also championed by another group of humanists such as Andrew West of Princeton and Irving Babbitt of Harvard. Their starting point was not the tradition of mental discipline but the devotion to literary studies—classical and modern—as the best way to develop the whole man and to provide standards of beauty and conduct for modern civilization. They objected to the emphasis on research, science, and practical studies on the grounds that it made narrow competence the test of education. And they saw the elective system as the vehicle of these tendencies.[22]

Unlike the defenders of Protestant scholasticism and literary culture, the communitarians welcomed science, research, and utility as important parts of culture. But they often shared the

traditionalist's concern for the unity of knowledge, a fact which
goes unnoticed by those who focus on the modernity of the late
nineteenth-century university.[23] Dewey was in fact as much a critic
of the elective system as McCosh or West. To his mind, it represented an abdication of all responsibility for order in education.
The problem of a congested curriculum, to which the elective
system was a response, was "a reflex of the lack of unity in the
social activities themselves, and of the necessity of reaching more
harmony, more system, in the direction of people's needs."[24] Cooley
was dismayed by the failure of the colleges to create a new common
culture to replace the classical tradition. No assortment of specialties, he contended, could substitute for a central intellectual
core. Finally, Royce, who thought of the university primarily as
a body of scholars, warned graduate students not to become pris-
oners of their special fields.[25] Although scholarship was important
to these men, they did not want to see narrow specialization
prosper at the expense of breadth.

Dewey's Ideal of Unity

At first glance, Dewey appears to be an unlikely representative of
the concept of intellectual unity.[26] As a Pragmatist he believed
in experimental inquiry rather than reliance on absolutes, an open
universe rather than one of design, and education as a process of
growth rather than the acquisition of a fixed cultural tradition.
In all three instances he took a stand against the notions of fixity,
teleology, and system. But the idea of knowledge as a unified
whole did not stand or fall with the Christian, natural law tradition of McCosh's generation in which Dewey was educated at
the University of Vermont and which he later came to attack.[27]
Other alternatives existed and Dewey found them.

The first alternative was Hegelian philosophy. As a graduate
student at Johns Hopkins in the 1880's, he found that Hegel's
thought "supplied a demand for unification that was doubtless an
intense emotional craving. . . . Hegel's synthesis of subject and
object, matter and spirit, the divine and the human,"[28] overcame

the dualisms of New England culture and natural law philosophy. Idealism gave intellectual weight to the view of the universe as "a perfect harmony, a unity in variety."[29] Although Dewey's response to Darwinism and the methods of science broke up his Hegelian philosophy during the 1890's, he later admitted that Hegel left a permanent mark on his thinking.[30]

The second influence on Dewey's ideal of unity, and one which mingled with the Idealist strand, was modern science. After 1891, science became the revelation of a harmony between man and nature once perceived in strictly Hegelian terms. Not dialectical reason but scientific inquiry revealed "the deeper truth of unity of law, the presence of one continuous living force, the conspiring and vital unity of all the world."[31] Following the lead of Franklin Ford and Ernest Renan, Dewey envisaged science as the new authority which would unify and direct a society afflicted by disintegrative individualism.[32] Thus Dewey's move from Idealism to Pragmatism, involving a rejection of Idealist metaphysics and a priori reason, did not signify the abandonment of an underlying bias toward unity. This preference merely found new expression in his philosophy of science.

When Dewey's view of science began to converge with his interest in education—an interest which began during his years of teaching at the University of Michigan (1884-1894), and which grew after his move to the University of Chicago in 1894—the stage was set for the full development of his concept of the unity of knowledge.[33] As he remarked in *The School and Society* (1899), the key to the unity of learning was the unity of man and nature. Without a sense of this unity, education would suffer from the chaos created by the advancement of knowledge and the conflict between traditional and modern learning. Neither tolerant eclecticism nor piecemeal additions to the curriculum could provide a way out of educational confusion.[34] The way out, Dewey argued, was through a single organizing principle.

The body of knowledge is indeed one; it is a spiritual organism. . . . The problem is not one of elimination, but of organization. . . .
Until the various branches of human learning have attained some-

thing like a philosophic organization, until the various modes of their application to life have been so definitely and completely worked out as to put even the common affairs of life under scientific direction, confusion and conflict are bound to continue.[35]

The philosophic organization of knowledge which Dewey sought was to grow from the study of man-in-nature. This philosophic organization would oppose itself to both the old split between the cultural and the useful and the new phenomenon of "over-specialized knowledge."[36]

Dewey criticized traditional forms of knowledge which exhibited a genteel disdain for the practical or the applied. Pointing to the long-standing preference for literary studies, he suggested that our notion of culture was still governed by the leisure-class ideal of the mind's separation from the workaday world. But in his view, experience knew no division between human concerns and nature. Man's home was the earth; his purposes depended on nature for their realization.[37] Nature, in turn, was "a rational thing, a unified intelligible system, that responds freely and fully"[38] to the application of man's intelligence. Modern times had implicated man and nature more than ever before: man in greater control of the environment; nature more "spiritualized and idealized"[39] by virtue of its hospitality to human aims.

This belief in a unified cosmos also animated Dewey's attack on the newer intellectual developments which threatened to fragment learning. He believed that the growing specialization in methods and the enormous accumulation of fact were dangerous tendencies.[40] Not that the accumulation of vast amounts of knowledge should or could be halted. Dewey after all believed with Bacon that knowledge was power. But until the diversity of method and of fact had been brought into an "organic unity," only intellectual confusion would result.[41]

The term organic unity was a slippery one in Dewey's hands; perhaps its meaning is best caught by examining its opposite— overspecialization. For Dewey, overspecialization meant more than concentration on a limited part of the whole body of knowledge. It meant the compartmentalization of knowledge which occurred when intellectual inquiry was separated from "the practical factor

—or, more truly speaking, the social factor, the factor of adaptation to the present need of the people."[42] Here modern science erred almost as much as traditional literary studies. Because the aristocratic preference for theory unsullied by practice lingered on, because knowledge was still treated as the private possession of the scholar, science too often divorced itself from its practical bearings. The result was "a science which . . . [was] remote and technical, communicable only to specialists, and a conduct of human affairs which . . . [was] haphazard, biased, unfair in distribution of values."[43]

Although Dewey joined with Positivists like Comte and Idealists like Münsterberg in condemning overspecialization, his notion of the organic unity of knowledge differed from theirs. Unlike Comte and Spencer, he did not seek a system of universal laws which governed nature and man. Unlike the Idealists, he did not look for the harmony of knowledge in the study of purposes as opposed to the study of casual laws.[44] Drawing on a Darwinian view of reality as the interactions of changing phenomena,[45] he thought of organic unity in terms of the interweaving of ends and means, values and facts, man's purposes and nature's processes. Because of this interaction, the course of studies which perpetuated the old dualisms was sterile. As he told his students in a course on "The Philosophy of Education" (1899) :

> The knowledge of nature without knowing what it leads to in human life, is blind, it is dead; . . . but a knowledge of humanities, culture, without a knowledge of its foundations, and a knowledge of its positive basis in nature, is superficial and comparatively speaking, empty. It tends all the time to become merely literary, and to lose its sense of vitality, its sense of its rights in the common earth through reference to which all these values have grown up.[46]

To see literature and art primarily in terms of personal expression was to court the danger of their isolation from the common earth. To avoid such isolation the humanities should be studied as expressions of the collective life of man. "The ultimate material of study is social life; . . . there is where the unity of history, and of literature, and of science . . . is really found."[47] For social life had its roots in nature, through which it maintained itself, and its ends in culture, through which it projected the values it had wrested from nature.[48]

Just as the foundation of the humanities lay in social life, so did that of the sciences. Nature should be studied from the viewpoint of man and not as a thing in itself, for by itself nature provided no unifying principle.[49] It was man who constituted "the center . . . from which the world radiates and expands."[50] Therefore man's experience and purposes should be the organizing principle in all scientific study.[51]

Dewey's stress on action as the focus of all learning accounted for many of his suggestions concerning educational practice. For example, it led him to insist that the secondary school and the college reconcile the need for more organized subject matter with the need to keep learning rooted in experience. One way to do this and also avoid a miscellany of unrelated specialties was through the use of the project or problem method. With this method "the central question acts as a magnet" drawing together material from areas of practice as well as theory and from many fields of study. Whatever the method of organizing the curriculum Dewey's aim was always to keep knowledge tied to action and available for use rather than compartmentalized and separated from the totality of experience.[52]

In its emphasis on man as the central organizing principle, Dewey's view of knowledge as a unified whole diverged from the natural law tradition of the early nineteenth century. His was an anthropocentric as opposed to a transcendental philosophy, but his belief in the need for intellectual unity was as strong as his predecessors'.

Dewey's ideal of the unity of knowledge becomes more concrete when his notion of the mission of science is examined more closely. For Dewey, as well as for many of the communitarians, the scientific method was more than a precise and reliable tool for discovering truth; it was also a source of authority for modern society.[53] Here he was consciously following in the footsteps of

Positivists such as Comte, Renan, and Mill who thought of science as the new regulative principle for society. Lecturing at the University of Michigan in 1893, Dewey reminded his students that these men were the first to see that intelligence must be organized so that science might direct human affairs.[54] But instead of starting from Comte's notion of science as the monopoly of a ruling oligarchy of sociologists or modern-day priests who would counteract the atomistic liberalism of the nineteenth-century bourgeoisie, Dewey expounded a more democratic form of scientism.[55] He wanted to see the truth distributed to the entire public, the scientific method of inquiry made the basis for an enlightened public opinion.[56] For the truth is fully freed, he explained in a semi-Hegelian address on "Christianity and Democracy" (1892), only when it "extends and distributes itself to all so that it becomes the Common-wealth, the Republic, the public affair."[57] Barriers of class, isolation, and ignorance must give way in order for this to occur.

It is no accident that the growing organization of democracy coincides with the rise of science, including the machinery of telegraph and locomotive for distributing truth. There is but one fact—the more complete movement of man to his unity with his fellows through realizing the truth of life.[58]

In the same year Dewey enthusiastically endorsed Renan's belief that science, by revealing the ultimate truths of metaphysics and morals, could effectively regulate social behavior. And Renan's faith in science as a new religion encouraged Dewey to move from a liberal Protestantism, couched in Hegelian terms, to an even more secular position.[59]

Since his renunciation of Congregational orthodoxy in the 1880's, Dewey's Idealistic theism had emphasized the immanence of God in man and of the kingdom of God in the world.[60] Now he was working his way toward the idea that science and "the community of truth" which it created was the kingdom come to earth.[61] In an article in *The Philosophical Review* of 1892 he contended that Christianity had originally meant that man is an . . . organ of the Reality of the universe. That, as such organ, he participates in truth, and through the completeness of his access to ultimate truth, is free, there being no essential barriers to his action either in his relation to the world or in his relations to his fellow-men.[62]

But for a long time, Dewey explained, the constraining forces of history prevented full consciousness of man's autonomy. With the rise of science and the conquest of nature, the meaning of man's freedom was finally becoming clear.[63] By 1894 Dewey explained its meaning in terms of a nontheistic, naturalistic view of revelation. "Science has made real to us . . . the actual incarnation of truth in human experience and the necessity for giving heed to it."[64] And he added, "The organs of grace, the means for lifting up the individual and binding men together in harmony are now found working in all forms of life."[65] From this time on Dewey was no longer a theist, but his notion of science as a revelation of the underlying harmony of nature and of the spiritual unity of mankind clearly represented the secularization of liberal theology.

Dewey's mature belief in the unity of knowledge grew out of the mixture of Hegelian, Christian, and Positivist ideas which formed a temporary though unstable compound during the 1890's. During these years, this set of ideas sustained the assumption that carried over into the instrumentalist phase of his philosophy, the assumption that the world was basically a harmony, that the facts of nature supported the values of human existence, and that man's mind could understand this natural order and use such understanding to promote human progress. Dewey's essay on the French writer, Ernest Renan (1892) contains perhaps the most concise statement of his early position. Here Dewey endorsed Renan's fusion of religion, metaphysics, and science.

"Has not the temple of our God been enlarged since science revealed to us the infinity of the worlds? . . . Are we not similarly justified in supposing that the application of scientific method to the metaphysical and moral region . . . will also simply shatter a narrow and paltry world to open another world of infinite marvels?"[66]

For Dewey, the answer was clearly yes. He went on to explain: "The truth is that either there is no ideal . . . or else this ideal is embodied in the universe and is to be found and drawn thence by science."[67] Elsewhere Dewey described this ideal as the unity of nature, that is, the absence of any hierarchy of higher and lower, ideal essence and material existence. The Darwinian theory of evolution had shown that unity was no longer a matter of philosophical speculation but one of fact; and the moral equivalent of the democracy of nature, he argued, was the democratic organization of society. Thus the facts of nature provided metaphysical and scientific support for Dewey's vision of the values of human community.[68]

After the 1890's, Dewey disavowed metaphysics in so far as it referred to a realm of ultimate ends beyond empirical investigation. But by 1915 he had returned to a kind of metaphysical inquiry which was in keeping with his pragmatic focus on experience. What he called a "naturalistic metaphysics" was not a shadowboxing with ultimate ends but a description of the irreducible traits of reality. And these traits included those which figured so prominently in his earlier thought—the unity of nature and the harmony of man with nature and with his fellow man. Dewey described the physical world in social terms as a rudimentary community characterized by interaction.[69] In human communication, he continued, "such conjunction and contact as is characteristic of animals . . . become symbols of the very culmination of nature."[70] According to Dewey, the culmination of nature lay in the "community of meanings," the community of "shared experience" which man created.[71] Moreover, he believed that the "is" of nature generated and supported the "oughts" of human growth, knowledge, fellowship, and love.[72]

By assuming a harmony between nature's processes and man's purposes, between facts and values, Dewey sustained his early belief in a common purpose in man and nature and in a corresponding unity of knowledge.[73] By the time he wrote *Reconstruction in Philosophy* (1920) he had, in a sense, come full circle. No longer a theist or Idealist, he nonetheless believed in the harmony of religion—now conceived as devotion to ideal ends—with science and community. He ended the book with a prophecy: "When the emotional force, the mystic force one might say, of communication, of the miracle of shared life and shared experience is spontaneously felt, the hardness and crudeness of contemporary life will be bathed in the light that never was on land or sea."[74]

•   •   •

Many of Dewey's contemporaries were attracted by the idea of knowledge as a unified whole. Not that their concept of unity or their animus against overspecialization took the same form. But the bias toward the harmony of all knowledge and the assumption that the results of specialized inquiry belonged in some inclusive system were common to several of them.

A comparison of the views of Addams, Giddings, and Royce on the nature of intellectual unity reveals the separate but parallel directions in which they moved. Jane Addams, who shared Dewey's Pragmatic notion of knowledge as a tool for action, was profoundly critical of the ideal of research which was gaining ground in academic circles. Not only were scholarly aims and practices, when translated into college extension courses, useless to the settlement, but they were also inappropriate for the university. For the habit of research was always in danger of degenerating into the pursuit of knowledge for its own sake. What would save higher learning from the sin of irrelevance was the ascendancy of applied knowledge; it alone could "rescue scholarship from the function of accumulating and transmitting to the higher and freer one of directing human life."[75] This higher function required above all a reorganization of knowledge already in man's possession. Intellectuals and reformers must organize knowledge "synthetically," joining parts into a whole so that ideas could give unity and direction to social life.[76] Although Addams moved close to Comte here, in the strict sense she was no more a Positivist than Dewey. She did not subscribe to Comte's rigid hierarchy of knowledge from mathematics up to sociology and its consequent application to society. Nonetheless she shared with Comte's English disciple, Frederic Harrison, whom she greatly admired, the same penchant for downgrading disinterested inquiry in favor of socially useful knowledge. Addams would have agreed with Harrison that "the problem of human life is not to secure the greatest accumulation of knowledge, or the vastest body of truth, but that which is most valuable to man."[77] According to Addams, this knowledge had to be molded into a unified whole before it could successfully regulate human affairs. With unity achieved, science would come into its own as the moral and intellectual authority for modern society. Moving beyond the domain of bricks and mortar, it would shape all our methods of thought and activity.[78]

Like Jane Addams, Franklin Giddings believed in the oneness of knowledge but supported the cause of research rather than that of utility. Giddings asserted that the proper goal of higher learning was neither service to society nor defense of moral orthodoxy but the unhampered search for truth. The colleges should not act as "the moral insurance agents of society"[79] but instead should function as the guardians of scientific inquiry, wherever that inquiry might lead.[80] As part of his own investigation of social behavior, Giddings delved into psychology, political science, philosophy, law, history, anthropology, ethnography, and zoology. But the diversity of his research and the wealth of detail which marks his studies does not disguise the fact that everything was grist for the mill of a distinctly cosmic sociology. The sociology explained both the history and the structure of society in terms of universal physical and psychic laws. Like Herbert Spencer, who inspired so much of his work, Giddings thought of reality as a seamless whole in which energy transformed itself in the physical and social realms to produce ever more complex forms of organization.[81] Corresponding to reality was a potentially unified science of society. To further the one science all the special sciences were to fall in line with what he claimed to be "the truths of a rational sociology."[82] With this goal in mind, Giddings criticized the specializing tendency of much modern research because it blocked the development of intellectual unity.[83] And the intellectual unity inherent in an integrated body of knowledge was necessary if science was to make good its claim to guide and regulate society.[84]

A third position on the unity of knowledge, neither Pragmatic like Addams nor Positivist like Giddings, can be seen in the work of the Idealist philosopher, Josiah Royce. Royce's views on the place of scholarship and the role of philosophy, together with his own philosophical writing, constitute a more complex statement than anyone's except Dewey's.

One facet of Royce's viewpoint emerges in connection with a talk he gave at Harvard to a group of graduate students. For Royce, the university was essentially a place for scholars and their graduate and undergraduate apprentices. But he by no means sanctioned a narrow professionalism. Instead Royce cautioned the students about the pitfalls of specialization and urged them to transform their specialties into advanced liberal studies. This they could do by self-conscious reflection on the methodology of their own fields of inquiry.[85] More was at stake in this line of argument than a plea for methodological sophistication. A philosophical Idealist, Royce spoke elsewhere of scholarship as a "spiritual construction"[86] of the mind. Reflection on one's methodology would inevitably testify to the common properties inherent in all mental constructs, whether they be scientific, historical, or literary.[87] The conflict between the scientific study of "things" and the literary study of "words," which had divided the academic world when Spencer's followers had set the terms of the debate, had given way to harmony. As Royce saw it, each overlapped the other. The study of nature required the use of "words" or organizing concepts to interpret phenomena; similarly literary and historical studies were moving toward the rigorous, scientific investigation of the "things" of the spirit.[88] The scholar, Royce contended, "works to understand truth, and the truth is at once Word *and* Thing, thought *and* object, . . . law *and* content, form and matter."[89] The two kinds of scholarship were further bound together, he believed, by the logical categories of thought which, like Kant's categories, ordered all empirical inquiry and unified mental life.[90] Thus the modern scholar did not need to be a captive of his specialty; he did not have to cut himself off from the whole body of truth because he investigated one segment of it.

Royce continued to develop his ideas on the harmony of knowledge when he addressed himself to the question of the proper role of philosophy. At the St. Louis Congress of Arts and Science, a meeting planned by his Harvard colleague and coworker Münsterberg, Royce gave a talk on "The Sciences of the Ideal." Here he expounded the synthesizing task of philosophy. The proper goal of philosophy was the unification of knowledge. The philosopher was interested in "the interrelations, in the common significance, in the unity, of all fundamental ideas, and in their relations both to the phenomenal facts and to life!"[91] And Royce went on to suggest that the unifying ideas of contemporary thought were the propositions of symbolic logic which were to play such an important part in his later philosophical work. The philosopher should not ignore the empirical work of the physical sciences, but he must direct most of his attention to the realm of "ideal truth," the realm of unverifiable and logical presuppositions.

> For the unity of things is never, for us mortals, anything that we find given in our experience. You cannot see the unity of knowledge; you cannot describe it as a phenomenon. It is for us now, an ideal. And precisely so, the meaning of things, the relation of knowledge to life, the significance of our ideals, their bearing upon one another— these are never, for us men, phenomenally present data.[92]

Although experience might suggest the explanatory concepts with which men interpreted the phenomenal world, it could not confirm or disprove them. Like the French philosopher of science, Henri Poincaré, who joined Kantian epistemology to the tradition of empiricism, Royce insisted on the a priori element in all hypotheses. Royce's Introduction to Poincaré's *The Foundations of Science* (1913) was an attempt to vindicate the right of "constructive reason" to formulate post-Kantian categories and unifying explanations for the historical, social, and physical sciences. Although not empirically verifiable, they were not arbitrary either. Not only did they conform roughly to experience, but they revealed "the nature of the knowable universe."[93]

Meanwhile Royce worked toward that "unity of the system of human ideas and ideals"[94] which he took to be the philosopher's task. Stimulated by his interest in the community as a philosophical as well as a social problem and aided by the logic of Charles Peirce, Royce moved from the abstract, monistic philosophy of the 1880's and 1890's to a concrete, pluralistic, and "social" Idealism.[95] By the time he wrote *The Problem of Christianity* (1913), he no longer conceived of the world as a fragment of an abstract unity, the Absolute. Instead he saw it as "a realm which is through and through dominated by social categories."[96] Peirce's logical doctrine of interpretation helped Royce formulate these categories.[97]

Peirce's logic of interpretation, which Royce freely admitted borrowing,[98] involved the idea that intrinsic to all thought were what he called signs, that is, objects requiring translation or elucidation before they could be understood. Signs ranged from a gesture or a word to a foreign language or a scientific explanation. All thought required a sign (A), an interpreter of its meaning (B), and one to whom the sign was interpreted (C). In short, knowledge was not just a matter of perception or conception but of communication.[99] "Interpretation," wrote Royce, "is a conversation, and not a lonely enterprise."[100]

Royce regarded the body of scientists, and later, the institutions of banking, law, and insurance, as communities of interpretation characterized by the triadic relationship mentioned above.[101] For instance, the community of scientists included those who advanced a new hypothesis (A), those who tested it by further experiments (B), and those who accepted it on the basis of public verification (C). An individual discovery was not a scientific fact until it became "the property and the experience of the community of scientific observers."[102] In the case of other types of communities, interpretation also played a reconciliatory role; it mediated between the conflicting interests of borrower and lender, plaintiff and defendant, insurant and beneficiary.[103] In each case, Royce reasoned, "the Will to Interpret undertakes to make of these three selves a Community."[104] Going beyond these communities,

Royce extended the category of interpretation to the meta-physical realm. He attempted to show that belief in the reality of the physical world required belief in the existence of one insight which spanned all temporal events. The Absolute was not an infinite thought which embraced all truth at a glance but an infinite sequential system or community of interpretation. It was the universal interpreter "who interprets all to all, and each individual to the world, and the world of spirits to each individual."[105] Thus man's finite communities of interpretation were part of the harmonizing nature of ultimate reality. They marked the point where the human and the divine converged. "In the Will to Interpret" Royce explained, "the divine and the human seem to be in closest touch with each other."[106] Like Dewey, Royce posited a universe whose true nature was social. And, like Dewey, he gave science the leading role in creating a human community where "we are members one of another."[107] By its devotion to securing the truth through public verification, by its ideal of full communication and by its dedication to the unity of mankind, the spirit of science had become the best hope of bringing to earth the Beloved Community—"man viewed as one conscious spiritual whole of life."[108] Thus Royce joined Dewey, Addams, and Giddings in the belief, so widely shared at this time, that science was the crucial unifying force in the life of the intellect and in the life of society.[109]

Behind the different intellectual orientations of the communitarians was the assumption, already discussed, that knowledge was one. Along with this went the belief that specialization and unity were compatible in a way that later generations found hard to accept. Granted that the intellectuals of the 1890's were at the beginning of the explosion of knowledge and the worship of research which has since become the watchword of the scholarly world; hence they could be justifiably optimistic about the way in which the parts of the intellectual universe could be held together. But when this has been said, it remains true that the organic bias, the tendency to regard all aspects of reality as parts of an interrelated whole, gave strong support to their conception of intellectual unity. For example, Mary Follett displayed a trust in the unifying properties of specialization which rested mainly on such a predisposition.

It is not a knowledge of his specialty which makes an expert of service to society, but his insight into the relation of his specialty to the whole. Thus it implies not less but more relation, because the entire value of that specialization is that it is part of something. Instead of isolating him and giving him a narrower life, it gives him at once a broader life because it binds him more irrevocably to the whole. But the whole works both ways: the specialist not only contributes to the whole, but all his relations to the whole are embodied in his own particular work.[110]

Such an unproblematical view of the question clearly grew out of a basic predilection for seeing the unitary, harmonious aspects of reality.

But no one better illustrates the relation between the organic bias and the belief in the oneness of knowledge than Cooley. In his eyes, specialization and breadth were not antithetical but complementary. The narrow specialist was as unnecessary as he was undesirable. For Cooley was quick to point out that specialization was not the same as isolation. A "specialty implies a whole to which the special part has a peculiar relation, while isolation implies that there is no whole," he argued.[111] And the relation of the part to the whole was above all a close one. Every phase of reality was bound into a visible, intelligible unity.

There is no such separation between general and special knowledge as is sometimes supposed. In what does the larger knowledge of particulars consist if not in perceiving their relation to wholes? Has a student less general knowledge because he is familiar with a specialty, or is it not rather true that in so far as he knows one thing well it is a window through which he sees things in general?[112]

Here Cooley joined Royce in describing the unifying effects that a larger knowledge of one's field produced. He pursued this line of argument not because of an Idealist epistemology but because of a belief in the intimate connection between the parts of knowledge and the whole.

As already suggested, the search for intellectual unity was not peculiar to this group but was, in fact, fairly widespread. It characterized not only the work of the communitarians but also the position of several other groups, including the new university presidents, the philosophical Idealists who organized and participated in the Congress of Arts and Science, and many of the scholars, especially social scientists, who took part in the Congress and argued for the unity of knowledge without subscribing to the tenets of Idealism.

The university presidents, though in favor of electives and concentration in a chosen field of study, opposed the move toward excessive specialization. Gilman, White, and Eliot have been identified so often with the trends toward electives, research, and vocationalism that their reservations about intellectual fragmentation have generally been overlooked. But reservations they had.[113] Gilman of Johns Hopkins warned his faculty about the dangers of specialization; White of Cornell proposed a union of practical and liberal studies which would reflect what he conceived to be the unity of truth; even Eliot, the most extreme advocate of the elective system, held on to the ideal of unity. To his mind, the universe was one orderly whole, the essence of which was uniformity and design. Therefore any specialty, he reasoned, could lead the student to an understanding of the unity of the whole. Indeed for all three men, the organic nature of reality, based in part on a religious concept of God's design, guaranteed a considerable degree of intellectual unity: by investigating the plan of the physical universe, science revealed the truths of religion; by studying man, the humanistic disciplines displayed the harmony between man and nature.[114] This belief in the harmony of the universe, a belief in many ways similar to that of the communitarians, led the university presidents to see in specialization a means for understanding the whole.

A similar belief in the unity of knowledge dominated the outlook of the Idealist philosophers who came together at the Congress of Arts and Science in 1904. As one of the organizers of the Congress, Münsterberg sought to counteract what he thought to be an ill-advised veneration of specialization by searching out the fundamental conceptions and methods in all fields of inquiry. Their discovery would pave the way for relating those fields where the study of values was supreme to those where the laws of causality predominated. Modern thought, Münsterberg argued, demanded that "sciences of purpose be coordinated with sciences of phenomena."[115] And it was philosophy, the Idealist George Howison contended, which could achieve this coordination by supplying the principles that connected the sciences in "one harmonious whole.[116]

The other leader of the Congress, the sociologist Albion Small, criticized its Idealist framework, but he too was sympathetic to the goal of integrating knowledge. Starting from the doctrine of evolution, Small viewed reality as a seamless web of forces which made the old division of the sciences obsolete. Although social scientists were specialists, he wrote shortly after the Congress, they were also "prophets of scientific synthesis" whose rightful work was to discover "the whole meaning of human experience."[117]

Many of the social scientists and historians who participated in the Congress shared Small's views on the unification of knowledge. Calling on scholars to synthesize the results of separate fields of inquiry, such men as G. Stanley Hall, Simon Patten, Franklin Giddings, James Harvey Robinson, and Frederick Jackson Turner suggested that the interrelationship of all human activities made it necessary to study all the sciences together. Often their belief in the validity of a unified approach came from the doctrine of evolution and from the organic bias.[118] Robinson spoke for this position when he claimed that the historian's task was to create, within an evolutionary framework, "nothing less than a synthesis of the results of the special sciences,"[119] including psychology, anthropology, economics, politics, sociology, religion, and history —hardly a modest proposal even in those days when "cultural organicism" was a widespread assumption.[120] Here again, the task of the specialist was to arrive at knowledge of the whole.

In assuming the existence of a unified intellectual sphere, these thinkers revealed the extent to which they believed order and harmony were properties of the world at large. To them, the province of thought was a unified system which reflected the nature of objective reality. Although parts of this world view have persisted into our own age—the social scientists in search of general laws being one example—the framework as a whole has not held up well. The generation of the 1890's spoke to the contemporary problem of fragmented and specialized knowledge, but it did so in a language which we cannot fully share.

9

The Ascendance
of Culture

The concept of culture employed by the communitarians represented an effort to deal with the problem of the division of labor, the specialization of knowledge, and the fragmentation of social life. As they conceived it, one of the main uses of culture was to give the individual a sense of connection with the largely unseen and complex environment in which he played a part. Its other major function was to foster a sense of solidarity which would mitigate conflict, selfishness, and indifference to the common good. "An education which should unify the disposition of the members of society would do much to unify society itself,"[1] Dewey asserted. What Cooley called a common culture would serve as a "medium of communication and spiritual unity"[2] at a time when occupational tasks were becoming more and more specialized. The notion of the unity of knowledge worked out by these thinkers provided the necessary intellectual framework for their ideal of a common culture.

The idea of culture not only occupied an important place in their social thought; it commanded the dominant place. This preeminence appeared in several ways. Economic problems were typically defined in spiritual or educational terms.[3] Thus these writers dealt with the question of work under the headings of creativity, passivity, and self-expression. What troubled them more than material deprivation was the absence of personal expression and social meaning in work. Their solution to the problem lay less in a restructured economic system than in a cultivated social imagination. Similarly, they dealt with the questions of social disorganization and conflict in psychological terms, putting great store by education as the fundamental cure for these problems.[4]

In their approach to the subject of work, some spiritualized the issues more than others. Royce clearly outdid Dewey and Addams in giving priority to subjective solutions to social ills. In *The Problem of Christianity*, Royce discussed the difficulty caused by large-scale organization and the division of labor: how to maintain personal devotion to social tasks where understanding was severely limited.[5] At first he seemed to insist on the importance and feasibility of a rationalistic answer to this dilemma. For he argued as follows:

> True community . . . depends for its genuine common life upon such coöperative activities that the individuals who participate in these common activities understand enough to be able, first, to direct their own deeds of coöperation; secondly, to observe the deeds of their individual fellow workers, and thirdly to know that, without just this combination, . . . just this deed could not be accomplished by the community.[6]

Royce further underlined the need for a cognitive answer by likening a community to an orchestra whose members were skilled in the conscious art of cooperation.[7] But then he quickly backtracked by reminding the reader that intricate deeds of cooperation defy comprehension and obstruct loyalty.

> When these deeds are hopelessly complex, how shall the individual member be able to regard them as genuinely belonging to his own ideally extended life? He can no longer understand them in any detail. He takes part in them, willingly or unwillingly. He does so because he is social, and because he must. . . . And the more complex the social order grows, the more all this coöperation must tend to appear to the individual as a mere process of nature, and not as his own work, . . .—unless indeed love supplies what individual wit can no longer accomplish.[8]

At this point, Royce abandoned intellect in favor of emotion. Love for the community, he was quick to note, was not unthinking mysticism;[9] but it is hard to discover in Royce's description of it much rational content either. We are told to rejoice "in the ancestors and heroes who have made the present life of this social group possible."[10] The suspicion that the problem of loyalty was finally going to be solved at the level of patriotic rhetoric was not entirely unfounded. For Royce turned to national holidays as a form of interpretation which would invest the routines of office and factory with heightened communal significance. The collective celebration was an interpreter of the past to the present, creating love for a community whose workings could no more be understood than they could be changed.[11]

Dewey differed from Royce in his insistence that the complexities of technology and the division of labor were subject to considerable modification and control. Yet, he too tended to overemphasize the psychological dimensions of the problem of work. Along with Addams and Cooley, Dewey typically focused his analysis on the consciousness of the individual rather than on the constraints of the system. When men possessed the requisite "intelligence and initiative in dealing with material and agencies of production,"[12] he reasoned, they would become creative and free. In part he meant that voluntary and skillful partnership with the machine freed men from the servitude which acquiescence in an incomprehensible necessity entailed.[13] But this Hegelian emphasis on inner accommodation to external conditions was not his major theme. For Dewey, freedom meant primarily the power to control events; a free man was one who had some control over the nature and conditions of his work. But the key to this control was first and foremost the intelligence and attitude of the individual. Material forces and economic conditions were less important than a special kind of personal experience.[14] As he explained in *The School and Society*:

How many of the employed are today mere appendages to the machines which they operate! This may be due in part to the machine itself, or the *régime* which lays so much stress upon the products of the machine; but it is certainly due in large part to the fact that the worker has had no opportunity to develop his imagination and his sympathetic insight as to the social and scientific values found in his work.[15]

Until an educational revolution had changed habits of mind, he argued, we could neither discover the real cause of our economic ills nor take steps to correct the situation. For until the full extent of human potentialities had been ascertained, it was difficult to discover which evils were caused by the economic system and which were caused by a failure to cultivate the powers of the individual. A generation whose impulses toward constructive and autonomous activity had been enlarged by education would be the best divining rod in the search for the conditions of meaningful work. Its members would be in a position to recognize the true obstacles to such work and to correct the remaining deficiencies of the economic system.[16] Thus Dewey managed to postpone judgment on the existing order by calling for a preliminary reform of men's habits and purposes. Such a postponement was quite in line with other aspects of his social philosophy, such as his failure to evaluate systematically the competing claims of socialism, capitalism, syndicalism, and guild socialism current in his day.[17] For Dewey did not rest his hopes primarily on institutional arrangements but on changes in thought and behavior. In comparison with the latter, "all reforms which rest . . . upon changes in mechanical or outward arrangements, are transitory and futile."[18]

The preference of the American communitarians for psychic rather than institutional solutions to the problems of work stands out more sharply when contrasted with the approach of a contemporary European social scientist who resembled them in many ways. Among those who concerned themselves with the division of labor and social solidarity, Emile Durkheim's program of reform was more in line with American thought than was the paternalism of Comte or the revolutionary socialism of Marx. Like his American counterparts, Durkheim put great store by education as a way to counter the effects of increasing specialization of function. Society, he wrote in *Moral Education*, was above all "a consciousness of the whole."[19] Both the health of society and of the individual depended upon a "collective consciousness" which lifted the individual out of his isolation.[20] Although threatened by the dangers of overspecialization, education could create the collective consciousness that would overcome the division of labor and bind the individual to the whole. But Durkheim balanced this emphasis on education with a concern for institutional arrangements which was at once more concrete and more systematic than were Dewey's or Addams' suggestions for a new order. In *The Division of Labor* (1893) and *Suicide* (1897), Durkheim combined a sociological analysis of solidarity with a proposal for the corporate organization of society in which occupational groups took on extensive welfare, educational, and recreational functions. Beyond this, he advocated a partnership of occupational groups and government to implement a moderate type of socialism.[21] Like Royce, Dewey, Cooley, and Addams, he was more interested in creating moral solidarity than in ending exploitation. Unlike them, however, he gave considerable attention to the institutional dimensions of the problem.

The tendency to subsume social and economic issues under cultural ones showed up not only in connection with the communitarians' approach to work but also in relation to the problems of individual detachment and social conflict. This tendency revealed itself in their concern with what Royce called estrangement, a feeling of separation from society which they discussed under the rubric of disorganization, impersonality, and isolation.[22] It also appeared in the premium they put on a spirit of cooperation and of individual identification with the whole. The two themes were not unrelated. For them, estrangement or alienation was primarily a psychological problem which required for its solution primarily a psychological answer—a shift toward greater moral commitment to the social order.[23]

Their focus on feelings of alienation involved a certain disregard for questions of social structure, economic power, and material rewards. In Cooley's writing, estrangement was a kind of intellectual and moral confusion about the meaning of social processes. His concern was primarily with failures of the mind.[24]

Understanding, he argued, had lagged behind technological progress, organizational complexity, and the growth of an interdependent economic order. Because "there . . . [was] a lack of vital thought and sentiment to keep the machinery pliant to its work"[25] social institutions had succumbed to "dead mechanism."[26] The discipline of corporation, church, and school was potentially moral, but was in reality completely external.[27] Formalism, bureaucracy, and routine prevailed because of a "lack of communication and social consciousness." Cooley summed up the problem: "There is always . . . a larger whole; the question is whether the individual thinks and feels it vividly through some sort of sympathetic contact; if he does he will act as a member of it."[28] To get the individual to identify himself with the whole was basic to the moral regeneration of society.[29]

Cooley's devotion to the cause of moral regeneration was accompanied by the feeling that too much attention to economic problems was vulgar and materialistic. Materialism, he agreed with Addams, had been America's fundamental defect.

The excessive preoccupation of the nineteenth century with material production and physical science may be regarded as a partial enslavement of the spiritual and aesthetic sides of humanity, from which we are now struggling to escape.[30]

An escape from materialism required a social criticism which emphasized the lack of moral standards in economic life, the excesses of self-seeking, and the demoralization which afflicted both the beneficiaries and the victims of an inequitable economic system. Material deprivation was bad but moral deprivation, the lack of an "authoritative canon for life"[31] was worse. The most serious problem was not inequality or injustice but intellectual and moral detachment.

Although the individual, in a merely mechanical sense, is part of a wider whole than ever before, he has often lost that conscious membership in the whole upon which his human breadth depends: unless the larger life is a moral life, he gains nothing in this regard, and may lose. When children saw the grain growing in the field, watched the

reaping and threshing and grinding of it, and then helped their
mother to make it into bread, their minds had a vital membership in
the economic process; but now that this process, by its very enlargement, has become invisible, most persons have lost the sense of it. And
this is a type of modern industry at large: the workman, the man of
business, the farmer and the lawyer are contributors to the whole, but
being morally isolated by the very magnitude of the system, the whole
does not commonly live in their thought.[32]

The remedy, he concluded, was to make "life a moral and spiritual as well as a mechanical whole."[33] As noted earlier, Cooley
assigned much of this task to education. But he also looked to
group solidarity to overcome isolation.

It was the effort to end the moral isolation of the individual
which shaped Cooley's views on industrial organization and
economic conflict. Union organization was necessary, he acknowledged, because workers were weaker than employers; they
needed group solidarity in order to redress grievances. But Cooley's occupational groups were not organized primarily for group
struggle. Rather, they were organized to envelop the individual
in an intimate association where fellowship, security, and standards of workmanship led him to identify with the common
good. Thus the main purpose of unions was to foster the sense
of belonging so necessary for moral health.[34]

In Cooley's view, the conquest of moral isolation would pave
the way for a society where "full and harmonious personal development"[35] was more important than material success, and
where social conflict was mitigated by devotion to the common
good.

Similarly, Dewey, Park, Addams, and Royce regarded estrangement as the fundamental defect of their society.[36] "The greatest
evil of the present regime," Dewey asserted, "is not found in
poverty and in the suffering which it entails, but in the fact that
so many persons have callings which make no appeal to them.
. . . Neither men's hearts nor their minds are in their work."[37]
Foreshadowing the psychological approach to industrial relations
of Elton Mayo and his followers in the 1930's, Park suggested that

the basic struggle in the economic realm was not between classes but between the individual and the mechanical, impersonal system.[38] And when he came to review Mayo's *Human Problems of an Industrial Civilization* (1933), he endorsed Mayo's idea that the answer to the problem was a set of "industrial folkways."[39] The communitarians went on to imply that if men could be made to see the social and moral significance of their work, their vision would somehow give birth to a better order. An illuminating, if extreme, statement of this belief shows the direction which their thinking took.

> The question of the amount of wages the laborer receives, . . . of the hours and conditions of labor, are, after all, secondary. The problem primarily roots in the fact that the mediating science does not connect with his consciousness, but merely with his outward actions. He does not appreciate the significance and bearing of what he does; and he does not perform his work because of sharing in a larger scientific and social consciousness. If he did, he would be free. All other proper accompaniments of wage, and hours . . . would be added unto him, because he would have entered into the ethical kingdom.[40]

Although they rarely underlined the primacy of the cultural as unequivocally as Dewey did here, the communitarians tended to argue in a similar vein. They thought that much of the mechanical and degrading aspects of work could be counteracted by scientific and social insight; they believed that an impersonal and complex social order could be humanized by understanding it. Not only did this kind of analysis push aside questions of institutional change, but it also ignored such values as the pursuit of culture for its own sake. The weight which they gave to education as the means to social salvation, the efficacy which they assigned to communication, or what Royce called interpretation, in building the good society bore witness to their primary concern—the creation of a sense of belonging.

Part III
Politics

10

Politics and the Small-Town Fetish

The importance which these intellectuals gave to psychic solutions to the problem of community leads inevitably to the question of the role which politics played in their thought. Their idea of democratic capitalism as the political form of the Great Community rested on the premise that education and communication would create the cooperation necessary to limit conflict and make the system work. Thus the aversion to structural change discussed in connection with their notion of culture appeared again in their political thought.

From the 1890's through the 1920's their views on industrial legislation, business regulation, and political organization reflected their support of reforms which regulated capitalism but stopped short of government control of the economy. Their belief in liberal reform was combined with an antibureaucratic bias which limited their enthusiasm for big government and the expertise which a rationalized economy required. Sharing with one wing of Progressivism a suspicion of large-scale organization, these intellectuals wanted to bring centralization and rationalization into harmony with the values of the small community.[1] As a result they tried to combine expertise with the town-meeting ethos and to halt the decline of the local community.

137

Political Solutions

The political position of the communitarians centered on the
desire to regulate capitalism without capitulating to state socialism. Representing different aspects of the Progressive movement,
they agreed on the need to correct economic and social injustice
while protecting property rights. Such "socialized individualism"
put a premium on harmonizing interests and mitigating class
conflict within the existing system.[2] They generally favored government protection of workers but not labor's own combative
tactics, such as the closed shop.[3] Where they supported labor
unions, they coupled this support with an eye toward their
eventual disappearance or diminished importance. Jane Addams
defended the union's current role in protecting the worker, but
she criticized the idea of a permanent organization of employers
and employees as too divisive. The labor movement was "to include all men in its hopes. It must have the communion of universal fellowship."[4] Therefore, instead of relying on contending
groups of capital and labor to redress grievances, she looked forward to a time when legislation would accomplish this "without
a sense of division or of warfare."[5] Like Addams, Mary Follett
backed collective bargaining, but she objected to it insofar as it
posited two different sets of interests; she preferred to think of
it as one step toward the harmony of capital and labor.[6] "Not
bargaining in any form, not negotiation, is the key to industrial
peace and prosperity,"[7] she argued. Instead "community is the
keyword for all relations of the new state."[8] And this meant that
capital and labor ought to become one decision-making group.[9]
Not surprisingly, then, these reformers had no sympathy for any
sort of class politics. They thought that class-based parties and
political appeals to class interest were inimical to the common
good.[10] Cooley's enthusiasm for nonpartisan activity typified this
attitude at the same time that it reflected the anti-conflict orientation which characterized American sociology. He wanted each
occupational group, including industrial workers, to function as
a profession "with *esprit de corps,* emulation and standards within

itself, and all animated with a spirit of loyalty and service to the whole."[11] Conflict between classes and groups could be resolved by recognizing the moral unity which transcended different interests and by basing a political program on this unity.[12]

What their liberal reform program meant in terms of legislation was the regulation of trusts, the protection of labor by child labor laws, workman's compensation, and support for collective bargaining.[13] To further these and other reforms, several became active in state and national politics: Addams worked for the passage of industrial legislation in Illinois and was a member of the national Progressive committee in 1912; White and Dewey campaigned for Theodore Roosevelt; Howe was an aide to Cleveland's reform mayor, a member of the city's tax commission from 1909 to 1910, and a La Follette supporter in the election of 1924.[14]

What their reform program meant in terms of political organization was a greater role for government at all levels—city, state, and federal—with the use of commissions of experts for what Giddings called "societal engineering."[15] As Cooley stated it, the modern era needed "a comprehensive 'scientific management' of mankind, to the end of better personal opportunity and social function in every possible line."[16] And these reformers envisaged a political system where the expert, both elected and appointed, worked with a well-informed and interested public toward this end. They often counted on the instruments of direct democracy to cement the alliance between expert and citizen. The direct primary, for example, would break the power of the boss and the party machine, enabling the people to elect to, say, the city council, men who qualified by virtue of special training. These men in turn would appoint other experts to the administrative positions below them. According to the communitarians, political parties themselves were not superfluous, but the regular party organizations were. The other devices of direct democracy, such as the initiative and the referendum, were also intended to by-pass the machine and to give greater power to both the people and to the experts who drafted the bills.[17] That the complexity of the "unseen reality" which stretched beyond the citizen's milieu might upset the balance of power in favor of the expert and the circle of administrators which he served, as Walter Lippmann argued in the 1920's, did not seem a real possibility until after the war.[18] In the area of public opinion, as elsewhere, they assumed that there was "no essential conflict between democracy and specialization."[19] The public would set the ends, the experts would devise the means. The difficulty of dividing general and technical matters was not even considered.[20] For the communitarians continued to view public opinion from the standpoint of the town-meeting model: the citizen who engaged in face-to-face discussion of the issues acquired the understanding and competence which enabled him to set policy if not to implement all its aspects. Accelerating the exchange of ideas, the large-scale communication created by the new media simply duplicated the virtues of small-scale discussion. As Cooley put it:

> Communication must be full and quick in order to give that promptness in the give-and-take of suggestions upon which moral unity depends. Gesture and speech ensure this in the face-to-face group; but only the recent marvelous improvement of communicative machinery makes a free mind on a great scale even conceivable.[21]

Nowhere in his writing did Cooley express concern about the rise of a system in which a small number of people delivered opinions and a large number received them. Instead he continued to think of the public as an entity containing as many givers as receivers of opinion.[22] In the same way, William Allen White, as the editor of a small-town newspaper, saw the press as a transmitter of face-to-face values. The newspaper was essentially a continuation of conversations begun in the small group. He made a point of insisting that it neither initiated, swayed, nor dominated public opinion; it merely provided an enlarged forum for the discussion of public issues.[23] Thus these writers defended the importance of local publics in an increasingly bureaucratic society. Such publics would dovetail with the expert because of their common allegiance to rational decision-making.

Working together, the public and the expert were meant to rationalize American society while preserving a large measure of individual liberty in the market place. Only Howe's single tax scheme, designed by Henry George to tax the unearned increment on land, represented a departure from this position by giving the public greater control of the distribution and use of wealth.[24]

World War I intensified rather than changed the direction of their reform impulse. Here they belonged to the main stream of Progressive reform in welcoming the collectivism of wartime.[25] The communitarians bore witness to the increased acceptance of government control and themselves participated in the celebration of an intensified public spirit. "The whole nation is aroused, as it has never been before, to the necessity for wider and wiser control of the common interests of the community,"[26] Park reported approvingly in 1918. In the same year Mary Follett noticed how wartime conditions fanned people's desire for "union and communion."[27] Out of these conditions a new era of social progress was coming to life.

> Democracy then is a great spiritual force evolving itself from men, utilizing each, completing his incompleteness by weaving together all in the many-membered community life which is the true Theophany. The world to-day is growing more spiritual, and I say this not in spite of the Great War, but because of all this war has shown us of the inner forces bursting forth in fuller and fuller expression.[28]

These forces included the exhilaration of participating in a common cause, which might survive in peacetime if men refused to return to "the deadly separateness of . . . ordinary life."[29] They included the mobilization of neighborhoods for selling Liberty Loans, doing Red Cross work, and teaching food conservation, all of which might lead to greater local patriotism after the war. Finally, the forces leading to a new community life were strengthened by the need for more regulation of industry in the interests of the common good.[30]

During the war these intellectuals moved further toward what Follett referred to as "coöperative collectivism."[31] Both their prewar bias toward a rationalized economy and the innovations of Woodrow Wilson's war government pushed them in this direction. Putting greater stress on efficiency and government regulation than before, they also described their views on reform with more precision than they employed before 1917.

The theme of efficiency which marked their wartime writing predated the struggle with Germany; ironically it often took the form of praise for Germany's methods of administration, social welfare system, and municipal government by experts. At the same time, these American reformers criticized the absence of political democracy together with the excess of paternalism. In Howe's words, Germany was both "a menace and a model."[32] After 1917, the emphasis on efficiency became even more noticeable. Commenting on the upsurge of public spirit, Park linked the cause of war and of scientific reform.

War work is everything that contributes to national efficiency and the measure of social efficiency is the extent to which rational methods have been applied to the problems of poverty, crime and disease.[33]

He took this opportunity to point out to "class-conscious reformers"[34] that most of their programs could be justified on the grounds of national efficiency, a goal which served the interests of all classes. John Dewey joined Park in tying the issue of domestic reform to the war. Dewey regarded World War I as a demonstration of the weaknesses of American society. These weaknesses were by no means new, but the strains of a war economy had fully exposed them. Most obvious was the inefficiency of production and distribution in an economy organized for private rather than public need. Less obvious but just as important was human inefficiency, which included not only low output but also waste of talent because of boredom on the job. A war economy required what was already long overdue—intelligent planning for both economic and human efficiency. Once set in motion by the war, Dewey insisted, "the movement will never go backward."[35]

For many of these intellectuals the domestic achievements of America during these years provided a map for the future. Writing in the Emporia *Gazette* in 1917, William Allen White cautioned the country not to revert to the "individualism" of the prewar period. He argued for conserving the gains of the war years, such as price controls and higher income taxes.[36] In the same vein, Franklin Giddings predicted the peacetime consolidation of recent accomplishments.

> The war will end, and the necessity for centralized command will once more be less imperative. It is improbable, however, that the old individualism will come back in all its irresponsibility and inadequacy. We shall demand coördination and correlation. We shall demand conservation and economy. We shall insist upon a more equitable distribution of the net product of toil.[37]

After the war, Giddings himself gave increased attention to the possibilities of social engineering. In contrast to the unions and "the phosphorescent ignorati" of radicalism, whom he accused of ignoring the scientific method, he relied on scientific planning by the expert to cure social ills.[38]

Despite Howe's opposition to American entry and his disgust with the curtailment of civil liberties during the war, when he held the difficult post of Commissioner of Immigration at Ellis Island, the war turned out to be far from a total loss in his eyes either. Not only did it swell the spirit of community, but it prompted the government to undertake public housing and the operation of the railroads. Against those who wished to return to greater laissez faire, Howe argued that the war had already made us "a semi-socialistic state";[39] moreover, it has shown us that a measure of collectivism was workable. The path toward the future seemed obvious—it led in the same direction. In a book about cooperative communities called *Land and the Soldier* (1919), he described how one part of the path might look. Still supporting the single tax, he explained how it could be used to open up land for agricultural cooperatives to men weary of the city and the factory. Modeled on Ebenezer Howard's garden suburb, built by the planners responsible for America's wartime housing projects, they would be small and self-sufficient, "real home communities."[40] Handicraft production would balance farming. Most important, through cooperative buying, marketing, and ownership of machinery, these communities would "socialize agriculture."[41]

Like Howe, Mary Follett endorsed the new collectivism, but her interests centered on the corporate organization of the state. Influenced by English guild socialism and by American thinkers like Herbert Croly, she wanted a larger role for the occupational group in government.[42] In this connection, wartime developments became a source for her political ideas. Adjustment boards, with representatives from labor and management to adjudicate disputes in industries with defense contracts, pointed toward joint control of all industries in the future. The War Labor Policies Board, where labor was represented in the making of national economic policy, led the way toward joint management of the economy after the war. Processes such as collective bargaining were merely way stations on the road to a national state based on harmony of interest: "If we want harmony between labor and capital, we must make labor and capital into one group: we must have an integration of interests and motives, of standards and ideals of justice."[43] The ideal state must avoid both the central control of state socialism and the decentralization of guild socialism, which denied sovereignty to the state. What Follett wanted was the integration of all groups with the state, so that the latter "should have no authority *as a separate* group, but only so far as it gathers up into itself the whole meaning of these constituent groups."[44] By 1918 Dewey joined her in advocating the corporate organization of society. He too held out for a flexible system of federated, self-governing industries controlled by labor and management, with the central government acting as an occasional arbiter rather than as the manager or the owner of industry.[45] Cooperation without statism remained the guiding principle of their political thought.

What the war did for their political thought concerning domestic issues, it did also for Royce's views on the international community. Working on the social application of the idea of interpretation when the fighting began in Europe, he turned the idea into an insurance plan for furthering peace and loyalty.

Under this plan, all nations would insure themselves against the losses due to war; a potential aggressor would be deterred by withholding compensation; other nations would cooperate to avoid war. Just as Royce saw the social and industrial insurance of Bismarck's Germany as an alternative to socialism, so he saw international insurance as an alternative to international socialism:

> It is not at all necessary to look towards the triumph of Socialism or of any other equally revolutionary social tendency, whether political or non-political, in order to foresee possible modes of international unification, which, if they were once tried . . . would almost certainly prove to be . . . conducive to a mutual understanding amongst the nations.[46]

Insurance, Royce believed, would "begin to make visible to us the holy city of the community of all mankind";[47] it thus made socialism obsolete. Royce's allegiance to capitalism on an international level paralleled the others' support of its more rational organization at home.

The Anti-Bureaucratic Bias

Before and after 1917 the political philosophy of these thinkers underlined the need for organization and expertise in modern American society. They welcomed the use of trained administrators in the fields of industrial regulation, transportation, and education; they recognized that in a large and interdependent society many problems exceeded the limits of old local boundaries, boundaries of neighborhood, city, and state. In the city, the ascendance of functional over geographical organization meant the rejection of ward-based politics for a commission or small council system with members elected at large rather than from local neighborhoods. It was the small council, assisted by a large number of appointed experts, which Howe advocated in *The City: The Hope of Democracy* (1905).[48] The reason for such innovations, Park noted, was an awareness of "the fact that the form of government which had its origin in the town meeting and was well suited to the needs of a small community based on primary relations is not suitable to the government of the changing and heterogeneous populations of cities of three or four millions."[49] A similar trend toward the functional organization of government on the state level was the "Wisconsin idea," also endorsed by Howe, which emphasized administrative efficiency, regulatory commissions, and the widespread use of experts.[50]

Despite their acceptance of functional organization, specialization of tasks, and planning, characteristics of what they called bureaucracy, these reformers had strong misgivings about such developments. Often their aversion to bureaucratic organization emerged as a plea for the kind of participation associated with the communities of the past. For instance, Park saw that the professionalization of welfare work was a logical response to the complexity of city life and to the decline of the neighborhood. But he regretted the decrease in civic participation which such expertise in this and other fields entailed.

In politics, religion, art and sport, we are represented now by proxies where formerly we participated in person. All the forms of communal and cultural activity in which we . . . formerly shared have been taken over by professionals and the great mass of men are no longer actors, but spectators.[51]

The results, Park reasoned, were the restlessness and the search for novelty on the part of people deprived in the "artificial" environment of the city of "natural" outlets for participation which small-town and rural society had once provided. He bolstered his argument with Jane Addams' testimony to the "contrasts between the warmth, the sincerity, and the wholesomeness of primary human responses and the sophistication, the coldness . . . of the secondary organization of urban life."[52] To satisfy the "baffled wish to participate"[53] required that urban neighborhoods and social institutions find ways for people to engage, both imaginatively and practically, in communal activities.[54]

A similar connection between their nervousness about bureaucracy and their attachment to the values of face-to-face community appeared in the attitude of Royce and Cooley toward public opinion. For Royce, "the small company of thoughtful individuals"[55] who met to discuss public affairs was an antidote to the mechanism of those large-scale organizations which dominated business and government. Face-to-face discussion counteracted feelings of helplessness and lack of initiative in the face of vast aggregations of power; it thus made possible responsible loyalty to a cause of one's own choosing. Cooley agreed with Royce on the importance of local publics as a remedy for institutional rigidity. In addition, he argued that the quick exchange of ideas within the larger public created by the communications revolution enabled this larger group to serve the same purpose as local publics did.[56]

Like their ideas on participation and public opinion, the political philosophy of the communitarians reflected their anti-bureaucratic bias. Dislike of remote, impersonal government led them to oppose statism of both the right and the left. Neither state capitalism, where government managed the economy, nor state socialism, where government owned the means of production, met their demands for flexibility, response to public opinion, and a sense of intimacy with social institutions.[57]

Most often they directed their criticism toward the left as the immediate danger, rejecting the socialist form of government while applauding its spirit of cooperation. According to Cooley, a "deadening uniformity and obliteration of alternatives [was] involved in the blanket socialism of the central state."[58] He encouraged experiments in municipal socialism precisely because they escaped that "remoteness from the fresher needs of the people"[59] which infected similar undertakings on the national level. Along with Cooley, Mary Follett's aversion to bureaucracy colored her views on reform. She always insisted that a cooperative social order begin at the grass roots lest the larger community become too mechanical. Political progress began on the local level where spontaneous cooperation flourished and provided the groundwork for political institutions. "We shall never know how to be one of a nation until we are one of a neighborhood,"[60] she argued. "We begin with the neighborhood group and create the state ourselves. Thus is the state built up through the intimate intertwining of all."[61] Imposing schemes from above was not the way to true collectivism.

> That state must be grown—its branches will widen as its roots spread. The socialization of property must not precede the socialization of the will. If it does, then the only difference between socialism and our present order will be substituting one machine for another. . . . Some people's idea of socialism is inventing a machine to grind out your duties for you. But every man must do his work for himself. Not socialization of property, but socialization of the will is the true socialism.[62]

Once this had been achieved, a flexible system of cooperation between business, labor, and government could stave off a bureaucratic form of collectivism.[63]

As a follower of Henry George, Frederic Howe put forward the most radical program for reform, but he too coupled his proposals for change with a distrust of statism. In fact his single tax plan was meant to achieve the aims of socialism without the "immeasurable bureaucracy" which a socialist system would bring.[64] He thought that the choice lay between the "industrial socialism" of Marx and the "industrial freedom" of George. Although the single tax would have radical consequences—public control of land, redistribution of wealth, and more spending for education, recreation, and transportation—it would require "no complicated organization of society, no bureaucracy, no increase in the functions of the state."[65] Howe occasionally thought that such administrative simplicity might be difficult to achieve in a modern industrial society, but this was a minor note. The main direction of his thought was toward reform without complexity. Indeed, his postwar enthusiasm for the cooperative movement in Denmark was linked to the ideal of collective effort without control by a remote government. In Howe's eyes the cooperative movement had the advantages of leaving most decisions to local producers and of fostering the "intimacy of the people with politics."[66] In contrast socialism meant a "mechanical justice"[67] which left no room for individual variety or local initiative. On this point, the others concurred.

The Retreat to the Small Community

The opposition to bureaucracy on the part of these reformers made them critical of socialist forms of community; it also led them to retreat to the local community. Their antipathy to the coldness of the larger society, together with their attachment to face-to-face communication and grass-roots democracy, made them cling to the small community as the *sine qua non* of a humane social order. Although they supported the drive to rationalize the functional organization of society, they also wanted a counterweight to its dangers. They tried to preserve the integrity of the small locality because it encouraged a sense of belonging; they tried to perpetuate the importance of local politics because it fostered civic and political participation. In many cases, however, their defense of the locality ran counter to their analysis of social trends. Generally, the communitarians contended that the factory, the city, and the new means of communication were destroying the vitality of the local community.[68] For instance, Howe maintained that the fate of the Cleveland-Pittsburgh corridor was an omen of the future. This strip would soon "become a vast semi-urban community interdependent and closely connected in its activities";[69] this pattern would repeat itself all over America. He also predicted the dispersion of the city population into the suburbs. These developments meant declining self-sufficiency for the separate units within the spreading metropolitan areas.[70] At the same time, Howe described the ideal city in terms of the more self-contained cities of the past. Except for areas like transportation, "the city [was] complete within itself."[71] Such a self-sufficient entity deserved the advantages of home rule and direct democracy, political devices which Howe explicitly equated with the town meeting.[72] These innovations, involving local control of health, education, taxation, and industry—some of which were in fact already coming under state control—would create a "city republic . . . a republic like unto those of Athens, Rome, and the mediaeval Italian cities."[73] The citizens of the modern Florence would be as loyal to their city as the burghers of the Middle Ages were to their towns; the modern city-dweller would participate as fully in public life as his counterpart in the colonial towns of New England.[74] Thus analysis and prescription conflicted in Howe's writing. Sharing with Howe this double perspective, White, Park, Dewey, and Royce also noted the forces which loosened the hold of the local community, while they continued to call for a more compelling local life.[75]

Among those who valued intimate community, William Allen White was the spokesman for the small town. Along with Royce, he was also the strongest critic of the city. Whereas Howe, Addams, Park, and Follett wanted to remake the city in the image of smaller and more cohesive forms of community, White, a lifelong resident of a midwestern town, wrote off the city. For him, intimate community equalled small-town community; both were threatened by the inroads of urbanization and industrialization.

In the *Gazette,* in articles and in novels, White carried on his crusade in behalf of small-town America. As he described it, the town had many virtues. It was small enough for people to feel that they knew each other; they were not isolated as they were in the crowded city or on the lonely farm. The small town exhibited fewer disparities of wealth than the city did; moreover the disparities which did exist in Emporia were more visible than those in New York and therefore more likely to arouse sympathy.

Only as we know each other well can we treat each other justly, and the city is a wilderness of careless strangers whose instincts of humanity are daily becoming more blunted to suffering, because in the nature of things suffering in cities must be impersonal. It is not the suffering of friends and neighbors . . . as it is in the smaller town.[76]

Not only did the town foster fraternity, but it also facilitated civic and political participation on the part of the citizenry. The average man knew more of the candidates and elected officials than his urban counterpart; his opinion carried more weight than the city-dweller's. Here the town, in contrast to the urban melting pot, had the benefit of a homogeneous population with an Anglo-Saxon tradition of self-government. White clearly equated what he deemed the American virtues—fraternity, equality, and civic participation—with the virtues of small-town life. Moreover, he was uncertain that they could survive the decline of the small community; the American town had nourished these virtues and in comparison all other forms of living together were barren ground.[77]

The key to the importance of the small locality in White's writing went beyond questions of size and homogeneity, however. The archetypical town was the "country town," a settlement which served as a service center for the farmer and had little or no industry.[78] As editor of the Emporia *Gazette,* White himself exhibited the booster spirit, encouraging population growth, the coming of a canning factory and an iron foundry; but after 1906, his editorials were less enthusiastic about more factories for Emporia.[79] At the same time, a jaundiced view of industrialization appeared in his novels. The story of two country towns, Sycamore Ridge in *A Certain Rich Man* (1909) and Harvey in *In the Heart of a Fool* (1918), was the story of an industrial assault on the fabric of community. In both cases the towns were ruined by the domination of the factory, whose headquarters were in the city—the city whose god was Mammon. As Sycamore Ridge and Harvey were trapped in "the spider web" of pipes and rails, the inhabitants lost their local pride and the inclination to temper the profit motive with considerations of local loyalty or social sympathy.[80] But White was no latter-day Luddite. Elsewhere he accepted the industrial order of twentieth-century America and supported Theodore Roosevelt's efforts to reform it along the lines of the New Nationalism.[81] Perhaps the clue to the puzzle lay in the setting of the novels. Both stories were set in the Midwest, and as he argued in his Harvard lectures on *The Changing West* (1939), the rural civilization of farms and country towns was the backbone of America. While the industrial sector was being tamed, the small-town society of the Midwest which gave us "the gospel of a fraternal equality"[82] had to be preserved as the guarantee of true community.

Whereas White defended the small town against the city, Park tried to foster "a new parochialism," a return to neighborhood loyalty within urban society. This effort was complicated by his sure grasp of the conflict between the bureaucratic-functional organization of human life and the local or neighborhood organization which he wished to see revived.[83] In "The City" (1915), Park diagnosed the kind of social order produced by mobility, technology, and the division of labor. By freeing the individual from the close supervision of the neighborhood, these forces paved the way for new forms of social control—the school, the courts, the press. Their political equivalents were the commission government, the bureau of municipal research and the good government association, institutions which "have sought to represent the interests of the city as a whole and have appealed to a sentiment and opinion neither local nor personal."[84] Park saw the logic and the utility of this development clearly enough, but he sometimes refused to accept his own corollary—the eclipse of the local community. Witnessing the decline of the neighborhood in the city, he continually looked for ways to revive it.

The survival of local community in an urban environment was a matter of considerable urgency for Park for a number of reasons. Secondary groups were too impersonal to fulfill the need for personal response and self-expression; for this reason, they did not compel the allegiance or affection of the urbanite, who slipped away from their grasp and was "everywhere hunting the bluebird of romance, . . . hunting it with automobiles and flying machines."[85] The romantic impulse, in short, made men neglect their duty to the community when this duty was too impersonal. In addition, Park's hope for larger communities, both nationwide and citywide, declined sharply in the 1920's. His pessimism stemmed in part from the postwar collapse of public spirit; Park used Lippmann's *Public Opinion* (1922) to confirm his sense that the people could not be constantly aroused about issues beyond their immediate circle. But he was also disturbed by the conversion of the enlightening potential of publicity into propaganda and "the subtle tyranny of the advertising man."[86] The legacy of Creel's paper bullets, which had won the war, was obstructing rational public opinion in the larger community.

Disillusioned about the prospects of the Great Community, Park turned back to the small one. In 1923, the same year that he echoed Lippmann's views on the national mind, Park called for "more attention and interest for the little world of the locality."[87] In "Community Organization and the Romantic Temper" (1923) and in *Old World Traits Transplanted* (1921) he pointed to the immigrant colonies of the city as the model for neighborhood building. Their mutual aid societies, newspapers, recreational centers, and churches made an intimate local life possible.[88] And such local inclusiveness should be imitated.

It represents the individual's responsibility to society which we have in a measure lost, and are consciously attempting to restore by the reorganization of the local community. It is a type of organization which can be made the basis of all kinds of co-operative enterprise— the basis, in fact, on which the local community will again function.[89]

Slighting the forces which he elsewhere saw undermining this type of community, ignoring for the moment the transitory nature of the immigrant enclaves, which he thought subject to the same dispersive forces as other local communities, Park sought salvation there.[90] But he was not to find it, either in theory or in practice.

An advocate of the small community in his writing, Park also took part in an unsuccessful attempt at community building. From 1922 to 1924, he was president of the National Community Center Association, whose headquarters were in Chicago.[91] Park saw the community center as an alternative to the ward organization of the urban machine, combining the latter's admirable emphasis on personal relationships with more participation by the citizenry than the boss system allowed.[92] However, the community center movement, which had been stimulated by the war, soon foundered in its attempt to strengthen neighborhood communities and to organize political interests outside the regular party machinery. And Park witnessed this failure on his own doorstep.

In *The Gold Coast and the Slum* (1929), one of Park's students documented the demise of the community council experiment on Chicago's Lower North Side.[93] Park's Introduction to the book noted "the difficulty of maintaining in the city the intimate contacts which in the small town insured the existence of a common purpose and made concerted action possible."[94] The Introduction was an epitaph for a cause which by then seemed hopeless.

John Dewey made his final case for the local community in the same decade that Park entered his final plea. In *The Public and Its Problems* (1927), Dewey juxtaposed the functional, large-scale mode of association and the local community. "In developing the Great Society," he wrote, "[the machine age] has invaded and partially disintegrated the small communities of former times."[95] The result was the "eclipse of the public";[96] the public, that is, the individuals affected by the consequences of an act, could no longer understand or control the economic, technological, and social forces impinging upon it because the industrial age aligned these forces "on an impersonal rather than a community basis."[97] Dewey's desire to strengthen local publics was at one with his desire to salvage the small community. Of course his attachment to this type of association was nothing new. Two decades before, he had described the ideal school as a face-to-face community designed to reincarnate in itself and in the surrounding society the values of the old local community.[98] But by the 1920's he had lost faith in the ability of education to reconstruct intimate community outside the walls of the school. A more direct solution was necessary, and it was all the more important because the prospects for community on the national level seemed so dim.

The solution involved the stimulation and organization of public opinion at the grass roots. Intent as always on the promise of the communications media for the larger community, he nonetheless allowed that the Great Community, as he called it, could never have what the small community had—warmth and immediacy. It followed that public opinion would be fully mobilized on issues of general or national importance only when it grew from "personal intercourse in the local community."[99] For "the connections of the ear with vital and out-going thought and

emotion are immensely closer . . . than those of the eye."[100] Dewey
did recognize that the kind of personal exchange which he referred to was not restricted to the local group; at one point he
even suggested that occupational associations be the focus of a
reorganized public. But because he feared their tendency toward
impersonality, he rejected them as alternatives to local community. Like Mary Follett, for whom the neighborhood had
more cohesion and cogency than occupational groups, Dewey
maintained that the locality best fostered the "vital, steady, and
deep relationships which are present only in an immediate community."[101] He even went so far as to say that "something deep
within human nature itself . . . pulls toward settled relationships."[102] Here Dewey's appeal to the innate ran parallel to Park's.
Both looked upon the restlessness, "the mania for motion" in
modern times as a substitute for the more satisfying gratifications
of primary group life.[103] But along with Park, Dewey gave up on
the local community as the foundation of a cooperative social
order before the decade ended. Following the failure of the communications revolution and of the schools to transform society in
anticipated ways, the appeal to a grass-roots movement was a last
attempt to save the system without resorting to basic changes.
With the crash of 1929, he gave up this attempt. In *Individualism
Old and New* (1929), written after the onset of the depression, he
finally argued the need for "some kind of socialism."[104]

Royce's prescription for provincialism represented a more serious retreat from the problems of the national society than did
Dewey's plea for local community, for Royce was more pessimistic
about changing the social order as a whole. Granted that his
writing on the province belonged to the years 1902 to 1909, and
that he later worked out ways of forming the bonds of wider
community; still, he did not move as far from his original position as one might think. For one thing, he never explained the
relation between his early views on local community and his
later views on the communities of interpretation represented by
the banking, judicial, and insurance communities.[105] More important, at the time he spelled out the philosophy of interpretation as a means to social loyalty, Royce still regarded the larger

society as a source of estrangement.[106] The province continued
as the guarantee of a sense of belonging and initiative if only by
default. Thus the answer of 1902 was still applicable to the later
period.

> I should say to-day that our national unities have grown so vast, our
> forces of social consolidation have become so paramount . . . that we,
> too, must flee in the pursuit of the ideal to a new realm. . . . It is the
> realm of the province. . . . There we must flee, I mean, not in the
> sense of a cowardly and permanent retirement, but in the sense of a
> search for renewed strength. . . . Freedom, I should say, dwells now
> in the small social group, and has its securest home in provincial life.
> . . . The province must save the individual.[107]

Nowhere in his later writings did he revise this estimate.

In his philosophy of provincialism, Royce was defending more
than regionalism; he was, in fact, implicitly defending the small
community. Although he put no upper limit on the size of a
province—it could be a city, a county, or a region so long as it
was conscious of its unity—he described it in terms which often
precluded bigness. Large cities, for example, did not lend themselves to the growth of local pride because they were often in-
habited by "wanderers without a community, sojourners with a
dwelling-place, but with no home, citizens of the world, who have
no local attachments."[108] He then contrasted the mob spirit, which
fed on metropolitan newspapers and the instability of urban life,
with the thoughtful discussion of civic issues by the small group.
It was the latter which contributed to a wise provincialism by
counteracting "the discipline of an impersonal social order"[109] and
by making the individual feel a moral responsibility for the
affairs of his own community.[110]

The province, then, was the small community and small communities were the building blocks of national loyalty. Unions and
political parties were too partisan to further the general good, or
what Royce called loyalty to loyalty. Grand schemes for reform,
such as the single tax, free silver, or socialism were too vague and
millenial to do anything but divert energies which might better

be directed to modest but effective efforts to improve public life.[111] In an address "On Certain Limitations of the Thoughtful Public in America," he noted that "our greatest national danger now lies in an extravagant love of ideally fascinating enterprises, whose practical results are . . . hard to foresee."[112] Provincial loyalty avoided this futile humanitarianism while it built up devotion to the common good. The province, in Royce's view, was "the best mediator between the narrower interests of the individual and the larger patriotism of our nation."[113] It was the way to overcome the *"self-estranged spirit"*[114] of the larger society.

Although Royce was the most politically conservative member of the group, his retreat to a local solution was shared by all. The Progressive intellectuals regarded the small community as the remedy for estrangement and rootlessness, the antidote for bureaucratic collectivism, and the prescription for moral commitment to the common good. Along with their faith in technology, however, their reliance on the curative powers of the local community blunted the edge of their social criticism and drew their attention away from the need for a basic transformation of American society.

Postscript

The communitarians of the Progressive era sought the answer to the problems of the national society in the intimate, face-to-face relations of the small group. By making local community a prerequisite for all wider forms of community, by insisting that only there could one truly "belong," they turned away from the possibility of a major restructuring of their society on the national level. In addition, their belief that the communications revolution would extend the values of the small community to the larger society and thereby solve many social problems simply reinforced their indifference to fundamental change. These intellectuals put great store by the right kind of communication; the key to the Great Community seemed to lie in the knowledge and sympathy created by face-to-face exchange and in the extraordinary scope given to these forces of solidarity by the new communications media. But this focus left the social structure untouched insofar as it assumed the continued hegemony of a market economy. The important question facing Progressive intellectuals was how to create community on such a foundation. That question was not answered adequately by their recourse to the small locality. In the decades that followed, the question still did not receive a satisfactory answer, but the ideal of decentralization and of the small group has again gained support as the best solution to the elusive problem of community. The ideal has much to recommend it in view of the increasing anonymity, impersonality, and rationalization of modern life, but it presents some of the same difficulties today that it did in the earlier period. The new localism raises again the issue of conflicting kinds of social organization; radical decentralization may be too much at odds with rational planning, and functional organization to be an acceptable alternative to what we have. That remains to be seen.

More serious are the political implications. As Royce's provincialism once ignored the larger outlines of his society, so too do contemporary arguments for decentralization and community control ignore the larger society in which local community is supposed to flourish. But unless there is a fundamental change of priorities in the society as a whole, decentralization will tend to perpetuate the conflicts and inequalities which already exist. It is discomforting to hear suggestions that the New Left, the old right, the black militants, and the liberal center should close ranks behind the cause of decentralization, because—whatever its attractiveness and ultimate workability—at this stage it cannot deal adequately with poverty, racism, and an environment which everywhere undercuts the physical basis for community. An ideal of community which does not do justice to these problems may have very important things to say, but it is far from being the total answer it sometimes claims to be.

Notes

1. This attitude is best expressed by Louis Hartz in *The Liberal Tradition in America,* New York, 1955, pp. 239–243. Hartz contends that the Progressives moved in the direction of European thinkers like T. H. Green and Mazzini but "could not follow through, for to arrive at the communitarian doctrines of the new European liberals, let alone of the socialists, would have spelled the end of the Alger taboo." *Ibid.,* p. 238. Recently, there has been some interest in the idea of community in late nineteenth- and twentieth-century America. See Morton White and Lucia White, *The Intellectual versus the City: From Thomas Jefferson to Frank Lloyd Wright,* Cambridge, Mass., 1962; R. Jackson Wilson, *In Quest of Community: Social Philosophy in the United States, 1860–1920,* New York, 1968. Wilson, who treats the idea of community directly, is less interested in social theory, however, than in the psychological and moral meaning for certain thinkers of the late nineteenth-century critique of individualism.

2. I certainly do not claim an invariable connection between this generation's small-town background and a particular set of attitudes toward community. Not only were other forces at work which influenced the ideas of the group under consideration here, but there were men such as Thorstein Veblen, E. H. Howe, and Hamlin Garland, who were from similar, if not identical backgrounds, but who were critical of the small town and its values.

3. Their dates are: White (1868–1944), Howe (1867–1940), Addams (1860–1935), Follett (1868–1933), Dewey (1859–1952), Royce (1855–1916), Giddings (1855–1931), Cooley (1864–1929), Park (1864–1944). Although Giddings, Cooley, and Park are sometimes assigned to different phases of American sociology, the evolutionary approach to the study of sociology and the interest in similar kinds of reform link them together.

4. William Allen White, *The Autobiography of William Allen White,* New York, 1946, p. 484; Lewis S. Feuer, "John Dewey and the

Back to the People Movement in American Thought," *Journal of the History of Ideas*, XX, October-December, 1959, 555–557; James Weber Linn, *Jane Addams: A Biography*, New York, 1935, p. 234; Jane Addams, *Democracy and Social Ethics*, New York, 1902, pp. 180–192; *The Spirit of Youth and the City Streets*, New York, 1909, pp. 108–109, 135–146; Robert E. Park and Ernest W. Burgess, *Introduction to the Science of Sociology*, Chicago, 1921, pp. 328–329.

5. Charles Horton Cooley, Journal, 1897, Charles Horton Cooley Papers, Michigan Historical Collections, The University of Michigan.

6. Charles Horton Cooley, Student Notebook, 1894, Cooley Papers.

7. Feuer, *JHI*, XX, 549–553; Ralph B. Perry, *The Thought and Character of William James*, Boston, 1935, II, 518–519; Robert E. Park, *Race and Culture*, ed. Everett Cherrington Hughes, *et al.*, Glencoe, Ill., 1950, v.

8. Mary Parker Follett, *The New State*, New York, 1918, pp. 58–59. Follett studied at Radcliffe from 1888 to 1898 and may have worked with Royce. Frederick T. Persons, "Follett, Mary Parker," *Dictionary of American Biography*, 1944, XXI, Supplement One, 308–309; *The Harvard University Catalogue: 1889–1890*, Cambridge, Mass., 1889, p. 48. Addams praised Follett's *Creative Experience*, a book about communication as a social process in Jane Addams, *The Second Twenty years at Hull-House: September 1909 to September 1929*, New York, 1930, pp. 202–203.

9. Frederic C. Howe, *The Modern City and Its Problems*, New York, 1915, pp. 305–306.

10. Franklin H. Giddings, *Studies in the Theory of Human Society*, New York, 1922, pp. 61–62; Park, *Science of Sociology*, pp. 31–42, 285–287.

11. According to the census of 1880, the population of these towns was as follows: Sherman, Conn. (Giddings) 828; El Dorado, Kan. (White) 1,411; Red Wing, Minn. (Park) 5,876; Meadville, Pa. (Howe) 8,860; Quincy, Mass. (Follett) 10,570; Burlington, Vt. (Dewey) 11,365. *Compendium of the Tenth Census, June 1, 1880*, Washington, D. C., 1883, I, 80, 141, 175, 186, 189, 269, 311. Cedarville, Ill., (Addams) had a population of 300 in 1900. Before 1900 it was listed under three townships. *Twelfth Census of the United States taken in the year 1900*, Washington, D. C., 1901, I, 131. There are no census figures for Grass Valley, Cal. (Royce). By 1854, the town had three churches and a school. John Clendenning, "Introduction," *The Letters of Josiah Royce*, Chicago, 1970, pp. 10–11.

12. Anselm L. Strauss, *Images of the American City*, New York, 1961, p. 194; Lewis Atherton, *Main Street on the Middle Border*, Bloomington, Ind., 1954, pp. 181–182.

13. Frederic C. Howe, *The Confessions of a Reformer*, New York, 1925, pp. 11–13.

14. *Ibid.*, p. 5. For evidence on this point see Atherton, *Main Street*, pp. 181–185. The nineteenth-century American town did not have the physical isolation or economic self-sufficiency of the medieval village, but density of interaction in the small and relatively isolated American town was sufficient to create a sense of mutual identification. Scott Greer, "Individual Participation in Mass Society," in *Approaches to the Study of Politics*, ed. Roland Young, Evanston, Ill., 1958, pp. 330–341.

15. William Allen White, "The Country Newspaper," *Harper's Magazine*, CXXXII, May, 1916, 891.

16. Atherton, *Main Street*, pp. 181–185; Page Smith, *As a City upon a Hill: The Town in American History*, New York, 1966, pp. 183–213.

17. Jane Addams, *Newer Ideals of Peace*, New York, 1907, p. 215.

18. Howe, *Confessions*, pp. 5, 12, 17, 320–321; Atherton, *Main Street*, pp. 181–183. For a critique of Riesman's concept of the inner-directed man of the nineteenth century, see Carl Degler, "The Sociologist as Historian," *The American Quarterly*, XV, Winter, 1963, 483–497.

19. George Dykhuizen, "John Dewey: The Vermont Years," *Journal of the History of Ideas*, XX, October-December, 1959, 518; William Allen White, "Emporia and New York," *American Magazine*, LXIII, January, 1907, 261; Merle Curti, *The Making of an American Community: A Case Study of Democracy in a Frontier County*, Stanford, Cal., 1959, pp. 109–110; Atherton, *Main Street*, pp. 101–105. The larger, older, and more industrialized the town, the more stratification there was. Smith, *City upon a Hill*, pp. 157–182; Stephan Thernstrom, *Poverty and Progress: Social Mobility in a Nineteenth Century City*, Cambridge, Mass., 1964, pp. 9, 33, 169–171.

20. Stanley Elkins and Eric McKitrick, "A Meaning for Turner's Frontier Thesis: Part I: Democracy in the Old Northwest," *Political Science Quarterly*, LXIX, September, 1954, 321–353; "A Meaning for Turner's Frontier Thesis: Part II: The Southwest Frontier and New England," *Political Science Quarterly*, LXIX, December, 1954, 565–602; Solon T. Kimball and James E. McClellan, *Education and the New America*, New York, 1962, pp. 84–85; Atherton, *Main Street*, p. 190.

21. White, *Autobiography*, pp. 4–5, 74–75. See also Howe, *Confessions*, p. 12; Jane Addams, *Twenty Years at Hull-House*, New York, 1910, pp. 1, 13–14.

22. White, *Autobiography*, p. 74.

23. Dykhuizen, JHI, XX, 515–518; Jane Dewey, ed. "Biography of John Dewey," *The Philosophy of John Dewey*, ed. Paul Arthur Schilpp, Evanston, Ill., 1939, p. 3.

24. Hartz, *Liberal Tradition*, p. 55.

25. Elkins and McKitrick, *PSQ*, LXIX, 321–353, 583–601.

26. The town meeting had disappeared in many places by the midnineteenth century. Constance McLaughlin Green, *American Cities in the Growth of the Nation*, New York, 1965, p. 34.

27. Giddings, *Studies in Theory*, p. 64. See also "The American People," *International Quarterly*, VII, June, 1903, 293; *Democracy and Empire: With Studies of Their Psychological, Economic, and Moral Foundations*, New York, 1900, p. 245. The essay referred to here was first published in 1898. Hereafter the date of an essay which appears in a collection of essays by the same author will be placed in parentheses at the end of the note.

28. Follett, *New State*, pp. 212, 223, 256.

29. Jane Addams, *Twenty Years*, p. 38. See pp. 38–42. Cedarville was settled in 1849. Linn, *Addams*, p. 15.

30. Linn, *Addams*, pp. 11–16; Addams, *Twenty Years*, pp. 13–14, 30, 34–36.

31. White, *Autobiography*, p. 138. See pp. 42, 51, 66. El Dorado was settled in 1867. Similarly, Park's youth coincided with the early days of Red Wing, Minn., which was settled in 1852. C. A. Rasmussen, *A History of the City of Red Wing, Minnesota*. Privately printed, 1933, pp. 37–45.

32. White, *American Magazine*, LXIII, 260, 264; *The Changing West*, New York, 1939, pp. 2, 9, 12, 81–86.

33. Josiah Royce, "Autobiographical Sketch," *The Hope of the Great Community*, New York, 1916, pp. 122–123. See also Clendenning, ed. *Letters of Royce*, pp. 65, 77, 93.

34. Josiah Royce, "Provincialism," *Putnam's Magazine*, VII, November, 1909, 235.

35. *Ibid.*, p. 234.

36. Josiah Royce, *California: From the Conquest in 1846 to the Second Vigilance Committee in San Francisco; a Study in American Character*, New York, 1948, p. 366. See also pp. 3, 182, 221, 250, 339–344.

37. Royce, *California,* xii.

38. Royce, *Putnam's,* VII, 237.

39. Royce, *Hope,* p. 129.

40. White, *Autobiography,* p. 105; Howe, *Confessions,* p. 16; Addams, *Twenty Years,* pp. 14–15, 49–50.

41. Cooley, Journal, 1882; Dykhuizen, *JHI,* XX, 521; John L. Gillin, "Franklin Henry Giddings," in *American Masters of Social Science,* ed. Howard W. Odum, New York, 1927, p. 196.

42. Sarah Royce, *A Frontier Lady: Recollections of the Gold Rush and Early California,* ed. Ralph Henry Gabriel, New Haven, Conn., 1932, p. 44. Italics Royce's.

43. Howe, *Confessions,* p. 17.

44. Richard Hofstadter, *The Age of Reform: From Bryan to F.D.R.,* New York, 1955, p. 205.

45. Cooley, Journal, 1890; Howe, *Confessions,* pp. 16–17; White, *West,* pp. 28–33; Addams, *Twenty Years,* pp. 3, 5, 13–14.

46. Howe, *Confessions,* p. 17.

47. H. Richard Niebuhr, *The Kingdom of God in America,* New York, 1937, pp. 172–181.

48. Sydney E. Ahlstrom, "Theology in America: A Historical Survey," in *Religion in American Life,* eds. James Ward Smith and A. Leland Jamison, Princeton, N. J., 1961, I, 280–286; Herbert Wallace Schneider, *Religion in 20th Century America,* Cambridge, Mass., 1952, pp. 117–119; Winthrop S. Hudson, *The Great Tradition of the American Churches,* New York, 1953, pp. 160–161; Daniel Day Williams, *The Andover Liberals,* New York, 1941, pp. 69–74, 114–132.

49. Theodore Munger, *The Freedom of Faith,* Boston, 1893, p. 24.

50. White, *Autobiography,* p. 107.

51. Gillin, *American Masters,* p. 176.

52. Jane Dewey, *Philosophy of John Dewey,* p. 17.

53. White, *Autobiography,* p. 105.

54. Howe, *Confessions,* p. 58.

55. Addams, *Twenty Years,* pp. 49–50. Cooley refused to join the Congregational Church in Ann Arbor. Cooley, Journal, 1882.

56. Royce, *Hope,* pp. 279–280; *The Problem of Christianity,* New York, 1913, I, 8, 10–12.

57. Dykhuizen, *JHI,* XX, 528–536; John Blewett, S. J., "Democracy as Religion: Unity in Human Relations," in *John Dewey: His Thought and Influence,* ed. John Blewett, S. J., New York, 1960, p. 47.

58. Paul E. Johnson, "Josiah Royce: Theist or Pantheist?", *Harvard Theological Review*, XXI, July, 1928, 197–205.

59. Gillin, *American Masters*, p. 197.

60. Giddings, *Democracy*, pp. 319–320 (1899); *International Quarterly*, VII, 293; Addams, *Twenty Years*, p. 50; White, *Autobiography*, pp. 105–108; Cooley, Journal, 1882; Charles Horton Cooley, *Human Nature and the Social Order*, New York, 1902, pp. 211–214; *Social Organization: a Study of the Larger Mind*, Introduction by Philip Rieff, New York, 1962, pp. 374–381; Edward C. Jandy, *Charles Horton Cooley: His Life and His Social Theory*, New York, 1942, pp. 43–46.

61. John Dewey, *On Experience, Nature and Freedom: Representative Selections*, ed. Richard J. Bernstein, New York, 1960, pp. 10–12 (1930).

62. Howe, *Confessions*, p. 5.

63. Royce, *Hope*, pp. 128–129; Josiah Royce, *Fugitive Essays*, ed. J. Loewenberg, Cambridge, Mass., 1920, pp. 69, 111–129 (1880); Vincent Buranelli, *Josiah Royce*, New York, 1964, pp. 84–87.

64. Park, *Race*, vi; *Science of Sociology*, pp. 331, 349–350; Don Martindale, *The Nature and Types of Sociological Theory*, Boston, 1960, pp. 253–255. Meanwhile Giddings began to study economics as part of the social organism and this led him to sociology. Letter from Franklin Giddings to J. B. Clark, October 24, 1886, John B. Clark Papers, Columbia University, New York; Franklin H. Giddings, "The Sociological Character of Political Economy," *Proceedings of the American Economic Association*, III, March, 1888, 29–47.

65. Persons, *DAB*, XXI, 308; Follett, *New State*, pp. 261–262, 267, 308–309, 326, 330.

66. Addams, *Twenty Years*, p. 37. John C. Farrell, *Beloved Lady: A History of Jane Addams' Ideas on Reform and Peace*, Baltimore, 1967, pp. 44–65.

67. Jandy, *Cooley*, p. 29; William Seagle, "Thomas McIntyre Cooley," *Encyclopedia of the Social Sciences*, 1931, IV, 357; O. Douglas Weeks, "Some Political Ideas of Thomas McIntyre Cooley," *The Southwestern Political and Social Science Quarterly*, VI, June, 1925, 30–39; Charles Horton Cooley, *Sociological Theory and Social Research*, New York, 1930, pp. 117–118 (1894).

68. White, *Autobiography*, pp. 162–171, 187, 286, 297–299, 325; Walter Johnson, *William Allen White's America*, New York, 1947, pp. 7, 107–109.

69. Maurice R. Stein, *The Eclipse of Community: An Interpretation of American Studies, Princeton, N. J.,* 1960, pp. 88–92, 107; Atherton, *Main Street,* pp. 217–242.

70. Blake McKelvey, *The Urbanization of America: 1860–1915,* New Brunswick, N. J., 1963, pp. 139, 196; Robert C. Wood, *Suburbia: Its People and Their Politics,* Boston, 1959, p. 103. These developments had begun at least as early as the second decade of the century. Richard C. Wade, *The Urban Frontier: Pioneer Life in Early Pittsburgh, Cincinatti, Lexington, and St. Louis,* Chicago, 1964, pp. 203–230.

71. Feuer, *JHI,* XX, 545-568; Stein, *Eclipse,* p. 16.

72. Jane Addams, "The Subjective Necessity for Social Settlements," in *Philanthropy and Social Progress,* ed. Henry C. Adams, New York, 1893, p. 4.

73. *Ibid.,* p. 23.

74. John Dewey, "The School as Social Center," *Proceedings of the National Education Association,* 1902, p. 381.

75. Robert E. Park, "The City: Suggestions for the Investigation of Human Behavior in the Urban Environment," in *The City,* by R. E. Park, E. W. Burgess, and R. D. McKenzie, Chicago, 1925, pp. 1–46 (1915).

76. Sam B. Warner, *Streetcar Suburbs: The Process of Growth in Boston, 1870–1900,* Cambridge, Mass., 1962.

77. *Ibid.,* pp. 19–46; Persons, *DAB,* XXI, 308.

78. Henry C. Metcalf and L. Urwick, "Introduction," *Dynamic Administration: The Collected Papers of Mary Parker Follett,* New York, 1940, p. 11.

79. Richard C. Cabot, "Mary Parker Follett, An Appreciation," *Radcliffe Quarterly,* April, 1934, p. 81. See Follett, *New State,* pp. 363–373 for a description of her early work with community centers.

80. Follett, *New State,* p. 240. Italics Follett's.

81. Howe, *Confessions,* p. 113.

82. *Ibid.,* pp. 6, 113–114.

83. *Emporia Gazette,* Feb. 1, 1912.

84. Franklin H. Giddings, *The Principles of Sociology: An Analysis of the Phenomena of Association and Social Organization,* New York, 1896, pp. 350–351; *Readings in Descriptive and Historical Sociology,* New York, 1906, pp. 296, 496–498; *The Elements of Sociology,* New York, 1898, pp. 6–8, 180–181, 193–200; Cooley, *Social Organization,* pp. 20, 25–26, 45, 193, 305, 349, 352–355; Robert E. Park, *Society: Col-*

lective Behavior, News and Opinion, Sociology and Modern Society, ed. Everett Cherrington Hughes *et al.,* Glencoe, Ill., 1955, pp. 283–284 (1931); "Community Organization and Juvenile Delinquency," in *The City,* by R. E. Park, E. W. Burgess, and R. D. McKenzie, Chicago, 1925, pp. 103, 107 (1923); pp. 1–14 (1915); Josiah Royce, *Race Questions, Provincialism and other American Problems,* New York, 1908, pp. 55–108 (1902); Dewey, *Proceedings of the NEA,* 1902, pp. 373–383; Follett, *New State,* pp. 49, 74, 80–81, 200–201; Frederic C. Howe, *The City: The Hope of Democracy,* New York, 1905, p. 45; Addams, *Spirit of Youth,* pp. 109, 141, 146; William Allen White, *The Old Order Changeth,* New York, 1910, pp. 4–5, 7.

85. Cooley, *Social Organization,* p. 247.

86. Graham Wallas, *The Great Society: A Psychological Analysis,* New York, 1914. See Park, *Science of Sociology,* pp. 162, 422; *Society,* pp. 311–313 (1940), 327 (1942); John Dewey, *The Public and Its Problems,* New York, 1927, p. 142; Follett, *New State,* p. 14.

87. For the influence of Tönnies and Simmel on this generation of American sociologists, see Roscoe C. Hinkle and Gisela J. Hinkle, *The Development of Modern Sociology: Its Nature and Growth in the United States,* Garden City, N.Y., 1954, p. 17, n. 4. Durkheim's distinction between mechanical and organic solidarity and its influence on Giddings, Park, and E. A. Ross is noted by Roscoe C. Hinkle, Jr., "Durkheim in American Sociology," in *Emile Durkheim, 1858–1917: A Collection of Essays with Translations and a Bibliography,* ed. Kurt H. Wolff, Columbus, Ohio, 1960, pp. 268–269, 276. The dominance of the *Gemeinschaft-Gesellschaft* schema from this time through the 1930's is mentioned by Edward Shils, "The Contemplation of Society in America," in *Paths of American Thought,* eds. Arthur M. Schlesinger, Jr., and Morton White, Boston, 1963, pp. 392–410.

88. Sir Henry Maine, *Ancient Law: Its Connection with the Early History of Society, and Its Relation to Modern Ideas,* New York, 1884, pp. 109–165; first published in 1861; Herbert Spencer, *The Principles of Sociology,* Westminster edition, New York, 1896, I–2, 556–571, II–2, 572–573, 603–608; first published 1876–1897; Ferdinand Tönnies, *Fundamental Concepts of Sociology,* trans. and ed. Charles P. Loomis, New York, 1940, pp. 37, 58, 74–88, 120, 154, 223–224; first published in 1887; Emile Durkheim, *The Division of Labor in Society,* trans. George Simpson, Glencoe, Ill., 1960, pp. 127–129, 130–131, 167, 172, 366; first published in 1893; Georg Simmel, *The Sociology of Georg Simmel,* trans. Kurt H. Wolff, Glencoe, Ill., 1950, pp. 409–423 (1902–1903).

89. The shift from a society of small intimate groups to a large-scale urban, industrial society was central to the works read and mentioned by the three Americans. Maine's work was cited by Giddings in *Principles,* pp. 265, 431 and read by Cooley. See Cooley, *Sociological Theory,* p. 5 (1930). Spencer was cited frequently by all, but figured most prominently in Giddings' work. Cf. Spencer, *Principles,* I–2, 452–453, 472–473; II–2, 618–638 and Giddings, *Principles,* pp. 300–302; *Elements,* pp. 6–8, 180–200, 267–289, 302–307. See also Cooley, *Sociological Theory,* pp. 4–5 (1928), 263–279 (1920); *Social Organization,* p. 92; Park, *Science of Sociology,* pp. 24–27. Tönnies was mentioned by Park, *Ibid.,* pp. 100–102, 940, but his *Gemeinschaft und Gesellschaft,* Leipzig, 1897, was not discussed by Park until much later. Park, *Race,* p. 12 (1931). Park's essay is an instance of the rare borrowing of terminology as opposed to the frequent borrowing of ideas. Durkheim was discussed by Giddings in *Principles,* p. 15, and in *Studies in Theory,* pp. 61–62, by Cooley in *Social Process,* New York, 1922, p. 400. His discussion of the notion of solidarity in French sociology also suggests acquaintance with Durkheim, though Cooley's reluctance to cite sources makes the origins of his ideas difficult to pin down. Park mentioned Durkheim in *Science of Sociology,* but Simmel was the greatest influence on him. *Science of Sociology,* pp. 33–34, 286, 322–327, 349–350, 714. Park also used the Americans, Sumner and W. I. Thomas, as well as Cooley on the primary group. Park, *Science of Sociology,* pp. 285–287, 420–421, 488–490; *Society,* pp. 244–248 (1931).

90. Cooley, *Social Organization,* p. 23, 26. Robert E. Park and Herbert E. Miller, *Old World Traits Transplanted,* New York, 1921, p. 38. Park, in *The City,* p. 23.

91. Park, *Science of Sociology,* p. 287. See Giddings, *Principles,* pp. 347–351; *The Western Hemisphere in the World of Tomorrow,* New York, 1915, pp. 31–33; Cooley, *Social Organization,* pp. 352–355, 357–369; Park, *Society,* p. 341 (1942); *Old World,* p. 262; *The City,* p. 22.

92. Some of the sources which they drew on included Graham Wallas, whose *Great Society* described the eclipse of small communities. He was cited by Follett, *New State,* p. 14, and by Dewey, *Public,* p. 142. Royce used Hegel in *The Philosophy of Loyalty,* New York, 1908, pp. 238–241. The writings of Howe, Addams, and Follett show traces of the germ theory of history, which sought the origins of American democratic institutions like the town meeting in the folkmootes of Teutonic villages and in the local institutions of English towns and parishes. Howe was greatly influenced by Albert Shaw, a colleague at

Johns Hopkins of Herbert Baxter Adams, the founder of the germ theory. Shaw, like Adams, stressed the Anglo-Saxon origins of local self-government in America. Howe, *Confessions,* pp. 5–6; Albert Shaw, "Local Government in Illinois," *Johns Hopkins University Studies in Historical and Political Science,* III, Baltimore, 1883, 5–19; Jane Addams discussed folk-motes and mirs as models for a revitalized local life in *Newer Ideals,* p. 121, and in "Problems of Municipal Administration," *The American Journal of Sociology,* X, January, 1905, 426–428. Follett also incorporated the germ theory in her philosophy of localism in *New State,* pp. 256–257.

93. Howe, *The City,* pp. 17, 19, 32, 45; Addams, *Second Twenty Years,* p. 412; White, *American Magazine,* LXIII, 258–264; Follett, *New State,* pp. 200–201; Royce, *Putnam's,* VII, 234; Dewey, *Proceedings of the NEA,* 1902, p. 373–383.

94. Royce, *Race Questions,* p. 61. See p. 97 (1902); *Loyalty,* pp. 241–242.

95. Park, *Science of Sociology,* p. 287; *Society,* pp. 147–148. (1918).

96. Addams, *Newer Ideals,* p. 216. See Giddings, *Principles,* pp. 350–351; *Elements,* pp. 7–8, 220–221; White, *Harpers,* CXXXII, 887–891; Howe, *The City,* pp. 164, 303.

97. The term was used by Royce in *The Hope of the Great Community,* ch. III, and by Dewey in *Public,* p. 142. The others, while not using the term, stressed the importance of imbuing the emerging industrial order with spiritual and moral purpose. See Follett, *New State,* pp. 49, 74; Howe, *The City,* pp. 22–23; Addams, *Philanthropy,* p. 1; White, *Old Order,* pp. 30–31, 147, 232–234; Park, *Science of Sociology,* pp. 162, 422; Charles Horton Cooley, "The Process of Social Change," *Political Science Quarterly,* XII, March, 1897, 76, 81–82; Giddings, *Elements,* pp. 203, 323, 328–329.

98. Cooley, *Human Nature,* pp. 111–114; *Social Organization,* pp. 25–26, 99–100, 178; Park, *Old World,* pp. 296–308; *Society,* pp. 93–94 (1923); Royce, *Christianity,* II, 83–90; *Race,* pp. 74–77; Dewey, *Public,* pp. 139–142; Mary Parker Follett, *Creative Experience,* New York, 1924, pp. 3–9, 27–30; Addams, *Democracy,* pp. 209–211; William Allen White, *In the Heart of a Fool,* New York, 1918, pp. 69, 346, 388; *American Magazine,* LXIII, 259–263; *West,* pp. 52, 57–58, 61, 81–89; Howe, *The City,* pp. 17–19.

99. Robert E. Park, "Community Organization and the Romantic Temper," in *The City* by R. E. Park, E. W. Burgess, and R. D. McKenzie, Chicago, 1925, p. 122 (1923).

CHAPTER 2: PATTERNS OF THOUGHT

1. Recent discussion of urban society reveals how the ingredients of an earlier theory of community have become separated out in much of contemporary sociological analysis. In this view, urban society is a spatial but not a spiritual community, and interdependence exists without individual identification with the whole. See Greer, *Approaches to the Study of Politics,* pp. 330–352; Carl J. Friedrich, ed., *Community,* New York, 1959.

2. John Dewey, *Democracy and Education: An Introduction to the Philosophy of Education,* New York, 1916, p. 5.

3. Howe, *The City,* p. 22.

4. Addams, *Democracy,* p. 211.

5. Royce, *Christianity,* II, 85–86.

6. Cooley, *Social Organization,* p. 40; Dewey, *Public,* pp. 98, 151–152. Reversing the usual meaning, Park used community to refer to physical cohesion and society to refer to a system of shared values. Robert E. Park, *Human Communities: The City and Human Ecology,* ed. Everett Cherrington Hughes, *et al.,* Glencoe, Ill., 1952, p. 181 (1929). Giddings, *Principles,* pp. 79, 376–377. For similar contrasts, see Addams, *Democracy,* pp. 210, 214; White, *Old Order,* pp. 34–57, 232; Howe, *The City,* pp. 22, 45; Follett, *New State,* p. 117.

7. Howe, *The City,* pp. 17, 22–23, 45. See Dewey, *Democracy and Education,* pp. 98–99; Addams, *Philanthropy,* pp. 4, 23; *Democracy,* pp. 213–215; Cooley, *Social Organization,* pp. 133–134, 244, 408–409.

8. Howe, *The City,* p. 45.

9. Royce, *Loyalty,* p. 242.

10. *Ibid.,* p. 239. See also Giddings, *Studies in Theory,* p. 59; Cooley, *Human Nature,* p. 399; *Social Organization,* pp. 114, 116; Student Notebook, 1894. This analogy seemed to be a popular one at this time. See also Josiah Strong, *The New Era or the Coming Kingdom,* New York, 1893, p. 39; Wallas, *The Great Society,* p. 9.

11. Dewey, *Public,* p. 98.

12. *Ibid.,* pp. 125–126.

13. Wallas, *The Great Society,* pp. 3–65, 305–314.

14. Park, *Society,* pp. 310–311 (1940); *Human Communities,* pp. 121 (circa 1939), 182 (1929), 260 (1939). Park agreed with Wallas that the need for belonging was stifled by the impersonality of modern society.

Along with Wallas and the Chicago sociologist, William Ogburn, Park spoke of "the cultural lag" between material changes and changes in customs and morals which were required if a feeling of community were to persist. See Park, *Science of Sociology,* p. 925; *Society,* p. 327 (1942); *Human Communities,* p. 169 (1925); Wallas, *The Great Society,* pp. 3–14, 172–174; William F. Ogburn, *Social Change with Respect to Culture and Original Nature,* New York, 1922, pp. 200–203, 280, 341–351.

15. Dewey, *Democracy and Education,* pp. 5–6. Park often quoted and paraphrased this passage. Park, *Science of Sociology,* pp. 36, 183–184; *Race,* p. 40 (1938); *Human Communities,* pp. 173–174 (1925).

16. The word consensus referred to like-mindedness as opposed to a sense of functional interdependence. In the sociological tradition, the theory of solidarity via consensus has been associated with Comte, that of solidarity via interdependence with Durkheim. Cf. Auguste Comte, *The Positive Philosophy of Auguste Comte,* trans. Harriet Martineau, London, 1896, II, p. 222, and Durkheim, *Division of Labor,* pp. 1–29, 200–228. Park and Dewey, both familiar with Comte, used the terms consensus and common purpose. Park, *Science of Sociology,* pp. 33, 42; Dewey, *Democracy and Education,* pp. 5–6, 96–98. Giddings and Cooley referred to like-mindedness. Giddings, *Elements,* pp. 125–126, 320–321; Cooley, *Social Organization,* p. 389. Royce's use of the term loyalty was similar to the concept of common purpose. Royce, *Loyalty,* pp. 138–141, 247–248. Follett spoke of integrating interests. Follett, *New State,* p. 27; *Creative Experience,* p. 42. Howe and Addams spoke of solidarity. Frederic C. Howe, *Denmark: the Coöperative Way,* New York, 1936, xiv; Addams, *Philanthropy,* p. 23; *Second Twenty Years,* p. 367. White used the word fraternity. *Gazette,* Feb. 1, 1912; *West,* p. 32.

Park criticized Giddings for his nominalist view of society as a collection of similar individuals. According to Park, that view gave undue importance to like-mindedness as a means to solidarity in modern society. Here Park explicitly followed Durkheim. Park, *Science of Sociology,* pp. 30–34, 37–41.

17. Dewey, *Proceedings of the NEA,* 1902, p. 383.

18. Cooley, *Human Nature,* pp. 86–93, 152–157; James Mark Baldwin, *Social and Ethical Interpretations in Mental Development,* New York, 1902, pp. 13–15, 42; George Herbert Mead, *Mind, Self, and Society: From the Standpoint of a Social Behaviorist,* ed. Charles W.

Morris, Chicago, 1934, pp. 144–164, 273–328; Peter Fuss, *The Moral Philosophy of Josiah Royce,* Cambridge, Mass., 1965, pp. 65–68; Giddings, *Elements,* pp. 341–343; Dewey, *On Experience, Nature,* pp. 15–17 (1930); Jane Dewey, *The Philosophy of John Dewey,* pp. 25–26; C. Wright Mills, *Sociology and Pragmatism: The Higher Learning in America,* ed. Irving Louis Horowitz, New York, 1964, p. 296; Follett, *New State,* pp. 29, 60, 264; John Mogey, "Follett, Mary Parker," *International Encyclopedia of the Social Sciences,* 1968, V, 500–502. Addams, Howe, and White shared the general view of the others insofar as they assumed social influences molded human nature. Addams, *Twenty Years,* p. 432; Howe, *Confessions,* p. 93; *The City,* pp. 232–234; White, *Old Order,* 172–173; "The Reorganization of the Republican Party," *Saturday Evening Post,* CLXXVII, December 3, 1904, 1–2.

19. Cooley, *Social Organization,* p. 52.

20. Follett, *New State,* pp. 44–47; Cooley, *Human Nature,* pp. 102–103; John Dewey and James H. Tufts, *Ethics,* New York, 1908, pp. 187–189; Giddings, *Studies in Theory,* pp. 94–116.

21. Cooley, *Social Organization,* p. 5.

22. *Ibid.,* p. 20.

23. Royce, *Race Questions,* pp. 92–93 (1902); *Loyalty,* pp. 219–220; Addams, *Democracy,* pp. 8–10; Cooley, *Social Organization,* p. 90; Follett, *New State,* pp. 44, 47, 81; *Creative Experience,* p. 225; Howe, *The City,* pp. 20–22; *Confessions,* p. 322; Park, *Human Communities,* p. 260 (1939); White, *Old Order,* pp. 234–236; *Post* CLXXVII, 2.

24. Giddings, *Principles,* p. 390. See also *Elements,* pp. 67–70; *Descriptive Sociology,* pp. 311–312; *Studies in Theory,* pp. 61–64, 177–178.

25. Giddings, *Principles,* p. 399. See also *Elements,* pp. 60–66. Consciousness of kind meant sympathetic identification based on the perception of likeness and it is for this concept that he is known among sociologists. Pitirim Sorokin, *Contemporary Sociological Theory,* New York, 1928, p. 727.

26. Dewey, *Democracy and Education,* p. 141; Cooley, *Human Nature,* pp. 102–110.

27. Dewey, *Democracy and Education,* p. 141. See also p. 101; *Ethics,* p. 255.

28. Josiah Royce, *War and Insurance,* New York, 1914, iii, pp. 44–45, 52; *Christianity,* I, 405; II, 173, 183, 208–209; *Hope,* pp. 57–59.

29. For its prevalence in different fields of thought see Stow Persons, ed., *Evolutionary Thought in America,* New Haven, Conn., 1950; Morton White, *Social Thought in America: the Revolt against Formal-*

ism, Boston, 1957. The organic bias cut across political divisions; for example, it accompanied the laissez faire philosophy of William Graham Sumner and the more interventionist views of some Hegelians. William Graham Sumner and Albert Galloway Keller, *The Science of Society,* New Haven, Conn., 1927, I, 87; III, 2220; Frances Harmon, *The Social Philosophy of the St. Louis Hegelians,* New York, 1943, p. 103. Although the organic framework does not determine a particular political position, it does affect the arguments used to defend a position because of its emphasis on unity, continuity, and inter-relation. On this, see W. T. Jones, *The Romantic Syndrome: Toward a New Method in Cultural Anthropology and the History of Ideas,* The Hague, 1961.

30. Albion Small, *General Sociology: An Exposition of the Main Development in Sociological Theory from Spencer to Ratzenhofer,* Chicago, 1905, p. 74.

31. Cooley, *Social Process,* p. 28. On the organic bias of the communi-tarians see White, *Old Order,* pp. 7, 135, 147, 167; *West,* pp. 28–33; Frederic H. Howe, *Wisconsin: An Experiment in Democracy,* New York, 1912, pp. 40, 159; *Modern City,* p. 194; *Confessions,* p. 114; *The City,* pp. 17, 22, 45, 294; Addams, *Philanthropy,* p. 23; *Twenty Years,* p. 452; *Second Twenty Years,* p. 412; Mary Parker Follett, "Community is a Social Process," *The Philosophical Review,* XXVIII, November, 1919, 582; *New State,* pp. 21–23, 75–78, 81–84, 95–99; *Creative Experi-ence,* pp. 54–74, 98, 113, 116, 128, 134; Giddings, *Proceedings of the NEA,* III, March, 1888, 29–47; *Principles,* pp. 15–20, 388–390; *Studies in Theory,* pp. 94–116; Cooley, *Sociological Theory,* pp. 54–76 (1894); *PSQ,* XII, 73–75; *Human Nature,* pp. 100–101, 115, 134; *Social Organi-zation,* pp. 4–5; *Social Process,* pp. 19–26; Park, *Science of Sociology,* pp. 33–42; *Human Communities,* pp. 180–182 (1929); John Dewey, *The Ethics of Democracy,* Ann Arbor, Mich., 1888, pp. 4–27; *Recon-struction in Philosophy,* Boston, 1955, pp. 187–199, 205–207; *Public,* p. 22; Josiah Royce, *The Spirit of Modern Philosophy,* Boston, 1892, p. 225; *The Religious Aspect of Philosophy,* Boston, 1885, pp. 163–196; *The World and the Individual,* New York, 1959, Second Series, p. 183; *Fugitive Essays,* pp. 111–112, 125–126; *Christianity,* I, 61–65.

32. Spencer, *Principles,* I-2, 447–462, 471.

33. Spencer's laissez faire philosophy has generally received more attention than has his organic philosophy. See for example Richard Hofstadter, *Social Darwinism in American Thought,* Boston, 1955, pp. 31–50; Bernard Crick, *The American Science of Politics: Its Origins*

and Conditions, Berkeley, Cal., 1959, pp. 37–44. The organic aspect of Spencer's thought is stressed by Stow Persons, *American Minds: A History of Ideas,* New York, 1958, pp. 225–229.

34. Sumner and Keller, *Science of Society,* II, 2217–2220; Lester Frank Ward, *Psychic Factors of Civilization,* Boston, 1893, p. 289; Crick, *American Science of Politics,* p. 56.

35. See for example, Richard T. Ely, *Studies in the Evolution of Industrial Society,* New York, 1903, pp. 7–8, 12, 21–22; John B. Clark, *The Philosophy of Wealth: Economic Principles Newly Formulated,* Boston, 1886, pp. 37–39, 44–45, 176–203, 225–226; Small, *General Sociology,* pp. 121, 134–135, 585.

36. For Darwin and his influence see David F. Bowers, "Hegel, Darwin and the American Tradition," in *Foreign Influences in American Life: Essays and Critical Bibliographies,* ed. David F. Bowers, Princeton, N.J., 1944, pp. 148–158; Cooley, *Sociological Theory,* p. 5 (1928); Park, *Human Communities,* pp. 240–262 (1939); John Dewey, "The Influence of Darwinism on Philosophy," in *American Thought: Civil War to World War I,* ed. with an Introduction by Perry Miller, New York, 1954, pp. 214–225; Follett, *New State,* pp. 95–97. For Spencer's usefulness and inadequacies see Giddings, *Principles,* pp. 8–18; Cooley, Journal, 1895, 1897; *Sociological Theory,* pp. 5 (1923), 40, 104 (1894), 263–279 (1920); *Social Organization,* p. 92; Park, *Human Communities,* pp. 179–180 (1929), 259 (1939); John Dewey, *Characters and Events: Popular Essays in Social and Political Philosophy,* ed. Joseph Ratner, New York, 1929, I, 45–62 (1904); Royce, *Fugitive Essays,* pp. 110, 112; *Spirit of Modern Philosophy,* pp. 297–300; Follett, *New State,* pp. 75–78.

37. Cooley, Journal, 1882, 1897; *Sociological Theory,* p. 6 (1928); *Social Organization,* pp. 211–214, 350–351; *Social Process,* p. 418; Giddings, *Principles,* pp. 10–15, 302–303; Royce, *Spirit of Modern Philosophy,* pp. 102, 138, 201, 275; *Hope,* p. 275; Dewey, *On Experience, Nature,* pp. 10–12; Follett, *New State,* pp. 29, 226–227. The influence of Idealism and its fusion with the empirical method in nineteenth-century social science is described by Martindale, *Sociological Theory,* pp. 52–53, 62–64, 81–89.

38. David W. Noble, *The Paradox of Progressive Thought,* Minneapolis, Minn., 1958, pp. 78–79, 87, 91, 93, 96; Giddings, *Democracy,* pp. 32–35, 40 (1889); *Elements,* pp. 60–65; Cooley, *Human Nature,* p. 90, n.; Fuss, *Moral Philosophy of Royce,* pp. 60–70, 71–75, 98–99.

39. Cooley, *Human Nature,* p. 100.

40. Giddings, *Principles,* pp. 359–360, 388–390, 420; *Elements,* pp. 6–8, 83–86, 180–215, 255–292, 331–340.

41. Follett, *New State,* p. 66.

42. *Ibid.,* p. 81. See also Cooley, *Social Process,* p. 28; Giddings, *Principles,* p. 399. Park and Royce were less optimistic than the others about this process of identification. For Park, advances in communication were offset by the impersonality of modern society. Robert E. Park, *The Principles of Human Behavior,* Chicago, 1915, p. 44; *Science of Sociology,* p. 957; *Society,* pp. 283–284 (1931). For Royce, society bred its own enemies in the process of social training. Royce, *Loyalty,* p. 34; *Christianity,* I, 140–141.

43. White, *Old Order,* pp. 63, 234–236, 247, 252–253; *West,* pp. 28–33, 115–121; Howe, *The City,* pp. 24, 27, 30; *Modern City,* pp. 2–3, 37; *Wisconsin,* pp. 188–190; Addams, *Philanthropy,* p. 10; *Twenty Years,* p. 432; *Newer Ideals,* p. 236; Follett, *New State,* pp. 57, 95–97, 156; *Creative Experience,* pp. 113–114; Giddings, *Principles,* p. 16–20, 359–378, 388–390; *Elements,* pp. 6–8, 83–86, 180–215, 255–292, 332–340; Cooley, *Sociological Theory,* pp. 40–104 (1894); *Social Organization,* pp. 4, 92, 113; *Social Process,* p. 28; Park, *Science of Sociology,* pp. 33–42; *Human Communities,* pp. 180–182 (1929), 253–262 (1939); John Dewey, *John Dewey on Education: Selected Writings,* ed. Reginald D. Archambault, New York, 1964, p. 427 (1897); *Ethics,* p. 255; Royce, *Fugitive Essays,* pp. 111–112, 125–126; *Christianity,* I, 143–158, 172–173, 405; II, 220, 430; *Hope,* pp. 37–39.

44. Addams, *Philanthropy,* p. 1. See also pp. 34–35, 53–54; *Twenty Years,* pp. 366–367; *Spirit of Youth,* pp. 120–124; John Dewey, *The School and Society,* Chicago, Ill., 1899, p. 32; John Dewey and Evelyn Dewey, *Schools of Tomorrow,* New York, 1915, pp. 205–228; Frederic C. Howe, *The British City: The Beginnings of Democracy,* New York, 1907, p. 342; *Wisconsin,* pp. 159–161; White, *Post,* CLXXVII, p. 2; *Old Order,* pp. 137, 234, 250–253; Cooley, "A Primary Culture for Democracy," *Publications of the American Sociological Society,* XIII, Chicago, 1918, 1–10; Park, *Society,* pp. 93–94 (1923); Royce, *Race Questions,* pp. 86–93 (1902); Mary Parker Follett, "Evening Centers—Aims and Duties Therein," A Paper Given to Managers and Leaders of the Evening Centers of the Boston Public School System, printed, January, 1913, pp. 3–19; Giddings, *Descriptive Sociology,* pp. 344–345.

45. The importance of the communications revolution was first suggested to me by Warren Susman. These figures did not use this term, which first appeared in the 1930's. For the history of the concept, see

Lee Benson, "The Historical Background of Turner's Frontier Essay," *Agricultural History*, XXV, April, 1951, 59–82.

46. George Rogers Taylor, *The Transportation Revolution: 1815–1860*, New York, 1951, pp. 150–151; Daniel J. Boorstin, *The Image or What Happened to the American Dream*, New York, 1962, pp. 12–13, 22–36; Frank Luther Mott, *American Journalism: A History of Newspapers in the United States through 260 Years: 1690 to 1950*, New York, 1950, pp. 478–507. Sociologists began to study the mass media in the 1940's and communication research gathered momentum in the 1950's and 1960's. See Otto N. Larsen, "Social Effects of Mass Communications," in *Handbook of Modern Sociology*, ed. Robert E. Faris, Chicago, 1964, pp. 348–381, for a review of this research, much of which goes counter to the hopes of an earlier generation. The social and psychological effects of speech, print, and electronic communications have been studied by Harold Innis, a one-time student of Park's. Marshall McLuhan, "Introduction," Harold A. Innis, *The Bias of Communication*, Toronto, 1951, xiv-xv; Innis, *Communication*, pp. 156–189, 190–192. They have also been studied by his colleague, Marshall McLuhan, *The Gutenberg Galaxy: The Making of Typographic Man*, Toronto, 1962, pp. 85–86, 93, 256–257, 284–299, 306–307; *Understanding Media: The Extensions of Man*, New York, 1964. Whereas the communitarians saw the telegraph, the radio, and the motion picture as essentially similar to print, McLuhan stresses the differences between them. Both he and Innis prefer oral to written communication for reasons not unlike those given by the earlier writers—immediacy and involvement. Innis, *Communication*, pp. 190–192; McLuhan, *Understanding Media*, p. 86; Dewey, *Public*, p. 179; Park, *Society*, p. 144 (1918); Franklin H. Giddings, "World Tendencies and China," *Chinese Students' Monthly*, XVIII, January, 1923, 8–10.

47. White, *Old Order*, p. 250.

48. Gardiner Spring, midnineteenth-century revivalist and editor, quoted in Perry Miller, *The Life of the Mind in America, from the Revolution to the Civil War*, New York, 1965, p. 48.

49. Curti, *American Loyalty*, pp. 116–121.

50. Quoted in Ford's "Draft of Action," p. 28.

51. Miller, *Life of the Mind*, pp. 48, 52–58.

52. Edward Bellamy, *Looking Backward: 2000–1887*, Boston, 1917, p. 134.

53. Vernon Louis Parrington, Jr., *American Dreams: A Study of American Utopias*, New York, 1964, p. 76.

54. Chauncy Thomas, *The Crystal Button*, Boston, 1891, p. 33.

55. Morrison I. Swift, *A League of Justice or Is It Right to Rob Robbers?*, Boston, 1893, pp. 19–21, 40.

56. Ford, "Draft of Action," p. 21.

57. Ford, "Draft of Action," p. 21.

58. David A. Wells, *Recent Economic Changes and Their Effect on the Production and Distribution of Wealth and the Wellbeing of Society*, New York, 1889, v-vi, p. 465. Benson puts Wells and the concept of the communications revolution in the setting of the agricultural depression of 1873–1896 in *Agricultural History*, XXV, 59–82.

59. Ely, *Evolution of Industrial Society*, pp. 89–90, 426–429, 431.

60. Giddings, *Outline of Lectures on Political Economy, Delivered in the Bryn Mawr College*, 1891, Philadelphia, 1891, p. 18. In "Internal Improvements," *The Chautauquan*, IX, May, 1889, 461–462, Giddings noted the historic importance of the communication and transportation network in unifying America.

61. Spencer, *Principles*, I-2, 498–517. The idea of the communications revolution and its unifying effect on modern society appeared in Europe at about the same time. See Albert Schäffle, *Bau und Leben des Socialen Körpers*. Tübingen, 1896, II, 178–183; first published in 1876, See also Gabriel Tarde, *L'Opinion et la Foule*, Paris, 1901, p. 75; Tönnies, *Fundamental Concepts*, p. 256; first published in 1887.

62. Giddings, *Principles*, 1893, p. 194. The French sociologist, Tarde, also influenced his ideas on communication and imitation, he acknowledged in *Descriptive Sociology*, 1911, pp. 5, 311.

63. Letter quoted in Perry, *James*, II, 518–519. Ford mentioned Dewey's conversion in "Draft of Action," p. 3.

64. Ford, "Draft of Action," pp. 25, 39, 56.

65. Cooley, Student Notebook, 1894. Under Ford's influence, Dewey started a newspaper in 1892 called *Thought News* but it soon failed. This incident, together with Ford's relation to Dewey, is discussed by Feuer, *JHI*, XX, 545–568. On this, see also Willinda Savage, "The Evolution of John Dewey's Social Philosophy at the University of Michigan," unpublished Ph.D. dissertation, University of Michigan, 1950; Earl James Weaver, "John Dewey: A Spokesman for Progressive Liberalism," unpublished Ph.D. dissertation, Brown University, 1963.

66. Dewey, *Characters*, I, 59–60 (1904). See John Dewey, "Ethics and Physical Science," *Andover Review*, VII, June, 1887, 587–590, and *Characters*, I, 45–62 (1904).

67. Park, *Race*, v-vi.

68. Park, *Race,* vi.

69. Robert E. Park, *Masse und Publikum: eine methodologische und sociologische Untersuchung,* Bern, 1904, pp. 7, 12–13, 17–18, 78–79, 82.

70. For Cooley's acknowledgement of his debt to Schäffle and Dewey, see Journal, 1897. Schäffle had also discussed the press, the mail, the telegraph, and books as extensions of "the motor-nerve apparatus of the organic body." *Bau und Leben,* II, 178–180. (My trans.)

71. Cooley, *Sociological Theory,* pp. 40, 64–65, 86 (1894); *PSQ,* XII, 74–81.

72. Albion W. Small and George E. Vincent, *An Introduction to the Study of Society,* New York, 1894, pp. 215–266. They draw on Spencer and Schäffle among others; Small, *General Sociology,* pp. 121, 134–135, 141, 361–362; Ely, *Evolution of Industrial Society,* pp. 426–442; Strong, *New Era,* pp. 19, 27–29; Herbert Croly, *Progressive Democracy,* New York, 1914, pp. 264–265; Walter Lippmann, *Drift and Mastery,* New York, 1914, pp. 144–145, 281–284.

73. Royce, *Race Questions,* pp. 86–93 (1902); Addams, *Democracy,* pp. 8–9; Howe, *The City,* pp. 20–23; Follett, *New State,* pp. 153–155; White, *Post,* CLXXVII, p. 2; *Old Order,* p. 191.

74. White, *Old Order,* pp. 252–253.

CHAPTER 3: MARY PARKER FOLLETT AND FACE-TO-FACE COMMUNICATION

1. Suggestions about the importance of small communities and face-to-face relations for American intellectuals have been made by Anselm Strauss and Morton and Lucia White. The Whites' exclusive preoccupation with the anti-urban impulse among American intellectuals should be balanced by David R. Weimer's *The City as Metaphor,* New York, 1966.

2. Park, in *The City,* p. 106.

3. Follett, *New State,* pp. 195–205, 211–212, 256–257; Giddings, *Principles,* pp. 138–139, 255–256; *Democracy,* pp. 244–245; *International Quarterly,* VII, 298; *Studies in Theory,* pp. 63–64; John Dewey, "Public Opinion," review of *Public Opinion,* by Walter Lippmann, in *The New Republic,* XXX, May 3, 1922, 286–288; *School and Society,* pp. 22–24, 28; *Proceedings of the NEA,* 1902, p. 381; *Characters,* II, 776–781 (1922); Royce, *California,* pp. 220, 361, 366; *Putnam's* VII, 239–240; *Loyalty,* pp. 239, 243; Howe, *The City,* pp.

170–172, 303; *Wisconsin*, p. 156; Addams, *Newer Ideals*, pp. 121, 215–216; *Twenty Years*, pp. 38–41, 186–187; Park, in *The City*, pp. 105–106; *Old World*, pp. 261–262, 294–295; *Race*, p. 259 (no date); Cooley, *Social Organization*, pp. 24–26, 54, 352, 415; *Publications of the ASS*, XIII, 7–8; William Allen White, "Kansas: A Puritan Survival," in *These United States: A Symposium*, ed. Ernest Gruening, New York, 1923, pp. 7–10; *West*, pp. 28–33.

4. Addams, *Newer Ideals*, p. 215.

5. *Ibid.*, pp. 215–216.

6. The number of large cities (above 100,000) and small cities (above 10,000) grew three times as fast between 1840 and 1880 as it did between 1790 and 1840. Strauss, *Images of the City*, pp. 91–92. On suburban growth in the cities where the communitarians lived, see Warner, *Streetcar Suburbs;* Bessie Louise Pierce, *A History of Chicago*, Chicago, 1957, Vol. III; Edmund H. Chapman, *Cleveland: Village to Metropolis: A Case Study of Problems of Urban Development in Nineteenth-Century America*, Cleveland, 1964. Studies of suburbanization in this period are few. On the effect of immigration on urban neighborhoods, see Charles N. Glaab and A. Theodore Brown, *A History of Urban America*, New York, 1967, ch. VI.

7. Park, *Science of Sociology*, p. 768.

8. Park, *Society*, p. 314 (1940). See also Park, in *The City*, p. 40; Cooley, *Social Organization*, pp. 93–97; *Social Process*, p. 249; Addams, *Newer Ideals*, p. 216; *Second Twenty Years*, pp. 367–368, 412.

9. Cooley, who formulated the classic definition of the primary group, described it as a group characterized by face-to-face relations, cooperation, and mutual identification, the main forms being family, play group, and neighborhood. *Social Organization*, p. 23. The term has undergone some modification since then. See Ellsworth Faris, "The Primary Group: Essence and Accident," *The American Journal of Sociology*, XXXVIII, July, 1932, 41–50; Robin M. Williams, Jr., *American Society: A Sociological Interpretation*, New York, 1960, pp. 491–492.

10. Dewey, *Public*, pp. 218–219.

11. Cooley, *Social Organization*, p. 415.

12. *Ibid.*, pp. 23–25.

13. Warner shows that it was not until the late nineteenth century that class and ethnic segregation appeared in Philadelphia, and he suggests that this might be true for other cities. Sam Bass Warner, Jr., "If All the World Were Philadelphia: A Scaffolding for Urban History,

1774–1930," *American Historical Review,* LXXIV, October, 1968, 26–43.

14. Follett, *New State,* pp. 200, 240.

15. Park, in *The City,* pp. 113–114.

16. Metcalf and Urwick, "Introduction," Follett, *Administration,* p. 11. Follett has been neglected in the literature of this period, although interest has increased in the 1960's. No mention of her is made in two major studies of Boston social thought and politics, Arthur Mann's *Yankee Reformers in the Urban Age,* Cambridge, Mass., 1954, and J. Joseph Huthmacher, *Massachusetts People and Politics: 1919–1933,* Cambridge, Mass., 1959. Curti's *American Loyalty,* pp. 218–219, briefly discusses her advocacy of local community. Roy Lubove's *The Professional Altruist: The Emergence of Social Work As a Career: 1880–1930,* Cambridge, Mass., 1965, does the same. Henry S. Kariel has an interesting analysis of her philosophy of politics and business management in the *Western Political Quarterly,* VIII, September, 1955, 425–440, and in *The Decline of American Pluralism,* Stanford, Cal., 1961. Samuel Haber's *Efficiency and Uplift: Scientific Management in the Progressive Era: 1890–1920,* Chicago, 1964, treats her as part of the elitist wing of Progressivism.

17. Warner, *Streetcar Suburbs,* pp. 1–44, 93–97, 153–166. The flight from slums to suburbs in Boston, under way by the 1870's, is also described by Huthmacher, *Massachusetts People,* pp. 5–12. Warner's book is especially useful for understanding Follett. He has studied the process of suburban growth and the patterns of settlement in Roxbury, West Roxbury, and Dorchester and also analyzed the obstacles to community there.

18. Follett, *New State,* pp. 197–199, 201.

19. *Ibid.,* p. 200.

20. *Ibid.,* p. 257.

21. *Ibid.,* pp. 200–201, 211–212. Her civic and political work is described by Metcalf and Urwick in the "Introduction" to her papers on business administration, *Administration,* pp. 11–15. Her own paper on "Evening Centers" also shows something of her work during the period 1900–1917. At this time she was also engaged in vocational guidance and labor arbitration. Persons, *DAB,* XXI, 308–309. Her private papers are in England. Information in a letter to the author from L. F. Urwick, 83 Kenneth St., Longueville, N.S.W., Australia, December 31, 1969. On the community center movement see Jesse Frederick Steiner, "Community Centers," *Encyclopedia of the Social Sciences,* 1931, IV, 105–106; Lubove, *Professional Altruist,* pp. 171–179; E. J. Ward, ed., *The Social Center,* New York, 1914.

22. According to one of her friends, *The New State* began as an account of the Boston school centers. When the focus of the book changed, the description of the centers went into the appendix. Cabot, *Radcliffe Quarterly,* April, 1934, pp. 80–81.

23. Follett, *New State,* p. 212.

24. Follett, *New State,* pp. 86–89, 209, 346, *Creative Experience,* p. 212.

25. Follett, *New State,* p. 44. Italics Follett's.

26. *Ibid.,* p. 37.

27. *Ibid.,* pp. 249–253, 346, 354–357.

28. Follett, "Evening Centers," p. 17; *The Philosophical Review,* XXVIII, 576; *New State,* pp. 23–24, 26–29, 86–87; *Creative Experience,* pp. 111–112, 156–157, 164.

29. Follett, *New State,* p. 28.

30. *Ibid.,* p. 29.

31. Follett, *The Philosophical Review,* XXVIII, 581.

32. Follett, *New State,* pp. 194, 205–208, 240, 366–372.

33. Follett, "Evening Centers," p. 33. See *New State,* pp. 363–366.

34. Follett, *New State,* p. 367.

35. *Ibid.,* pp. 144–145, 152, 166–167, 180–181, 205, 207, 245–251, 254–257; *Creative Experience,* pp. 225–226. On the issue of grass-roots democracy, it is interesting to compare the main body of her work with her first book on politics. There she emphasized the need for leadership and efficiency while criticizing the town meeting ideal as impractical. See Mary Follett, *The Speaker of the House of Representatives,* New York, 1896, pp. 303, 308, 310, 313–316. That book was written before her period of community work and before her encounter with the philosophy of decentralization espoused by English pluralists like Harold Laski, a philosophy which figured prominently in *New State,* pp. 262–273.

36. Follett, *New State,* p. 194.

37. *Ibid.,* pp. 3–11, 160–161, 320–324, 337–339.

38. Follett, *The Philosophical Review,* XXVIII, 578; *New State,* pp. 6, 65, 69, 77, 81–82, 255–256. See Park, in *The City,* pp. 117–118; Addams, *Philanthropy,* p. 10; *Democracy,* p. 75; Cooley, *Human Nature,* pp. 8–11, 115, 396–401; *Social Organization,* pp. 34–38; Giddings, *Principles,* pp. 302–306, 384–386; *Democracy,* pp. 60, 72–73, 321–327, 338–340; Dewey, *Ethics,* pp. 391–397; *Democracy and Education,* pp. 141–143, 415–418; Royce, *Loyalty,* pp. 143, 252–257.

39. Follett, *New State,* p. 69.

40. *Ibid.,* pp. 137–138.

41. Follett, *New State,* p. 62.

42. *Ibid.,* p. 62. See also pp. 66, 191.

43. *Ibid.,* p. 66.

44. *Ibid.,* pp. 213, 368. Cf. Addams, *Democracy,* pp. 73, 76–79.

45. Follett, *New State,* p. 42.

46. Follett, *New State,* p. 42.

47. Royce, *Loyalty,* pp. 252–256; Addams, *Democracy,* p. 76–79; Dewey, *Democracy and Education,* pp. 142–144.

48. Follett, *New State,* p. 75. See also pp. 37, 62, 75, 97; *Creative Experience,* pp. 54–55, 225. She used James' ideas extensively in her psychology, especially those from *A Pluralistic Universe* (1909).

49. Follett, *New State,* p. 97.

50. *Ibid.,* p. 81.

51. *Ibid.,* pp. 13, 81, 161, 194, 205, 240, 251, 338.

52. *Ibid.,* p. 65. See also pp. 156–157.

53. Follett, *New State,* pp. 33, 35, 57, 95–97, 103–104, 157; *Creative Experience,* pp. 54–56, 74–75, 116, 225. Like James she derived metaphysics from empirical observation, but she did not have the "leap of faith" which James thought all metaphysical statements required.

54. Follett, *New State,* p. 251.

55. *Ibid.,* pp. 245, 256–257.

56. *Ibid.,* p. 202. See also pp. 73, 202–203. Follett used the terms bureaucracy and bureaucratically, as well as synonyms. *Ibid.,* pp. 74, 203, 326, 330.

57. Follett, *New State,* p. 73.

58. *Ibid.,* p. 197.

59. *Ibid.,* pp. 196–200.

60. Morton Grodzins, *The Loyal and the Disloyal: Social Boundaries of Patriotism and Treason,* Chicago, 1956, p. 257.

61. Cooley, *Social Organization,* p. 349. See *Social Process,* p. 180.

62. *Gazette,* Feb. 1, 1912.

63. Park, in *The City,* p. 117; *Science of Sociology,* pp. 287, 328–329; Dewey, *Public,* pp. 213–214; Cooley, *Social Organization,* pp. 408–409; *Social Process,* pp. 180–184; Howe, *Modern City,* pp. 305–319; Addams, *Spirit of Youth,* pp. 4–7, 13–15, 19–20, 79, 82, 95, 97, 100–101; Royce, *Putnam's,* VII, 234–239; *Loyalty,* p. 243–244; White, *Old Order,* pp. 250–253.

64. Addams, *Spirit of Youth,* pp. 98. See also pp. 4–7, 13–15, 19–20, 79, 82, 95, 97, 100–101; Park, *Science of Sociology,* p. 329; Cooley, *Social Organization,* pp. 408–409; *Social Process,* pp. 71, 184, n., p. 184;

Howe, *British City*, p. 324; *Modern City*, pp. 305–319. Park, Cooley, and Howe cited Addams' *Spirit of Youth* on this subject.

65. Cooley, *Social Organization*, pp. 24–26, 33; *Social Process*, pp. 420–421; *Life and the Student*, New York, 1927, pp. 9–24; Giddings, *Principles*, pp. 396–398; Dewey, *Democracy and Education*, pp. 413–416; *Public*, pp. 213, 218–219; Park, in *The City*, pp. 117–122; Royce, *Race Questions*, pp. 96–98 (1902); White, *West*, pp. 28–33; Addams, *Philanthropy*, pp. 1, 4, 10; *Twenty Years*, p. 366; Howe, *Wisconsin*, pp. 156–157; *Denmark: The Coöperative Way*, viii–xiv.

66. Howe, *The City*, p. 22.

67. *Ibid.*, pp. 24–25; Howe, *Modern City*, pp. 5–7, 37, 316–319; *Confessions*, p. 324. Although Howe came to accept the variety of the city as a positive good, he wanted to see the cultural and civic institutions of the city strengthened to counteract lower forms of entertainment. For example, he wanted the social settlement to replace the saloon, and he pictured the settlement as the social center for each ward. Howe, *British City*, p. 342.

68. Park, in *The City*, p. 41.

69. Park, in *The City*, pp. 9, 12, 110–111, 116–118; *Old World*, pp. 41, 299; *Science of Sociology*, pp. 313–314. Park's mixed feelings about the freedom of the city are noted by Stein, *Eclipse*, pp. 17–19; White and White, *Intellectual versus City*, pp. 161–165.

70. Cooley, *PSQ*, XII, 78. See *Social Organization*, pp. 24–27; *Social Process*, pp. 181—184, 249.

71. Cooley, *Social Organization*, pp. 93–97; Addams, *Second Twenty Years*, pp. 367–368; Dewey, *School and Society*, pp. 25–26; Royce, *Race Questions*, pp. 105–107 (1902). Some interesting ideas have been put forward recently by social scientists concerning the perennial question of freedom versus community. Bramson argues that the tension between the values of social order and freedom are inevitable and appear in the work of American sociologists like Park. Leon Bramson, *The Political Context of Sociology*, Princeton, N.J., 1961, pp. 17, 30–32, 77–78. Greer contends that community is a product of isolation and constraint; that therefore mutual identification and intense participation cannot flourish in modern society. Greer, in *Approaches to the Study of Politics*, pp. 330–341. This view, of course, contrasts sharply with that of the writers in question.

72. Addams, *Twenty Years*, p. 151. See also 177–183, 366 and Jane Addams, "Objective Value of a Social Settlement," *Philanthropy and Social Progress*, ed. Henry C. Adams, New York, 1893, pp. 34–35, 54.

73. Addams, *Philanthropy*, p. 54. See *Newer Ideals*, pp. 214–216; *Twenty Years*, pp. 365–367; Jane Addams, "A Toast to John Dewey," *The Survey*, LXIII, November 15, 1929, 203; *Second Twenty Years*, pp. 407, 412.

74. Addams, *AJS*, X, 426–427; *Newer Ideals*, p. 121. Cooley also referred to these institutions in *Social Organization*, p. 25. Interestingly, the community center movement pictured itself in the tradition of the Teutonic mark, the Russian mir, and the New England town meeting. See Ida Clyde Clarke, *The Little Democracy*, New York, 1918, pp. 3, 32.

75. Jane Addams, "Why the Ward Boss Rules," *The Outlook*, LVIII, April 2, 1898, 880. See *Newer Ideals*, pp. 31–35, 51, 53; *Democracy*, pp. 260–267; *Twenty Years*, p. 335. For her increasingly sympathetic view of machine politics after 1895, see *The Outlook*, LVIII, 879–882; *Twenty Years*, pp. 315–317; *Democracy*, pp. 266–270.

76. Addams, *Democracy*, pp. 260–268; *Newer Ideals*, pp. 31–35; *Spirit of Youth*, pp. 108–111, 141, 146.

77. Dewey, *John Dewey on Education*, p. 427; *School and Society*, pp. 29–30, 44; *Democracy and Education*, pp. 5–6, 36–37, 272–273, 413, 416. The literature on Dewey's educational views is enormous. Useful on this point is Cremin's, *Transformation of the School*, pp. 60–68, which relates Dewey's ideas on education to other communitarian movements of the period, such as the settlement movement, and Kimball and McClellan's, *Education*, pp. 96–99, which suggests the importance for Dewey of the small town as the model for the school and for industrial organization.

78. Dewey, *Democracy*, p. 416.

79. *Ibid.*, p. 413.

80. Howe, *Wisconsin*, p. 162. Howe thought the school center would be the proper focus for civic and educational activity in both urban and rural areas. *Ibid.*, pp. 159–162; *British City*, p. 342; *Modern City*, pp. 311–319. Cooley had a similar idea in *Social Process*, pp. 73–75; see also Park, in *The City*, p. 117; White in Ward, ed. *The Social Center*, pp. 39–41.

81. Dewey, *Proceedings of the NEA*, 1902, p. 381. See his sympathetic account of an attempt to make an Indianapolis school into a community center. Deweys, *Schools of Tomorrow*, pp. 205–228.

82. Dewey, *Democracy and Education*, pp. 5–6, 23–25, 36–37, 97–101, 272–273, 413–418.

83. Dewey, *Public*, p. 218.

84. *Ibid.*, p. 219; See *Characters*, II, 537–541 (1920); "Practical

Democracy," review of *The Phantom Public* by Walter Lippmann, in *The New Republic*, XLV, December 2, 1925, 52–54.

85. Dewey, *Public*, p. 213.

86. Steiner, *Encyclopedia of the Social Sciences*, IV, p. 105.

87. Lubove, *Professional Altruist*, pp. 85–107, 157–180. The same failure attended the most ambitious experiment of this kind—the "Social Unit" plan for community organization, begun in Cincinnati in 1917. *Ibid.*, pp. 175–177. Follett supported the plan in *Creative Experience*, p. 214.

88. Cooley, *Life*, p. 10.

CHAPTER 4: CHARLES HORTON COOLEY AND THE COMMUNICATIONS
        REVOLUTION

1. One of the weaknesses of Morton and Lucia Whites' study of late nineteenth-century figures is their almost exclusive attention to the plea for small and intimate communities. They give scant attention to Dewey's and Park's ideas about the communications revolution. Whites, *Intellectual versus City*, pp. 165–174.

2. Dewey, *Public*, p. 184.

3. *Ibid.*, p. 183; White, *Old Order*, pp. 250–253; Royce, *Race Questions*, pp. 75–98 (1902); Follett, *New State*, p. 154; Park, *Society*, pp. 93–94 (1923); Cooley, *Social Organization*, pp. 54, 89; Addams, *Newer Ideals*, p. 216; Giddings, *Democracy*, pp. 242–244 (1898); Howe, *The City*, p. 123.

4. Park, in *The City*, p. 9.

5. *Ibid.*, pp. 2, 9, 15–18, 23–33; Park, *Science of Sociology*, p. 285.

6. Giddings, *Democracy*, pp. 69–96 (1893); *Descriptive Sociology*, pp. 496–498; Park, in *The City*, pp. 31–32, 41, 106–107, 109, 117–118; Addams, *Spirit of Youth*, pp. 6–7, 13; Cooley, *Social Organization*, pp. 357, 369; *Social Process*, p. 180; Howe, *The City*, pp. 34–37; Royce, *Loyalty*, pp. 220–228.

7. Cooley, *Social Process*, p. 181. See Cooley, *Social Organization*, p. 25; *Social Process*, p. 180; Dewey, *Proceedings of the NEA*, 1902, p. 376.

8. Giddings, *Principles*, pp. 105–112; *Elements*, pp. 67–74; *Studies in Theory*, pp. 61–62.

9. Dewey, *School and Society*, pp. 38–40; Cooley, *Social Organization*, pp. 52–53; Royce, *Race Questions*, pp. 93–94. (1902).

10. Follett, *New State,* p. 256; Cooley, *Social Organization,* pp. 25, 107; Giddings, *Principles,* pp. 355–356; Park, in *The City,* pp. 106–107; White, *American Magazine,* LXIII, 262–264.

11. Cooley, Student Notebook, 1894.

12. Dewey, *Democracy and Education,* p. 100. See Cooley, *PSQ,* XII, 63–81; White, *Old Order,* p. 234; Addams, *Twenty Years,* p. 452; *Second Twenty Years,* p. 412.

13. Howe, *The City,* pp. 123, 164–166, 170.

14. Aside from histories of American sociology, the literature on Cooley includes the biography by Jandy, *Cooley,* and a number of shorter pieces. G. H. Mead, T. V. Smith, and C. Wright Mills have criticized (1) the notion of preestablished harmony inherent in his sociological theory and (2) the overemphasis on the social self. See George H. Mead, "Cooley's Contribution to Social Thought," *The American Journal of Sociology,* XXXV, March, 1930, 695–697; T. V. Smith, *Beyond Conscience,* New York, 1934, pp. 112–117; C. Wright Mills, "The Professional Ideology of Social Pathologists," *The American Journal of Sociology,* XLIX, September, 1943, 166–175. Philip Rieff's "Introduction" to Cooley's *Social Organization* contains a sharp attack on Cooley's hopes for "a gigantic town meeting." Cooley's views on class and conflict are dealt with in Charles Hunt Page, *Class and American Sociology: from Ward to Ross,* New York, 1940, and more recently in Lewis A. Coser, *The Functions of Social Conflict,* Glencoe, Ill., 1956. Noble, in *The Paradox of Progressive Thought,* emphasizes the doctrine of progress and the rejection of historical and materialistic determinism which Cooley shared with other Progressive intellectuals.

15. Jandy, *Cooley,* p. 29; Richard Dewey, "Charles Horton Cooley: Pioneer in Psychosociology," in *An Introduction to the History of Sociology,* ed. Harry Elmer Barnes, Chicago, 1948, p. 833.

16. Cooley, *Sociological Theory,* pp. 17–118 (1894).

17. *Ibid.,* p. 276 (1920). See also pp. 263–274 (1920); Cooley, *Journals,* 1882, 1889; *Human Nature,* p. 211.

18. In his Journal of 1897 he singled out Schäffle's ideas on evolution, the organic nature of society, and the modern means of communication as guidelines for his own thought. He later mentioned Emerson, Goethe, and Darwin as major influences on his development. *Sociological Theory,* p. 10 (1928). Talcott Parsons argues that it was William James' concept of the pluralism of the self which was Cooley's theoretical starting point, leading him to the notion that there was no

hard dividing line between the individual and society. Talcott Parsons, "Cooley and the Problem of Internalization," in *Cooley and Sociological Analysis,* ed. Albert J. Reiss, Jr., Introduction by Robert Cooley Angell, Ann Arbor, Mich., 1968, pp. 48–62.

19. Cooley, *Sociological Theory,* pp. 55–61.

20. Cooley, Journal, 1897. He heard Dewey in 1893, finished his thesis in 1894, and started teaching that year. Richard Dewey, *Introduction to the History of Sociology,* p. 833.

21. Cooley, *PSQ,* XII, 74.

22. *Ibid.,* 74–75; Cooley, *Human Nature,* p. 399; *Social Organization,* pp. 114–116.

23. Cooley, *PSQ,* XII, 76.

24. *Ibid.,* 76.

25. Cooley, *Social Organization,* p. 82. See also pp. 81, 83, 85–87. Cooley, *PSQ,* XII, 75; *Sociological Theory,* pp. 170–171 (1899).

26. Cooley, *Social Organization,* pp. 54, 80–87, 107–112; 114–116; *PSQ,* XII, 76, 81–82.

27. Cooley, *Social Organization,* p. 81. See pp. 83, 93–97.

28. *Ibid.,* pp. 82–83, 91–97, 180; Cooley, *PSQ,* XII, 76–77; *Social Process,* p. 249; Giddings, *Democracy,* pp. 61–62 (1900). Cf. Alexis de Tocqueville, *Democracy in America,* New York, 1954, I, 48–54; II, 173–175, 227, 335–337.

29. Cooley, *Social Organization,* p. 116.

30. *Ibid.,* p. 193.

31. *Ibid.,* pp. 193, 242, 303–304, 342, 349, 352, 355; Cooley, *Social Process,* pp. 128–129.

32. Cooley, *Social Organization,* p. 243; see also pp. 351–352, 357–369, 374–380, 383–387; *Social Process,* p. 146. Cooley's discussion of social disorganization is similar to Durkheim's analysis of normlessness and perhaps owes something to his work. Cooley cited Durkheim's *Suicide* in *Social Process,* p. 400. He also discussed the French term *solidaire,* the notion of disorganization and the importance of occupational groups in *Social Organization,* pp. 242–245, 330-332, 342–349.

33. Park, in *The City,* p. 106.

34. Cooley, *Social Organization,* p. 244.

35. *Ibid.,* p. 180. See also pp. 242, 261, 284; *Sociological Theory,* pp. 177–178 (1899); *Social Process,* pp. 137–143, 329–337.

36. Cooley, *Social Organization,* p. 23.

37. Cooley, *Human Nature,* p. 366. See also pp. 114–115; *Social Organization,* pp. 23–24, 33.

38. Cooley, *Human Nature,* p. 125. See pp. 102–103, 113–115, 125–127; *Social Organization,* p. 89. Cooley took Goethe's notion of "elective affinities," combined it with the communications revolution and worked out a variation on the theme of communion. Cooley, *PSQ,* XII, 77–78.

39. Cooley, *Social Organization,* p. 90. See pp. 37–40, 88; *Human Nature,* p. 115. Whereas Cooley merged communion and community, political theory has recently emphasized the distinctions between them. Communion is characterized by intense emotional fellowship, as in sects and messianic political groups; community is characterized by a common commitment to certain rights and duties. Herbert W. Schneider, "Community, Communication and Communion," in *Community,* ed. Carl J. Friedrich, New York, 1959, pp. 216–224.

40. Cooley, *Social Organization,* pp. 54–55. 84–88, 97, 125.

41. Mead, *AJS,* XXXV, 705.

42. Cooley, *Social Organization,* pp. 25–27, 352, 357–369; *Social Process,* pp. 180–184; *Life,* pp. 9–10. Because the family and the neighborhood supposedly expressed a universal human nature, Cooley was convinced that they would survive intact.

43. Cooley, *Social Organization,* p. 33. See p. 24.

44. *Ibid.,* pp. 32–34, 36–38, 194, 257–258, 298, 345–349; *Social Process,* pp. 128–133.

45. White, *Old Order,* p. 247; Cooley, *Social Organization,* p. 37.

46. Cooley, *Human Nature,* p. 134. See n., p. 90 for the description of his debt to James and Baldwin.

47. Cooley, *Human Nature,* pp. 84–87, 152.

48. *Ibid.,* p. 87. Italics Cooley's.

49. Cooley, *Human Nature,* pp. 85, 89–90.

50. *Ibid.,* p. 273. A contemporary dissent from this view which had little influence on American sociology at this time can be found in the work of Simmel.

51. Cooley, *Human Nature,* p. 115. See *Social Process,* pp. 26–28, 128.

52. Cooley, *Sociological Theory,* p. 5 (1928), p. 40 (1894), pp. 170–171, 177–178, 189 (1899); *PSQ,* XII, 73–74. *Human Nature,* pp. 11, 399.

53. Cooley, *Human Nature,* pp. 111–114; *Social Organization,* pp. 99–101, 133–134, 232–233, 415; Park, in *The City,* p. 40.

54. Giddings, *Descriptive Sociology,* p. 311. See pp. 187–191, 205–208, 210, 213–214, 311–312, 344–350; *Democracy,* pp. 51–53 (1900), 213–214 (1896).

55. Giddings, *Descriptive Sociology,* p. 140.

56. Royce, *Race Questions,* pp. 75, 80–90, 92–93, (1902).

57. Park thought that the new communications increased men's susceptibility to imitation and suggestion, and the effectiveness of propaganda during World War I brought this home to him. Park, *Old World*, p. 262; *Science of Sociology*, pp. 829–833. Park's interest in crowd behavior dated back to his Ph.D. thesis, which dealt with the contrast between the crowd and the public. Here he argued, following Le Bon, that the disruption of established social ties encouraged crowd behavior. Park, *Masse und Publikum*, pp. 61–64.

58. Giddings, *Democracy*, pp. 60–63 (1900), 206–213 (1896), 306 (1899); *International Quarterly*, VII, 298; *Elements*, pp. 291, 328–329, 345–346.

59. Franklin H. Giddings, "The Greatness of Herbert Spencer," *Independent*, LV, December 17, 1903, 2961; *Principles*, pp. 111–112; *Elements*, pp. 74–75, 283–285, 347–348; *Chinese Students' Monthly*, XVIII, 8.

60. White, *Old Order*, pp. 235–236. See pp. 1–3, 7, 172–173, 232–233.

61. *Ibid.*, p. 253.

62. *Ibid.*, pp. 167, 173; White, *Post*, CLXXVII, 2; William Allen White, "The Glory of the States: Kansas," *American Magazine*, LXXXI, January 1916, 41; Cooley, *Human Nature*, pp. 179–180, 360; *Social Organization*, pp. 53, 90; Dewey, *Democracy and Education*, pp. 99, 101; Addams, *Democracy*, p. 5; Howe, *Confessions*, p. 322; *The City*, p. 306; Follett, *New State*, pp. 153–154, 249–251. Royce took greater account of the opposition between the individual and society. *Loyalty*, p. 34; *Christianity*, I, 140–141. Park thought that as communications improved, social relations became more casual, but he also thought communications increased consensus. Park, *Society*, pp. 283–284 (1931); *Human Communities*, pp. 121 (circa 1939), 182 (1929), 260 (1939).

63. Addams, *Democracy*, p. 9. See pp. 4–9, 22; *Philanthropy*, pp. 10–11; *Hull-House Maps*, p. 203; Jane Addams, "The Reaction of Modern Life upon Religious Thought," *Religious Education*, IV, April 1909, 26; *Second Twenty Years*, p. 407.

64. Addams, *Survey*, LXII, 203, and *Second Twenty Years*, p. 412. Cf. Dewey's formulation of this idea in *Characters*, I, 74 where he uses Emerson's idea of communication as the foundation of a democratic philosophy.

65. Addams, *Second Twenty Years*, p. 412.

66. John Dewey, *Outlines of a Critical Theory of Ethics*, Ann Arbor, Mich., 1891, pp. 206–208; *John Dewey on Education*, p. 427 (1897); *School and Society*, p. 59; *Ethics*, pp. 298–299, 416, 434, 446–449; *Democracy and Education*, pp. 58–59, 99–101.

67. Dewey, *Democracy and Education*, p. 59.

68. Dewey, *Ethics*, p. 163.

69. Cooley, *Social Organization*, p. 89.

70. William B. Hesseltine, "Four American Traditions," *The Journal of Southern History*, XXVII, February, 1961, 3–32.

71. Croly, *Progressive Democracy*, p. 264. See pp. 265, 316–319.

72. Strong, *New Era*, pp. 19–30.

CHAPTER 5: THE PROMISE OF TECHNOLOGY

1. Dewey, *School and Society*, p. 40.

2. Follett, *New State*, p. 154, n. 1; Addams, *Twenty Years*, pp. 153, 301–303; Park, *Society*, pp. 143–151 (1918). Park regarded Addams' *Survey* magazine as a kind of national press bureau for the social agencies. Park, *Society*, p. 148 (1918).

3. Follett, *New State*, p. 154, n. 1. See Park, in *The City*, p. 38.

4. Park, *Society*, pp. 101–103 (1923); White, *Old Order*, pp. 106–107, 133; Letter from White to John S. Phillips, April 9, 1900, in Walter Johnson, ed., *Selected Letters of William Allen White: 1899–1943*, New York, 1947, p. 32–33; Addams, *Twenty Years*, pp. 200–201, 298, 302–304, 322; *AJS*, X, 441–442; Frederick C. Howe, *Privilege and Democracy in America*, New York, 1910, p. 243; *Modern City*, pp. 174, 330; *Wisconsin*, pp. 151–155; Franklin H. Giddings, *The Scientific Study of Human Society*, Chapel Hill, N.C., 1924, pp. 145–167; Cooley, *Social Organization*, pp. 411–412; *Social Process*, p. 347. The term social motor was Dewey's. Dewey, *Characters*, I, 27 (1892).

5. Dewey, *Public*, p. 184.

6. It was not until after the war that Park came to see the ruinous effect of propaganda on public opinion. Park, *Science of Sociology*, pp. 831–837.

7. Park, *Society*, pp. 102 (1923), 145–148 (1918).

8. *Ibid.*, p. 149 (1918).

9. *Ibid.*, p. 148 (1918).

10. Park, in *The City*, p. 38. See also pp. 24, 106–107; *Science of Sociology*, pp. 284–287. Park used Cooley's concept of the primary group here.

11. Park, in *The City*, pp. 23–29, 38, 105–107; *Science of Sociology*, p. 286.

12. Park, in *The City,* p. 40. See also pp. 15, 19, 29, 39, 109; *Science of Sociology,* pp. 33–42, 714–736; *Human Communities,* pp. 88–90 (1929).

13. Park, in *The City,* pp. 113–122; *Old World,* pp. 294–295.

14. Park, *Society,* p. 93 (1923). See p. 94; *The City,* p. 39. Hofstadter mentions that the latent function of "sob-sister journalism" in this period was to create solidarity in the impersonal environment of the city. Hofstadter, *Age,* p. 190, n. 2.

15. Park, *Society,* pp. 71–77 (1940), p. 98 (1923).

16. Dewey, *Characters,* I, 21–29 (1892); *Ethics,* p. 448; *Democracy and Education,* pp. 25, 99, 256–263.

17. Dewey, *Ethics,* p. 191. See also p. 448; *Outlines of Ethics,* pp. 125–126; *Characters,* II, 552–553 (1918); John Dewey, *Experience and Nature,* New York, 1929, p. 205.

18. Dewey, *Ethics,* p. 448; *Public,* pp. 172–176.

19. Dewey, *Public,* p. 180.

20. *Ibid.,* pp. 180–181.

21. *Ibid.,* p. 184. See Dewey, *Characters,* I, 3–16 (1891); *Ethics,* p. 448.

22. *Ibid.,* pp. 184, 218–219.

23. Letter from White to Senator Brewster, February 18, 1911, William Allen White Papers, The Library of Congress, Washington, D.C.

24. Follett, *New State,* pp. 73–74; Franklin H. Giddings, *The Responsible State: A Reëxamination of Fundamental Political Doctrines in the Light of World War and the Menace of Anarchism,* Boston, 1918, p. 106; Howe, *Privilege,* pp. 255–256; Dewey, *Characters,* II, 559 (1918).

25. Lewis Mumford, *The Golden Day,* New York, 1926, p. 262.

26. Dewey, *Proceedings of the NEA,* 1902, p. 375.

27. *Ibid.,* p. 383.

28. Cooley, Student Notebook, 1894. Dewey's 1928 articles on the Russian Revolution revealed a similar way of thinking. He thought that the Revolution was more "psychic and moral" than it was political and economic. Dewey, *Characters,* I, 379 (1928). His later advocacy of socialism in *Individualism Old and New,* New York, 1930, pp. 118–119, and *Liberalism and Social Action,* New York, 1935, p. 88, was vague.

29. Park, *Society,* pp. 144–151 (1918).

30. Cooley, Journal, 1902.

31. John Dewey, "Christianity and Democracy," in *Religious Thought at the University of Michigan: Being Addresses Delivered at*

the Sunday Morning Services of the Students' Christian Association,
Ann Arbor, Mich., 1893, p. 68.

32. Dewey, *Characters,* II, 515. See also 504–516 (1908); *John Dewey on Education,* p. 439 (1897); *Human Nature,* pp. 330–332; John Dewey, *A Common Faith,* New Haven, Conn., 1934, pp. 83–85.

33. White, *Post,* CLXXVII, 2; *Old Order,* pp. 167, 172–173.

34. *Gazette,* Oct. 26, 1911.

35. Cooley, Journal, 1895; 1896; 1902; 1919; *Life,* p. 265; Jane Addams, "Introduction," Graham Taylor, *Religion in Social Action,* New York, 1913, xiv; *The Excellent Becomes Permanent,* New York, 1932, pp. 7–8; Royce, *Christianity,* I, 398–402; *Hope,* p. 35; White, *Autobiography,* pp. 107–108; Dewey, *Characters,* II, 506–516 (1908).

36. These terms often had a religious connotation in their writing. Addams, *Philanthropy,* p. 18; *Hull-House Maps,* p. 293; Jane Addams, "Religious Education and Contemporary Social Conditions," *Religious Education,* VI, June, 1911, 150; *Peace and Bread in Time of War,* New York, 1922, p. 238; Dewey, *Proceedings of the NEA,* 1902, p. 381; *Public,* p. 184; *Experience and Nature,* p. 205; Follett, "Evening Centers," pp. 7, 13; Cooley, Journal, 1882; 1919; *Social Organization,* pp. 35, 40; Royce, *Christianity,* I, xix-xxv, 92–95, 172–173. White and Giddings used the term brotherhood. White, *Old Order,* pp. 3, 234, 253; Giddings, *Principles,* p. 360; *Western Hemisphere,* pp. 26–32.

37. Cooley, Journal, 1919; *Social Organization,* p. 205. See *Social Process,* p. 76.

38. Cooley, *Social Process,* pp. 420–421. "Sociology is to me in so far a religion that it is a way of seeing life as an onward whole, as the manifestation of God." Cooley, Journal, 1914.

39. Dewey, *Ethics of Democracy,* p. 27; Addams, *Religious Education,* VI, 147–152; Follett, *New State,* pp. 43, 103–104; Giddings, *Principles,* pp. 353–360; White, *Gazette,* Oct. 26, 1911; *Old Order,* pp. 3, 163.

40. Royce, *Christianity,* I, 103, 405–406.

41. For example, the doctrine of Christ's atonement was interpreted as an act of creative will which reconstituted the community shattered by betrayal and enabled it to embody the spirit of love. Royce, *Christianity,* I, 278–322. On this see John E. Smith, *Royce's Social Infinite: The Community of Interpretation,* New York, 1950, pp. 152–160. It is Christ defined not as a supernatural person but as the spirit of the Christian community who saves men by overcoming their self-

will and enabling the individual to love the community. Royce, *Christianity,* I, xxvi, 92–95, 405–406.

42. Royce, *Christianity,* I, xix, 92–95, 172, 187–188, 398–402, 404–406, 409–410; II, 101–102; Josiah Royce, *The Sources of Religious Insight,* New York, 1912, p. 206. Grace was necessary for salvation, but the change of heart which it produced did not consist of faith in the saving power of Christ but in love for the community in which the divine spirit lived. On Royce's fusion of God, Christ, and the Christian Church and the preeminence of the latter in his thought see William Adams Brown, "The Problem of Christianity," in *Papers in Honor of Josiah Royce on his Sixtieth Birthday,* ed. J. E. Creighton, *The Philosophical Review,* XXV, 1916, 81–86.

43. Royce, *Christianity,* I, 54, 405; II, 220; *Hope,* pp. 57–59.

44. Royce, *Religious Insight,* pp. 206–288; *Christianity,* II, 335–336, 368, 372, 423–430; *War,* pp. 76, 80. Taken together, these three works show that Royce did not regard science as simply a source of morality or an instrument for actualizing the characteristics of the Beloved Community on earth. He saw science as a source of transfiguring grace. In the light of this merging of sacred and secular, statements like "it is not my thought that natural science can ever displace religion or do its work," Royce, *Christianity,* II, 430, do not separate the two spheres as much as they appear to. Royce's tendency to join the sacred and the secular is emphasized by John Wright Buckham, "The Contribution of Professor Royce to Christian Thought," *The Harvard Theological Review,* VIII, April, 1915, 219–237.

45. Here the term secularism does not mean worldliness or lack of religiosity but the deification of the worldly, as used for example by Gabriel Vahanian, *The Death of God: The Culture of Our Post-Christian Era,* New York, 1957, p. 67.

46. This deification can be seen in the absence, except in Royce, of a sense that the kingdom never could be fully identified with the world; that it always stood in judgment on man's achievements; that it required for its realization the transcendent power of grace. This kind of secularism was also widespread in the New Theology and the Social Gospel. See Lyman Abbott, *The Theology of an Evolutionist,* Boston, 1897, pp. 73–77, 83–84; Gerald Birney Smith, *Social Idealism and the Changing Theology: A Study of the Ethical Aspects of Christian Doctrine,* New York, 1913, pp. 13, 103, 113–117, 123–124.

CHAPTER 6: CULTURE AND COMMUNITY

1. See Laurence R. Veysey, *The Emergence of the American University*, Chicago, 1965, pp. 180–251, on the ideal of liberal culture. The term liberal humanist is his.

2. Matthew Arnold, *Culture and Anarchy: An Essay in Political and Social Criticism*, New York, 1883, xi. For Arnold's influence on American ideas of culture in the early twentieth century, see Henry F. May, *The End of American Innocence: A Study of the First Years of Our Own Time: 1912–1917*, Chicago, 1959, pp. 30–36 and John Henry Raleigh, *Matthew Arnold and American Culture*, Berkeley, Cal., 1957.

3. Meredith Nicholson, *The Valley of Democracy*, New York, 1918, p. 283.

4. *Ibid.*, pp. 54, 278–284; Bliss Perry, *The American Mind*, Boston, 1912, pp. 209–247; Irving Babbitt, *Literature and the American College*, Boston, 1908, pp. 94–95.

5. Veysey, *American University*, pp. 195–196, 243–251.

6. Their definition was similar to that of nineteenth-century anthropologists. Milton Singer, "The Concept of Culture," *International Encyclopedia of the Social Sciences*, 1968, III, 527. John Dewey, "Are the Schools Doing What the People Want Them to Do?" *Educational Review*, XXI, May, 1901, 459–474; Josiah Royce, "Present Ideals of University Life," *Scribner's Magazine*, X, July, 1891, 376–388; Giddings, *Democracy*, pp. 218–225; Howe, *Wisconsin*, pp. 152–161; Jane Addams, "The College Woman and Christianity," *The Independent*, LIII, August, 1901, 1852–1855; *Philanthropy*, pp. 5–10; *Twenty Years*, pp. 70–76; Cooley, *Publications of the ASS*, XIII, 1–10. Here the communitarians resembled Carlyle, Ruskin, and Morris. Raymond Williams, *Culture and Society: 1780–1950*, New York, 1960, pp. 77–93, 152–166.

7. Royce, *Scribners*, X, 387–388.

8. Cooley, *Social Process*, p. 67.

9. Addams, *Democracy*, pp. 88–89.

10. Dewey, *Democracy and Education*, p. 141. See pp. 141–143. Cf. Addams, *Twenty Years*, pp. 71–76, 359–360.

11. Cooley, *Publications of the ASS*, XIII, 9; *Social Process*, pp. 70–72; John Dewey, "Psychology and Social Practice," in *John Dewey: Philosophy, Psychology and Social Practice*, ed. Joseph Ratner, New York, 1963, p. 301 (1899); *School and Society*, pp. 27, 33–38; *Democ-*

racy and Education, pp. 98–99, 252, 268, 278, 302–303; *Human Nature,* pp. 143–144; Jane Addams, "The Humanizing Tendency of Industrial Education," *The Chautauquan,* XXXIX, May, 1904, 266–271; *Democracy,* pp. 141–145; *Spirit of Youth,* pp. 108–135; Royce, *Christianity,* II, 88–93; Howe, *Wisconsin,* pp. 151–161; *Modern City,* p. 318–319.

12. Cooley, *Social Process,* p. 418. See also pp. 342, 419.

13. Cooley, *Social Organization,* p. 305. See pp. 303–306; *Social Process,* pp. 304, 342; *Ethics,* p. 448; Dewey, *Democracy and Education,* pp. 142–143. Cooley acknowledged his debt to Veblen's ideas on these points. Cooley, *Social Process,* n, p. 134. On his use of Veblen see also pp. 314–345 and *Social Organization,* p. 304. Cf. Thorstein Veblen, *The Portable Veblen,* ed. with an Introduction by Max Lerner, New York, 1948, pp. 91, 117, 163, 184, 190.

14. Cooley, *Social Organization,* p. 306.

15. The revolt against formalism is the theme of White's *Social Thought in America.*

16. Cooley, *Social Process,* p. 318.

17. *Ibid.,* p. 418.

18. Quoted in Karl Marx and Friedrich Engels, *Basic Writings on Politics and Philosophy,* ed. Lewis S. Feuer, New York, 1959, p. 254.

19. Royce, *Christianity,* II, 88.

20. *Ibid.,* 87.

21. Dewey, *School and Society,* p. 22.

22. *Ibid.,* pp. 27–28. See also Howe, *Privilege,* pp. 274–282; *Land,* pp. 26–28, 38; Park, *Science of Sociology,* p. 287; *Society,* pp. 295–299 (1934); Addams, *The Chautauquan,* XXXIX, 266–272; Jane Addams, "The Present Crisis in Trade-Union Morals," *North American Review,* CLXXIX, August, 1904, 178–193; *Spirit of Youth,* pp. 108–109, 120–135; Franklin H. Giddings, "Profit Sharing," *Seventeenth Annual Report of the Massachusetts Bureau of Statistics,* Boston, March, 1886, pp. 231–234; *Democracy,* pp. 99–133; *The Responsible State,* p. 104; Cooley, *Social Organization,* pp. 383–385.

23. Addams, *The Chautaquan,* XXXIX, 266–272; *Democracy,* pp. 180–219; *Newer Ideals,* p. 121; *Twenty Years,* pp. 141–143; *Spirit of Youth,* pp. 106, 109, 124, 135, 146; *Second Twenty Years,* pp. 358–359; Dewey, *School and Society,* pp. 23–24, 28–30, 37–39; *Democracy and Education,* pp. 9, 36–37, 96–99, 302–305, 372–374; *Characters,* II, 746, 755 (1918); John Dewey, *Education Today,* ed. with a Foreword by Joseph Ratner, New York, 1940, pp. 178–183 (1923); Cooley, *Social Organization,* pp. 263, 304–305; *Social Process,* p. 142; *Publications of*

the *ASS,* XIII, 1–10; Howe, *Modern City,* pp. 318–319; *Land,* pp. 38, 70–71, 89–124; *Confessions,* p. 325; Park, *Science of Sociology,* p. 287; *Society,* pp. 295–299 (1934); Royce, *Christianity,* II, 88–93; Follett, *New State,* pp. 117–120, 320–325; *Administration,* pp. 71–94 (1925).

24. The term "the instinct of workmanship," appeared in Addams, *Spirit of Youth,* p. 134; Cooley, *Social Organization,* p. 304; Park, *Science of Sociology,* p. 287. The two other terms come from Addams, *Spirit of Youth,* p. 124, and Dewey, *School and Society,* p. 60.

25. Addams, *Spirit of Youth,* p. 124.

26. Addams, *Democracy,* p. 206; Park, *The City,* pp. 13, 117; Cooley, *Social Organization,* pp. 385–389; Dewey, *Proceedings of the NEA,* 1902, p. 379.

27. Persons, *American Minds,* pp. 189–195.

28. Royce, *Scribner's,* X, 376–388; Howe, *Confessions,* pp. 1–8; Cooley, *Publications of the ASS,* XIII, 1–10; Giddings, *Democracy,* pp. 218–226 (1894).

29. Dewey, *On Experience, Nature,* pp. 9–10 (1930); Royce, *Scribner's,* X, 383–384; Howe, *Confessions,* pp. 1–8.

30. Persons, *American Minds,* pp. 189–190.

31. Cooley, *Publications of the ASS,* XIII, 4.

32. *Ibid.,* 3–7; Dewey, *School and Society,* pp. 37–38; *Democracy and Education,* pp. 244–263; Royce, *Scribner's,* X, 379–380; Park, *Old World,* p. 271; *Science of Sociology,* pp. 267–268; *Society,* pp. 147–149 (1918); Addams, *Annals,* XIII, 330, 339–340; *Democracy,* pp. 210–214; Follett, *New State,* pp. 64–65. Veysey distinguishes between advocates of utility, research, and liberal culture. According to him, only the latter were concerned with overspecialization and the problem of cultural unity. However, on this point the figures in this study do not fit into these categories. Dewey's and Cooley's thought cuts across all three categories. Park and Giddings saw research and general culture as complementary. And Royce, as Veysey points out, upheld an ideal of breadth acquired through reflection on the methodology of the arts and sciences. Veysey, *American University,* pp. 143, 191–192, 198–199, 203. John Higham's "The Schism in American Scholarship," *The American Historical Review,* LXXII, October, 1966, 1–21, although not concerned with the question of specialization, suggests that a unifying framework, historical and evolutionary in emphasis, characterized the humanities and social sciences until World War I.

33. Cooley, *Social Organization,* p. 97. See also *Human Nature,* pp. 116–119; *Social Process,* pp. 19–26; Follett, *New State,* pp. 64–66; Howe, *Confessions,* pp. 113–114; *The City,* pp. 22–23, 45, 164–166; *Modern*

City, pp. 37, 48; Addams, *Philanthropy,* pp. 1–4; *Spirit of Youth,* pp. 122–127; Dewey, in *Religious Thought at Michigan,* pp. 64, 67–68; *John Dewey on Education,* pp. 427–429 (1897); *Ethics,* p. 416; *Democracy and Education,* pp. 36–37, 101.

34. Cooley, *Social Process,* p. 71.

35. *Ibid.,* p. 26. See Cooley, *Human Nature,* n., p. 116.

36. Follett, *New State,* p. 64. On their views about the compatibility of specialization and breadth, see Royce, *Scribner's,* X, 380; Addams, *Annals,* XIII, 330, 340; Giddings, *Principles,* pp. 67–68; John Dewey, *The Educational Situation,* Chicago, 1902, pp. 18, 19, 35, 45, 80–104.

CHAPTER 7: JANE ADDAMS AND THE DIVISION OF LABOR

1. Hofstadter, *Social Darwinism,* p. 33; Persons, *American Minds,* pp. 218–227; Sumner and Keller, *Science of Society,* III, 2217–2220; Ely, *Evolution of Industrial Society,* pp. 7–8; Small, *General Sociology,* pp. 134–135, 585.

2. Spencer, *Principles,* II-1, 245–247.

3. The point here is not the deliberate adoption of Durkheim's views but rather the similarity between his views and those of his American contemporaries. Several of the communitarians were at least familiar with his work. See Cooley, *Social Process,* p. 400; Park, *Science of Sociology,* pp. 30–34; Giddings, *Studies in Theory,* pp. 61–62; John Dewey, "The Need for Social Psychology," *Psychological Review,* XXIV, July, 1917, 273.

4. Durkheim, *Division of Labor,* pp. 1–26, 130–131, 256–258; *Suicide,* pp. 379, 388–390. "Mechanical solidarity" was based on common values.

5. Giddings, *Principles,* p. 396; *Elements,* pp. 6–8, 83–84, 214; Howe, *Modern City,* pp. 1–3, 37; Addams, *Democracy,* p. 210; Royce, *Fugitive Essays,* pp. 125–126; Cooley, *Sociological Theory,* pp. 93–104 (1894); *Human Nature,* pp. 118–119; Park, in *The City,* pp. 12–14; *Human Communities,* pp. 180–181 (1929); Dewey, *Ethics,* p. 430.

6. Giddings, *Elements,* pp. 6–8, 192–198; *Descriptive Sociology,* pp. 496–498; Howe, *Modern City,* pp. 37–48; Addams, *Democracy,* pp. 209–210; Royce, *Christianity,* II, 82–98; Cooley, *Sociological Theory,* p. 104 (1894) *Social Organization,* pp. 25–27, 243; *Life,* pp. 9–10; Park, in *The City,* pp. 13–14, 117–118; Dewey, *School and Society,* pp. 21–24; *Proceedings of the NEA,* 1902, p. 381.

7. Dewey, *Proceedings of the NEA,* 1902, p. 379.

8. Royce, *Christianity*, II, 85.

9. *Ibid.*, 87.

10. Sigfried Giedion, *Mechanization Takes Command: A Contribution to Anonymous History*, New York, 1948, pp. 90, 93, 121; C. Wright Mills, *White Collar: The American Middle Classes*, New York, 1951, pp. 170, 192–193; Thernstrom, *Poverty and Progress*, pp. 213–214.

11. Harold U. Faulkner, *The Decline of Laissez Faire, 1897–1917,* New York, 1951, p. 123; Giedion, *Mechanization,* pp. 96–99, 115–116, 121.

12. Frederick W. Taylor, *The Principles of Scientific Management,* New York, 1911, p. 140.

13. Cooley, *Human Nature,* pp. 118–119; Charles Horton Cooley, *Human Nature and the Social Order,* 2nd ed. revised, New York, 1922, n., p. 152; *Social Organization,* pp. 408–409; *Publications of the ASS,* XIII, 2; *Social Process,* p. 142; Jane Addams, "Child Labor and Pauperism," *Charities,* XI, 301–302.

14. Park, in *The City,* p. 117.

15. Dewey, *Democracy and Education,* pp. 98–99, 138–139, 303.

16. Follett, *Administration,* pp. 51–59 (1926), 80 (1925), 117–131 (1925).

17. Cooley, *Social Process,* p. 142.

18. The studies which illuminate Addams' views on work and education are Christopher Lasch, *The New Radicalism in America: 1889–1963: The Intellectual as a Social Type,* New York, 1965, which interprets her reaction to genteel culture in psychological terms and argues that her educational schemes were conservative in so far as they aimed at reconciling workers to the existing industrial situation; Cremin, *Transformation of the School,* and White and White, *Intellectual versus City,* which discuss her communitarian ideals and the ways in which education was meant to serve them. Daniel Levine's *Varieties of Reform Thought,* Madison, Wis., 1964, shows how her concept of the welfare state and her views of worker's education fit into her ideal of a harmonious society characterized by the individual's devotion to the social organism.

19. Green, *American Cities,* p. 100; Ray Ginger, *Atgeld's America: The Lincoln Ideal versus Changing Realities,* New York, 1958, pp. 15–34; Glaab and Brown, *Urban America,* pp. 86, 98, 102, 110.

20. Ginger, *Atgeld's America,* Ch. I.

21. Feuer, *JHI,* XX, 545–568; Jane Addams, *The Social Thought of Jane Addams,* ed. with an Introduction by Christopher Lasch, Indianapolis, 1965, pp. 176–177; letter from John Dewey to Jane

Addams, January 19, 1896, Jane Addams Papers, Swarthmore College Peace Collection; Dewey, *Proceedings of the NEA,* 1902, p. 381; Jane Dewey, in *The Philosophy of John Dewey,* pp. 29–30; Addams, *Annals,* XIII, 324; *Twenty Years,* pp. 236, 435–436; *Second Twenty Years,* pp. 345–358; *Survey,* LXII, 203–204. The similarity in the educational views of Addams and Dewey has been noted often. See Cremin, *Transformation of the School,* p. 63, n. 7. Lasch argues in Addams, *Social Thought,* pp. 176–177, that she contributed more to Dewey's educational ideas than is usually acknowledged.

22. Robert L. McCaul, "Dewey's Chicago," *The School Review,* LXVII, Summer, 1959, 261–275.

23. The similarity between the early writings of Veblen and Dewey is discussed by White, *Social Thought in America,* pp. 94–97 and by Feuer, *JHI,* XX, 567–568.

24. Addams, *Hull-House Maps,* p. 184; *Twenty Years,* p. 99; Ginger, *Atgeld's America,* pp. 26–27.

25. Addams, *Annals,* XIII, 335. See *Hull-House Maps,* pp. 183–204, Jane Addams, "Trade Unions and Public Duty," *The American Journal of Sociology,* IV, January, 1898, 450–458; *Twenty Years,* pp. 200–204, 211–212, 298, 300–304.

26. Addams, *Democracy,* p. 210.

27. *Ibid.,* pp. 180–181, 193, 210–211.

28. Addams, *Annals,* XIII, 334.

29. Addams, *Twenty Years,* pp. 61–76. Lasch argues that her revulsion against genteel culture and her subsequent decision to help the poor sprang less from a sense of outrage at their lot than from her psychological ties to the moralistic father whom she worshipped. Lasch, *New Radicalism,* pp. 15–25.

30. Addams, *Philanthropy,* p. 15. See also p. 14; *Independent,* LIII, 1852–1855; *Democracy,* pp. 83–86, 88–89.

31. Addams, *Annals,* XIII, 329–330, 334–337, 399; *Democracy,* pp. 196, 206; *Twenty Years,* p. 431.

32. Addams, *Democracy,* p. 202. Levine's *Reform Thought,* p. 27, notes that the effect of Addams' scheme would be to keep workers in their place and thereby reinforce the class divisions which she disliked.

33. Addams, *Democracy,* p. 193.

34. Addams, *Twenty Years,* pp. 41–42, 187–188.

35. Addams, *Democracy,* p. 213. See also Addams, *Annals,* XIII, 324, 335, 337; *Democracy,* pp. 16, 181, 204; *Second Twenty Years,* pp. 345–358.

36. Addams, *Spirit of Youth*, pp. 124, 135; *Second Twenty Years*, pp. 358–359.

37. Addams, *Democracy*, pp. 208–209.

38. Addams, *Twenty Years*, pp. 236–237, 242; Nancy Portia Pottishman, "Jane Addams and Education," unpublished Master's thesis, Columbia University, 1961, pp. 33–35.

39. Addams, *Twenty Years*, p. 236.

40. Addams, *Democracy*, pp. 192, 209, 212.

41. *Ibid.*, p. 206. See also Addams, *Annals*, XII, 330; *Twenty Years*, p. 236.

42. Addams, *Annals*, XIII, 323–345; *Twenty Years*, p. 436.

43. Addams, *Annals*, XIII, 339–340.

44. *Ibid.*, 336.

45. *Ibid.*, 330, 336.

46. Addams, *Democracy*, p. 206.

47. *Ibid.*, p. 212. See also pp. 211–213; Addams, *Philanthropy*, p. 10.

48. Addams, *Democracy*, p. 214.

49. *Ibid.*, p. 209.

50. *Ibid.*, pp. 209–210. See *Twenty Years*, pp. 237, 436, 440; Jill Conway, "Jane Addams: an American Heroine," *Daedalus*, XCIII, Spring, 1964, 768.

51. Addams, *Philanthropy*, p. 10. See also *Democracy*, pp. 180, 209, 212–214; *Twenty Years*, p. 427.

52. Addams, *Spirit of Youth*, pp. 109, 114, 122, 127; Dewey, *School and Society*, pp. 22–24, 27–30, 33, 37–38; *Democracy and Education*, pp. 98–99, 141, 304; *Human Nature*, p. 144; Cooley, *Human Nature*, 1902, pp. 115–116; *Social Organization*, pp. 385–387; *Social Process*, pp. 70–72.

53. Addams, *The Chautauquan*, XXXIX, 271; *North American Review*, CLXXIX, 191; *Twenty Years*, p. 374; *Spirit of Youth*, pp. 108, 124, 128, 135; *Second Twenty Years*, p. 359.

54. The influence of the Arts and Crafts movement on Addams is evidenced by her reliance on Ruskin's ideal of work in *The Chautauquan*, XXXIX, 266–272, and by Veblen's description of the Ruskinesque Chicago Arts and Crafts Society which she organized in 1897 and from which she recruited teachers for her Hull House workshops. Thorstein Veblen, *Essays in Our Changing Order*, ed. Leon Ardzrooni, New York, 1934, pp. 194–199 (1902); Addams, *Twenty Years*, p. 375. Farrell contends that the movement was also the inspiration for the Labor Museum. Farrell, *Beloved Lady*, p. 96. Addams had known of

Ruskin since her college years and of Morris, since her visits to England. Addams, *Twenty Years*, pp. 38, 47; Linn, *Addams*, pp. 88–89; Farrell, pp. 44–45. On Louis Sullivan and his Industrial Art League, also influenced by Ruskin and Morris, see Ginger, *Atgeld's America*, pp. 327–328, and a contemporary account of the League, Oscar Lovell Triggs, *Chapters in the History of the Arts and Crafts Movement*, Chicago, 1902, pp. 189–194.

55. Addams, *Annals*, XIII, 333; *North American Review*, CLXXIX, 173–181; *Spirit of Youth*, p. 124.

56. Addams, *Annals*, XIII, 332; *Twenty Years*, p. 374.

57. Addams, *The Chautauquan*, XXXIX, 266–271; *North American Review*, CLXXIX, 185, 191; *Twenty Years*, pp. 374–376; *Spirit of Youth*, pp. 127–128.

58. Addams likened their protest to Ruskin's plea for pleasure in work. Addams, *North American Review*, CLXXIX, 178–193. She often used Ruskin to criticize the division of labor and to stress the importance of art in labor. Addams, *Annals*, XIII, 331; *The Chautauquan*, XXXIX, 272.

59. Addams, *Spirit of Youth*, p. 124.

60. *Ibid.*, p. 135.

61. White and White, *Intellectual versus City*, p. 152.

62. Addams, *Twenty Years*, p. 374; *Spirit of Youth*, pp. 109, 122, 124, 135; *Second Twenty Years*, pp. 350, 358–359. She used Veblen's term in *Twenty Years*, p. 246. Cooley also used the term in *Social Organization*, p. 304, and his use of Veblen is markedly similar to Addams'. See Cooley, *Social Organization*, pp. 244, 304; *Social Process*, pp. 142, 304, 321, 342–345. Dewey refused to use the term "instinct of workmanship" because he thought it took attention away from the evils of the economic environment. He wanted to focus on the wrong use of the machine, and on this point, he too, along with Addams and Cooley, emphasized the desirability of personal control, initiative, and creativity. Dewey, *Human Nature*, pp. 142–148; *Democracy and Education*, pp. 371–374.

63. Thorstein Veblen, *The Instinct of Workmanship and the Industrial Arts*, New York, 1914, p. 241. See also pp. 31–34.

64. Addams, *Annals*, XIII, 331; *North American Review*, CLXXIX, 185; *Democracy*, p. 219; Veblen, *Instinct of Workmanship*, p. 234; J. A. Hobson, *Veblen*, London, 1936, pp. 100–101. Hannah Arendt has analyzed the confusion of "work" and "labor" in modern thought. Whereas labor is part of the biological metabolism between man and

nature, which produces things only for the purpose of consumption, work produces permanent objects. Work is not compatible with the division of labor (though it is compatible with specialization of function) or with standardized production. Nonetheless, Veblen, Marx, and others continued to attribute the qualities of work to labor. Hannah Arendt, *The Human Condition,* Chicago, 1958, pp. 102–103. So too did Addams, Cooley, and Dewey and those who tried to make individual creativity compatible with machine labor. Interestingly, Addams used the terms labor and work interchangeably. Addams, *The Chautauquan,* XXXIX, 266; *Democracy,* p. 192; *Spirit of Youth,* p. 122.

65. Jane Addams, "Arts and Crafts and the Settlement," *The Chautauquan Assembly Herald,* XXVII, July 9, 1902, 2–3, Jane Addams Papers; *Spirit of Youth,* p. 135. *Second Twenty Years,* p. 359.

66. Addams, *Spirit of Youth,* pp. 126–127.

67. *Ibid.,* p. 128.

68. Addams, *Democracy,* p. 219.

69. *Ibid.,* p. 207.

70. Cooley, *Social Process,* pp. 71–72.

71. Dewey, *School and Society,* pp. 21–32; *Democracy and Education,* pp. 23–25, 416. The relation between Dewey's educational ideals and his allegiance to an older form of social organization has only recently become an important theme in the literature on Dewey. See Kimball and McClellan, *Education,* pp. 96–107; White and White, *Intellectual versus City,* pp. 167–171; Arthur G. Wirth, *John Dewey as Educator: His Design for Work in Education (1894–1904),* New York, 1966, ix-x, pp. 291–293.

72. Dewey, *Proceedings of the NEA,* 1902, p. 379.

73. Dewey, *School and Society,* pp. 22–26; *Democracy and Education,* p. 278.

74. Dewey, *School and Society,* p. 44.

75. *Ibid.,* pp. 32–33, 37; Dewey, *Democracy and Education,* pp. 252, 256–262, 302–303.

76. Dewey, *Democracy and Education,* p. 254.

77. *Ibid.,* p. 244. See pp. 256–261; *School and Society,* p. 37; *Educational Review,* XXI, 471.

78. Dewey, *Democracy and Education,* p. 263.

79. *Ibid.,* pp. 36–37, 99, 304.

80. *Ibid.,* p. 304.

81. *Ibid.,* pp. 99, 302, 304, 370–372; Dewey, *Characters,* II, 752–757 (1918).

82. Cooley, *Social Process,* p. 73.

83. Cooley, *Social Organization,* pp. 384–385; *Social Process,* pp. 73, 418–419; *Publications of the ASS,* XIII, 7–8.

84. Cooley, *Publications of the ASS,* XIII, 2–7.

85. *Ibid.,* p. 7.

86. *Ibid.,* pp. 2–3, 5–6; Cooley, *Social Organization,* p. 97; *Social Process,* pp. 68, 70–71.

87. Cooley, *Social Process,* p. 143. Cooley attacked pecuniary values in the name of efficiency and service, but he too wanted to inject the values of craftsmanship and of self-expression into the system of production. Cooley, *Social Organization,* pp. 244, 304; *Social Process,* pp. 70–71, 142, 342, 345.

88. Cooley, *Social Organization,* pp. 385–387.

89. Cooley, *Publications of the ASS,* XIII, 4.

90. Cooley, *Social Process,* p. 344.

91. *Ibid.* Italics Cooley's.

92. *Ibid.* See also pp. 417–418.

93. Dewey, *Proceedings of the NEA,* 1902, p. 379.

CHAPTER 8: JOHN DEWEY AND THE SPECIALIZATION OF KNOWLEDGE

1. Charles William Eliot, *Educational Reform: Essays and Addresses,* New York, 1901, pp. 412–413.

2. Henry Adams, *The Education of Henry Adams,* New York, 1931, p. 455. See pp. 225–226, 342–343, 427–429, 458.

3. *Ibid.,* p. 472.

4. Hugo Münsterberg, "The Scientific Plan of the Congress," in *Congress of Arts and Science: Universal Exposition, St. Louis, 1904,* ed. Howard J. Rogers, Boston, 1905, I, 92.

5. Veysey, *American University,* pp. 180–200; Matthew Arnold, *Discourses in America,* London, 1889, pp. 72–137.

6. Examples of such attention include Veysey, *American University;* R. Freeman Butts, *The College Charts Its Course,* New York, 1939; Richard Hofstadter and Walter Metzger, *The Development of Academic Freedom in the United States,* New York, 1955.

7. Richard Hofstadter and Wilson Smith, eds., *American Higher Education: a Documentary History,* Chicago, 1961, II, 957.

8. The terms "seekers" and "conservers" are Hofstadter's and Metzger's. Adams and Hall represented the single-minded devotion to

research which captured the imagination of some postwar scholars. Jurgen Herbst, *The German Historical School in American Scholarship: A Study in the Transfer of Culture,* Ithaca, N.Y., 1965, pp. 99–128; Veysey, *American University,* pp. 142–144.

9. Giddings, *Democracy,* pp. 218–225 (1894); Royce, *Scribner's,* X, 376–388; Dewey, *Reconstruction,* pp. 161–186; Howe, *Confessions,* pp. 1, 5, 8, 15; Cooley, *Social Organization,* pp. 388–389; *Publications of the ASS,* XIII, 3–4; *Sociological Theory,* pp. 4–10 (1928).

10. Walter E. Houghton, *The Victorian Frame of Mind: 1830–1837,* New Haven, Conn., 1957, pp. 9–20, 32–35, 144–148.

11. Joseph L. Blau, *Men and Movements in American Philosophy,* New York, 1952, pp. 73–110; Persons, *American Minds,* pp. 189–195.

12. Hofstadter and Smith, *Higher Education,* I, 282.

13. *Ibid.,* 283–284.

14. Blau, *American Philosophy,* pp. 88–91.

15. John McVikar, *Outlines of Political Economy,* New York, 1825, n., p. 69.

16. Butts, *The College,* pp. 93–94, 99–115, 143–149, 176, 184–186, 198, 343–346, 360; Hofstadter and Metzger, *Academic Freedom,* pp. 292, 339–340, 345–346, 377.

17. Hofstadter and Smith, *Higher Education,* II, 706. See also Charles W. Eliot, *The Man and His Beliefs,* ed. William Neilson, New York, 1926, I, 197–198.

18. Eliot, *Educational Reform,* pp. 413–416.

19. Hofstadter and Smith, *Higher Education,* II, 699–700, 721.

20. *Ibid.,* 725–726.

21. *Ibid.,* 725.

22. Veysey, *American University,* pp. 180–181, 199–200.

23. *Ibid.,* pp. 67–68, 142–143.

24. Dewey, *Educational Review,* XXI, 464.

25. Cooley, *Social Organization,* pp. 388–389; *Publications of the ASS,* XIII, 7; Royce, *Scribner's,* X, 386–388.

26. On Dewey's notion of intellectual unity, the following are suggestive: Wirth, *Dewey as Educator,* pp. 172–177, 206–224, 283–284; Blewett, in *Dewey: Thought and Influence,* pp. 33–57; Albert William Levi, *Philosophy and the Modern World,* Bloomington, Ind., 1959, pp. 292–296.

27. John Dewey, "The Influence of Darwinism on Philosophy," in *American Thought: Civil War to World War I,* ed. with an Introduction by Perry Miller, New York, 1954, pp. 214–225; *Experience and*

Education, New York, 1938, pp. 107–108; Dykhuizen, *JHI,* XX, 527–531.

28. Dewey, *On Experience, Nature,* p. 10 (1930).

29. Dewey, *Andover Review,* VII, 590.

30. Dewey, *On Experience, Nature,* p. 12 (1930). Dewey's break with Idealism occurred primarily during the years 1891–1894; by 1903 it was complete. Darwinism helped him reject the Hegelian idea of fixed ends for man and society and the a priori logic which accompanied it. Morton White, *The Origins of Dewey's Instrumentalism,* New York, 1943, pp. 106–109.

31. Dewey, in *Religious Thought at Michigan,* p. 64. See also *Characters,* II, 515 (1908); *Reconstruction,* pp. 211–213; *Common Faith,* pp. 50–51.

32. Perry, *William James,* II, 518–519; Dewey, *Characters,* I, 21–29 (1892). On Ford's influence, see Feuer, *JHI,* XX, 545–568. On Renan's influence see Richard McClain Chadbourne, "Two Organizers of Divinity: Ernest Renan and John Dewey," *Thought: Fordham University Quarterly,* XXIV, September, 1949, 430–448.

33. Reginald D. Archambault, "Introduction," John Dewey, *Lectures in the Philosophy of Education: 1899,* ed. with an Introduction by Reginald D. Archambault, New York, 1966, xx–xxiv.

34. Dewey, *School and Society,* pp. 106–107; *Educational Review,* XXI, 462–474; *Educational Situation,* pp. 18–19, 35, 45; *Educational Confusion,* pp. 1–36.

35. Dewey, *Educational Review,* XXI, 466–467.

36. Dewey, *Ethics,* p. 448. See *School and Society,* pp 39–40; *Democracy and Education,* p. 5.

37. Dewey, *Lectures: 1899,* pp. 224–225, 284–285, 288; *School and Society,* pp. 32–33; *Educational Review,* XXI, 470; *Democracy and Education,* pp. 333–335.

38. Dewey, *Lectures: 1899,* p. 133.

39. *Ibid.,* p. 134.

40. Dewey, *Outlines of Ethics,* p. 26.

41. *Ibid.,* p. 126; Dewey, *Lectures: 1899,* p. 253; *Educational Situation,* p. 45; *Reconstruction,* pp. 28–76.

42. Dewey, *Educational Review,* XXI, 463. See also *Ethics,* p. 448; *Democracy and Education,* p. 289; *Characters,* II, 496–497 (1916); *Public,* pp. 176–177.

43. Dewey, *Public,* p. 174. See *Outlines of Ethics,* p. 126; *Democracy and Education,* pp. 268, 302; *Characters,* II, 552 (1918).

44. John Dewey, "The St. Louis Congress of the Arts and Sciences," *Science*, XVIII, August 28, 1903, 275–278; *On Experience, Nature*, p. 12 (1930); John Dewey, *Freedom and Culture*, New York, 1939, pp. 74–81. Dewey's differences with the educator and Idealist philosopher, William Torrey Harris, appear in his recently published lectures of 1899, where he agreed with Harris' insistence on the unification of learning but criticized him for dividing the study of nature from the study of man. Dewey, *Lectures: 1899*, pp. 187–199.

45. Dewey, in *American Thought*, p. 217.

46. Dewey, *Lectures: 1899*, p. 225.

47. *Ibid.*, p. 224. See pp. 223–225; Dewey, *Democracy and Education*, pp. 268–269; Wirth, *Dewey as Educator*, p. 181.

48. Dewey, *Lectures: 1899*, p. 225.

49. *Ibid.*, p. 216.

50. *Ibid.*

51. Dewey, *Experience and Education*, pp. 49, 87–89.

52. Dewey, *Educational Confusion*, pp. 10, 33; *Experience and Education*, p. 49.

53. Dewey, *Democracy and Education*, pp. 261–264; *Intelligence in the Modern World*, pp. 343–363 (1936); *Freedom and Culture*, pp. 134–135, 153. For similar ideas in the works of others, see Royce, *Religious Insight*, p. 273; *Christianity*, I, 423, II, 430; *Hope*, pp. 37–39; Giddings, *Democracy*, pp. 224–226 (1894), 247 (1898); *Studies in Theory*, pp. 62–63, 184; *Principles*, p. 418; Park, *Society*, pp. 143–151 (1918); Addams, *Annals*, XIII, 330; Howe, *Confessions*, pp. 317–322; *Wisconsin*, pp. 38–50, 153–156, 189–190; Cooley, *Social Organization*, pp. 87, 386, 389; *Social Process*, pp. 247, 347, 391–392; Follett, *New State*, pp. 245–257; *Creative Experience*, pp. 3–9.

54. By Positivism Dewey meant the reliance on science for valid knowledge and the emphasis on its role as a regulator of society. See Cooley, Student Notebook, 1894; John Dewey, "Some Stages of Logical Thought," *Philosophical Review*, IX, September, 1900, 486. Dewey was not a Positivist in the narrower sense, i.e., he did not subscribe to Comte's law of the three stages of history or to his idea of the hierarchy of the sciences. Neither did Renan and Mill, whom Dewey groups with Comte. See W. M. Simon, *European Positivism in the Nineteenth Century: An Essay in Intellectual History*, Ithaca, N.Y., 1963, pp. 95–98, 182–191 on the differences among these figures. Dewey's interest in Comte dated back to his undergraduate days, when, as he described it, he ran across "Harriet Martineau's exposition of Comte.

I cannot remember that his law of the 'three stages' affected me particularly; but his idea of the disorganized character of Western modern culture, due to a disintegrative 'individualism,' and his idea of a synthesis of science that should be a regulative method of an organized social life, impressed me deeply. I found, as I thought, the same criticisms combined with a deeper and more far-reaching integration in Hegel." Dewey, *On Experience, Nature*, p. 12. The role of Comte in Dewey's intellectual development is mentioned by Weaver, "John Dewey; Spokesman for Liberalism," p. 55, and by John Herman Randall, Jr., "The Religion of Shared Experience," in *The Philosopher of the Common Man: Essays in Honor of John Dewey to Celebrate His Eightieth Birthday*, Foreword by Sidney Ratner, New York, 1940, p. 115.

55. Comte recoiled from the individualism which he thought characterized modern society following the French Revolution. He wanted to reconstruct an organic society with the sociologists as the spiritual powers and the employers as the temporal powers. The moral education directed by the former would overcome the divisions between classes and between groups fragmented by the division of labor. Comte's idea of the proper organization of knowledge and of education was directed against the evil of specialization, which he thought contributed to social disorganization. What he wanted was a unified science of man. In contrast to Dewey, Comte's notion of science was dogmatic because he feared free inquiry as the harbinger of anarchy. Bramson, *Political Sociology*, pp. 11–14; Simon, *European Positivism*, pp. 4–6; Giorgio de Santillana, "Positivism and the Technocratic Ideal in the Nineteenth Century," in *Studies in the History of Science and Learning Offered in Homage to George Sarton on the Occasion of his Sixtieth Birthday*, ed. M. F. Ashley Montagu, New York, 1947, pp. 249–257.

56. Cooley, Student Notebook, 1894; Dewey, *Public*, p. 174.

57. Dewey, in *Religious Thought at Michigan*, p. 67.

58. *Ibid.*, pp. 67–68.

59. Dewey, *Characters*, I, 18–30 (1892).

60. For Hegel, the original meaning of Christianity was the unity of the divine and the human. The realization of the consciousness of this unity was the goal of history. G.W.F. Hegel, *The Philosophy of Hegel*, ed., with an Introduction by Carl J. Friedrich, New York, 1953, pp. 60, 120–121, 461–467, 511, 513–514; *Lectures on the Philosophy of Religion*, ed. E. B. Speirs, London, 1895, II, 346–347. Dewey's views on history as the secularization of the Absolute and of the idea of

freedom are remarkably like Hegel's. Cf. the above with Dewey, "Green's Theory of the Moral Motive," *Philosophical Review,* I, November, 1892, 610; *Ethics of Democracy,* p. 27; *Andover Review,* VII, 587–590.

61. Dewey, in *Religious Thought at Michigan,* p. 67.

62. Dewey, *Philosophical Review,* I, 610. In a talk to the Students' Christian Association during that year Dewey expounded the idea that the next religious prophet would be the man "who succeeds in pointing out the religious meaning of democracy, the ultimate religious value to be found in the normal flow of life itself." John Dewey, "The Relation of Philosophy to Theology," *The Monthly Bulletin* of the Students' Christian Association of the University of Michigan, XIV, January, 1893, 68.

63. Dewey, *Philosophical Review,* I, 610.

64. John Dewey, "Reconstruction," *The Monthly Bulletin* of the Students' Christian Association of the University of Michigan, XV, June, 1894, 154.

65. *Ibid.,* 152–153.

66. Ernest Renan, quoted in Dewey, *Characters,* I, 26 (1892).

67. *Ibid.,* 26. See also p. 27 (1892).

68. Dewey, in *Religious Thought at Michigan,* pp. 60–69; *Philosophical Review,* I, 593–612; *Philosophical Review,* IX, 485–486.

69. Dewey, in *American Thought,* pp. 214–225; John Dewey, "The Subject-Matter of Metaphysical Inquiry," *Journal of Philosophy,* XII, June 24, 1915, 337–345; *Human Nature,* pp. 331–332; *Experience and Nature,* pp. 110, 175, 185, 202; *Common Faith,* pp. 33, 51, 85. On Dewey's metaphysics see Levi, *Philosophy,* pp. 292–301.

70. Dewey, *Experience and Nature,* p. 202.

71. *Ibid.,* pp. 202, 205.

72. Dewey, *Reconstruction,* pp. 211–213; *Common Faith,* pp. 50–51, 85–87.

73. Dewey, *Characters,* I, 14 (1891).

74. Dewey, *Reconstruction,* p. 211.

75. Jane Addams, "A Function of the Social Settlement," *Annals of the American Academy of Political and Social Science,* XIII, May 1899, 340. See also 326, 336. This essay is similar to Albion Small's article on "Scholarship and Social Agitation," *The American Journal of Sociology,* I, 1895–1896, 567, 581–582. Small criticized the accumulation of knowledge divorced from practice. According to Farrell, Addams identified with the reform-minded social scientists at the Uni-

versity of Chicago where Small was chairman of the Sociology Department. Farrell, *Beloved Lady,* pp. 67–68.

76. Addams, *Annals,* XIII, 325.

77. Frederic Harrison, quoted in Simon, *European Positivism,* p. 55. On the influence of Positivism on Addams, see Merle Curti, "Jane Addams on Human Nature," *Journal of the History of Ideas,* XXII, April-June, 1961, 244, and Linn, *Addams,* pp. 75–77, 195. On her second trip to Europe in 1887–1888, she was much impressed with Harrison and the Positivists' religion of humanity. Her mature religious views centered on brotherhood and social justice rather than on personal communion, and she herself suggested a link with the Positivists. Addams, *Twenty Years,* pp. 82–83; *Philanthropy,* pp. 16–19. Others in this group were in varying degrees familiar with and influenced by different aspects of Comte. Park, *Human Communities,* pp. 179–182 (1929), 240–262 (1939); Giddings, *Principles,* pp. 6–7. The impact of Comte in America has not yet been adequately studied. There is some suggestion that the ideal of the unity of knowledge may have been transmitted by American Positivists of the midcentury such as John Draper. Donald Fleming, *John William Draper and the Religion of Science,* Philadelphia, 1950, pp. 125–131.

78. Addams, *Annals,* XIII, 330.

79. Giddings, *Democracy,* p. 219 (1894).

80. *Ibid.,* pp. 224–226 (1894).

81. Giddings, *Principles,* pp. 357–360, 423–442; *Elements,* pp. 330–343.

82. Giddings, *Principles,* p. 69.

83. *Ibid.,* p. 67.

84. Giddings, *Elements,* pp. 328–329; *Scientific Study,* pp. 35–36, 145–154, 171.

85. Veysey, *American University,* p. 203.

86. Royce, *Scribner's,* X, 388.

87. Josiah Royce, "The Sciences of the Ideal," in *Congress of Arts and Science: Universal Exposition, St. Louis, 1904,* ed. Howard J. Rogers, Boston, 1905, I, 152–167; Josiah Royce, "Introduction," Henri Poincaré, *The Foundations of Science,* New York, 1913, pp. 9–25.

88. Royce, *Scribner's,* X, 379–380.

89. *Ibid.,* 380.

90. Royce, "Introduction," *Foundations of Science,* pp. 9–25.

91. Royce, in *Congress,* I, 156.

92. *Ibid.,* 155.

93. Royce, "Introduction," *Foundations of Science,* pp. 14, 15. Examples of such explanations were the principles of Euclidean and non-Euclidean geometry, the principles of mechanics and parts of the theory of evolution. *Ibid.,* pp. 18–20. Royce, like Poincaré, rejected the Kantian idea that the categories were necessities dictated by the nature of the human mind. Royce, in *Congress,* I, 159–167.

94. Royce, in *Congress,* I, 159.

95. Royce's *World and the Individual* (1899) is the turning point in his movement away from monism and Peirce's influence is already evident here. But Peirce's greatest impact came after the publication of *The World and the Individual,* when he wrote a letter to Royce telling him he needed to study more logic. J. Harry Cotton, *Royce on the Human Self.* Cambridge, Mass. 1954, pp. 216–219, 261–265.

96. Royce, *Christianity,* II, 280. On the transition, see Cotton, *Royce,* pp. 261–265; Smith, *Royce's Social Infinite,* pp. 11–14. Smith's book is devoted to a study of Royce's theory of the community of interpretation and Peirce's influence on it. Royce's use of logic in *The Problem of Christianity* gave precision to the philosophy of community first developed in *The Philosophy of Loyalty.* Smith, *Royce's Social Infinite,* p. 8.

97. In *Christianity,* Royce used Peirce's doctrine (1) of signs, (2) of the triadic nature of knowledge, (3) of interpretation and (4) of the indefinite community. Cotton, *Royce,* pp. 216–237. Peirce's own idea of community as a precondition of knowledge is discussed in Smith, *Royce's Social Infinite,* p. 26.

98. Royce, "Introduction," *Christianity,* I, xi; II, 114–117.

99. *Ibid.,* II, 118–129, 140–141, 283, 287.

100. *Ibid.,* 148.

101. *Ibid.,* 231–250; Royce, *War,* iv, 44–49, 57–63. The most thorough exposition of Royce's theory of interpretation is Fuss, *Moral Philosophy of Royce,* pp. 102–133.

102. Royce, *Christianity,* II, 231.

103. *Ibid.,* 173, 183, 208–209, 217–220; Royce, *War,* pp. 51, 59–61, 71.

104. Royce, *Christianity,* II, 208.

105. *Ibid.,* 219. See pp. 264–284 for his metaphysical doctrine. Royce made a point of saying that here he diverged from Peirce. Peirce did expound what he called "a religion of science" in which the truths of science and religion were no longer in conflict. Charles Sanders Peirce, *Collected Papers of Charles Sanders Peirce,* eds. Charles Hartshorne and Paul Weiss, Cambridge, Mass., VI, 1935, 302–304 (1893).

106. Royce, *Christianity*, II, 220.

107. *Ibid.*, I, 194.

108. *Ibid.*, 406. See also 103, 172, 423–424; II, 368, 371, 430.

109. See for example, Wiebe, *Search for Order*, pp. 133–163.

110. Follett, *New State*, p. 64.

111. Cooley, *Human Nature*, 1902, n., p. 116. See pp. 115–116; *Sociological Theory*, p. 188 (1899).

112. *Ibid.*, p. 116.

113. Butts, *The College*, pp. 175–183, 184–188; Hofstadter and Metzger, *Academic Freedom*, pp. 357, 377; Veysey, *American University*, pp. 61–96, 122–143, 255. The best analysis of the presidents' ideal of intellectual unity is in Burton Bledstein, "Cultivation and Custom: The Idea of Liberal Culture in Post Civil War America," unpublished Ph.D. dissertation, Princeton University, 1967.

114. Bledstein, "Cultivation and Custom," pp. 351–360, 421–432, 504–534. A similar belief that God's design gives unity to all intellectual endeavors can be found among liberal Protestant figures such as Strong, *New Era*, p. 19, and Lyman Abbott, *The Evolution of Christianity*, Boston, 1892, p. 247.

115. Münsterberg, in *Congress*, I, 102.

116. George Holmes Howison, "Philosophy: Its Fundamental Conceptions and Its Methods," in *Congress of Arts and Science: Universal Exposition, St. Louis, 1904*, ed. Howard J. Rogers, Boston, 1905, I, 177.

117. Albion Small, "Points of Agreement among Sociologists," *Proceedings of the American Sociological Society*, I. 1907, 68. See A. W. Coates, "American Scholarship Comes of Age," *Journal of the History of Ideas*, XXII, July-September, 1961, 407.

118. See their addresses in *Congress*, II, 40–51, 183–194, 215–228; V, 577–589, 787–799. Several of the social scientists, such as Small, Patten, and Robinson, were much influenced by the German tradition of empirical Idealism which sought to relate many fields in one broad synthesis. On this see White, *Social Thought in America*, pp. 12–13, 27, 29, 285, n. 48, and Herbst's, *German Historical School*, pp. 53–231. On Hall's synthesis of psychology, biology, evolution, and Christianity, see Wilson, *In Quest of Community*, pp. 179–180.

119. James Harvey Robinson, "The Conception and Methods of History," in *Congress of Arts and Science: Universal Exposition, St. Louis, 1904*, ed. Howard J. Rogers, Boston, 1905, II, 51.

120. White, *Social Thought in America*, p. 12.

CHAPTER 9: THE ASCENDANCE OF CULTURE

1. Dewey, *Democracy and Education,* p. 305.
2. Cooley, *Social Organization,* p. 388.
3. Lasch has suggested how the "new radicals" of the Progressive period confused cultural and political issues. See Lasch, *New Radicalism,* pp. 141–180.
4. Park, *Science of Sociology,* pp. 284–285, 644; *Society,* pp. 143–151 (1918), 295–310 (1934); Royce, *Loyalty,* pp. 212, 248, 258–267, 271–276; *Christianity,* II, 82–99; *Race Questions,* pp. 111–159 (1899); Addams, *Newer Ideals,* pp. 147–150; *Democracy,* pp. 180–181, 192–214; *Spirit of Youth,* pp. 51–56, 108–146; Cooley, *Human Nature,* 1902, p. 119; 1922, n., p. 152; *Social Organization,* pp. 244–245, 284–289, 302–306, 384–389; *Social Process,* pp. 70–73, 125–146, 180–184, 322–327, 385–389; Dewey, in *Philosophy, Psychology and Social Practice,* p. 301 (1899); *Proceedings of the NEA,* 1902, pp. 379–381; *Democracy and Education,* pp. 5–6, 80–90, 98–99, 262, 302, 304, 370–372; *Characters,* II, 751–758 (1918); *Human Nature,* pp. 142–148.
5. Royce, *Christianity,* II, 87–88.
6. *Ibid.,* 88.
7. *Ibid.,* 88–89.
8. *Ibid.,* 90–91.
9. *Ibid.,* 97–98.
10. *Ibid.,* 91.
11. Royce, *Loyalty,* pp. 242, 268–269; *Christianity,* II, 60–61, 92–93.
12. Dewey, *Democracy and Education,* p. 372. See also Addams, *Spirit of Youth,* pp. 124, 127–128, 135; Cooley, *Human Nature,* 1902, pp. 115–116; *Social Process,* pp. 71–72, 131–141.
13. Dewey, *Democracy and Education,* p. 304.
14. Dewey, *School and Society,* p. 38; *Proceedings of the NEA,* 1902, pp. 373–383; *Human Nature,* pp. 143–148.
15. Dewey, *School and Society,* p. 38. Italics Dewey's.
16. *Ibid.;* Dewey, *Democracy and Education,* pp. 369–371.
17. Charles Frankel, "John Dewey's Legacy," *The American Scholar,* XXIX, Summer, 1960, 317.
18. Dewey, *John Dewey on Education,* p. 437 (1897). See also *Democracy and Education,* p. 370.

19. Emile Durkheim, *Moral Education,* trans. by Everett K. Wilson and Herman Schhurer, ed. with an Introduction by Everett K. Wilson, Glencoe, Ill., 1961, p. 277.

20. *Ibid.* See also Durkheim, *Suicide,* pp. 373–375.

21. Emile Durkheim, *Education and Sociology,* trans. with an Introduction by Sherwood D. Fox, Glencoe, Ill., 1951, pp. 77–81, 118, 140–141; *Moral Education,* pp. 228–246, 275–277. See also *Division of Labor,* pp. 1–26; Emile Durkheim, *Suicide: A Study in Sociology,* trans. John A. Spaulding and George Simpson, ed. with an Introduction by George Simpson, Glencoe, Ill., 1951, pp. 378–391; Melvin Richter, "Durkheim's Politics and Political Theory," in *Emile Durkheim: 1858–1917: a Collection of Essays with a Bibliography,* ed. Kurt H. Wolff, Columbus, Ohio, 1960, pp. 187–188, 194–197.

22. Only Royce used the Hegelian term estrangement (Entfremdung; also trans. as alienation); Royce, *Loyalty,* pp. 238–245. But others drew on the philosophical and sociological definitions of the idea which had developed in Europe, except for those of Marx which were unknown until the 1930's. Daniel Bell, "The Debate on Alienation," in *Revisionism: Essays on the History of Marxist Ideas,* ed. Leopold Labedz, New York, 1962, pp. 207–208. Park discussed Simmel's essays on "The Stranger" and "The Metropolis and Mental Life." Like Simmel, he described urban life in terms of impersonality, balked spontaneity, and reserve. Cf. Park, *Science of Sociology,* pp. 284–287, 322–331, *Society,* pp. 147 (1918), 318–319 (1940), *Human Communities,* pp. 175–176 (1925), and Simmel, *Sociology,* pp. 410–422. Cooley's discussion of lack of standards was similar to Durkheim's concept of *anomie* or normlessness. Cf. Cooley, *Social Organization,* pp. 308, 342–385, *Social Process,* pp. 180, 187, 400, and Durkheim's *Suicide.* Cooley used terms like "moral and intellectual isolation," "formalism," and "disorganization." Addams, whose ideas on self-expression were derived from Ruskin, spoke of "instinctive protest" against mechanical arrangements, of activity separated from "direct emotional incentive." See Addams, *Newer Ideals,* p. 52; *Spirit of Youth,* pp. 108–109, 122. Dewey also spoke of "mechanical" relations where the individual did not see the meaning of his activity. Dewey, *Proceedings of the NEA,* 1902, p. 379; *Democracy and Education,* p. 98. Because of his early Hegelianism and the similarity of Dewey's and Hegel's language on this subject, Dewey's ideas on alienation probably derived originally from Hegel. See Dewey, *Philosophical Review,* I,

593–612; Dewey, in *Philosophy, Psychology and Social Practice,* p. 301 (1889).

23. This emphasis on psychological or subjective factors, on the feelings of distance and estrangement, contrasts with the emphasis on objective conditions which is found in Marx. In the early Marx of the *Economic-Philosophical Manuscripts* alienation meant both a sense of estrangement and the externalization of the self through sale of one's labor as a commodity whereby one becomes an object used by others. In his later writings, the second meaning of the term was replaced by or merged with the notion of exploitation. See Bell, in *Revisionism,* pp. 195–196; Eugene Kamenka, *The Ethical Foundations of Marxism,* London, 1962, pp. 144–155.

24. Cooley, *Social Organization,* pp. 342–350.

25. *Ibid.,* p. 345.

26. *Ibid.*

27. *Ibid.,* p. 350. See pp. 357–385.

28. *Ibid.,* p. 350.

29. *Ibid.,* pp. 380, 385–386; Cooley, *Social Process,* pp. 71–73.

30. Cooley, *Human Nature,* 1902, p. 402. See also *Social Organization,* pp. 355, 380, 384; *Publications of the ASS,* XIII, 1–10.

31. Cooley, *Social Organization,* p. 352. See also pp. 349, 354, 384–386.

32. *Ibid.,* p. 385. See also pp. 304, 384–386; Cooley, *Social Process,* pp. 125–146, 322–327.

33. Cooley, *Social Organization,* p. 386.

34. *Ibid.,* p. 245; Cooley, *Social Process,* pp. 137–140, 143–149, 180–187.

35. Cooley, *Human Nature,* 1902, p. 394.

36. Dewey, in *Philosophy, Psychology and Social Practice,* p. 301 (1899); *Democracy and Education,* p. 370; Park, in *The City,* pp. 117–118; *Science of Sociology,* p. 644; *Society,* pp. 143–151 (1918), 295–299 (1934); Addams, *Democracy,* pp. 180, 192–193, 206–207, 211–214; *Spirit of Youth,* pp. 122–124; Royce *Christianity,* I, 142–154, 178–179, 396–397; II, 83–95.

37. Dewey, *Democracy and Education,* p. 370. See also *Characters,* II, 747 (1918), for a later statement of the same idea.

38. Park, *Science of Sociology,* p. 644.

39. Park, *Society,* pp. 293–300 (1934). Cf. Elton Mayo, *The Human Problems of an Industrial Civilization,* New York, 1933, pp. 164–185. Like Mayo, Park agreed that the primary problem was poor morale;

that the solution lay not in the realm of politics but in the realm of sentiments and loyalties. The conservative implications of Mayo's work and that of industrial psychology are developed in Loren Baritz, *The Servants of Power: A History of the Use of Social Science in American Industry*, Middletown, Conn., 1960. A connection also existed between the work of Follett and Mayo. Follett was familiar with some of the early experimental work which led up to his book. See Follett, *Administration*, pp. 183–209 (1927). That Follett had an influence on Mayo is suggested by Kariel, *Western Political Quarterly*, VIII, 427–428. In any case, they shared a psychological approach to work which valued harmony and cooperation. Kariel demonstrates how this emphasis has dominated American social science from the time of Follett and Mayo to the present. Kariel, *American Pluralism*, pp. 113–138.

40. Dewey, in *Philosophy, Psychology and Social Practice*, p. 301 (1899).

CHAPTER 10: POLITICS AND THE SMALL-TOWN FETISH

1. The populistic wing of Progressivism is discussed by Hofstadter, *Age*, pp. 176, 188–190, 215–216; Daniel Aaron, *Men of Good Hope: A Story of American Progressives*, New York, 1951, pp. 160–169; George E. Mowry, *The California Progressives*, Berkeley, Cal., pp. 89–91; *The Era of Theodore Roosevelt and the Birth of Modern America: 1900–1912*, New York, 1958, pp. 52–57. The elitist wing is analyzed by Charles Forcey, *The Crossroads of Liberalism: Croly, Weyl, Lippmann and the Progressive Era: 1900–1925*, New York, 1961, and by Haber, *Efficiency and Uplift*. Associated with the populistic school were direct democracy in government and individualism in economic affairs; with the elitist school, centralized government, the use of experts, and a more collectivist economic policy. What is often regarded as a split between the two schools is viewed in this book as a split within the minds of Progressive thinkers. This latter approach is also used by Levine, *Reform Thought*, p. 116. For a populistic interpretation of White see Hofstadter, *Age*, pp. 258–302; for an elitist one, see Russell B. Nye, *Midwestern Progressive Politics: A Historical Study of Its Origins and Development: 1870–1950*, East Lansing, Mich., 1951, pp. 220–222. Haber's *Efficiency and Uplift*, pp. 26–27, interprets Follett as an elitist.

2. Giddings used this term in *Studies in Theory*, p. 12, n. 2. Similar terms used by others were the "socialization of steam," White, *Old Order*, p. 233; "socialization of industry," Dewey, *Characters*, II, 558 (1918); "social efficiency," Park, *Society*, p. 146 (1918); Follett, *New State*, p. 160.

3. Addams, *North American Review*, CLXXIX, 183; Giddings, *Responsible State*, pp. 43–44; Cooley, *Social Organization*, p. 288; *Social Process*, pp. 44–45; Royce, *Loyalty*, p. 232.

4. Addams, *Hull-House Maps*, p. 204.

5. Addams, *AJS*, IV, 459.

6. Follett, *New State*, pp. 116–121.

7. *Ibid.*, p. 117.

8. *Ibid.*

9. *Ibid.*

10. White, *Gazette*, Sept. 18, 1919; *Autobiography*, p. 465; *Heart of a Fool*, pp. 60, 437; *West*, pp. 42–43; Franklin H. Giddings, "The American Idea," *Harper's Weekly*, XLVIII, November 5, 1904, 1702; *Principles*, pp. 350–351, 355–356; Park, *Society*, pp. 150–151 (1918); Addams, *Twenty Years*, pp. 186–188; Howe, *Confessions*, pp. 321–322; Royce, *Loyalty*, pp. 228–232, 247–248.

11. Cooley, *Social Process*, p. 143. On the anticonflict bias of this generation of sociologists, see Ralf Dahrendorf, "Out of Utopia: Toward a Reorientation of Sociological Analysis," *The American Journal of Sociology*, LXIV, September, 1958, 115–127 and Robert C. Angell, "The Sociology of Human Conflict," in *The Nature of Human Conflict*, ed. Elton B. McNeil, Englewood Cliffs, N.J., 1965, pp. 103–104.

12. Cooley, *Social Organization*, p. 201.

13. Giddings, *Democracy*, pp. 137–143 (1898); *Elements*, pp. 328–329; Franklin H. Giddings, "Mr. Bryan and Our Complex Social Order," *The Century*, LXXIII, November, 1906, 154–157; William Allen White, letter to Theodore Roosevelt, Feb. 1, 1900, White Papers; *Post*, CLXXVII, 2; *Autobiography*, pp. 485–486; *Gazette*, Feb. 24, 1910; Howe, *Wisconsin*, pp. 104–106; Follett, *New State*, pp. 216–217; *Administration*, pp. 168, 181 (1926); Dewey, *Characters*, II, 558 (1918); 756 (1918); Park, *Science of Sociology*, pp. 22, 50, 511, 644; Addams, *North American Review*, CLXXIX, 178–193; *Twenty Years*, pp. 202–206, 208–209, 302–303.

14. Addams, *Twenty Years*, pp. 202–206, 302–303; Jane Addams, "My Experiences as a Progressive Candidate," *McClures*, XL, Novem-

ber, 1912, 12–14; Nye, *Midwestern Progressive Politics,* p. 146; Johnson, *White's America,* pp. 196–198; Jane Dewey, in *The Philosophy of John Dewey,* p. 39; Landon Warner, "Howe, Frederic Clemson," *Dictionary of American Biography,* 1958, XXII, Supplement Two, 326–328.

15. Giddings, *Scientific Study,* p. 145.

16. Cooley, *Social Process,* p. 347.

17. White, *Old Order,* pp. 32–65, 110–121, 228–229; William Allen White, "A Democratic View of Education," *Craftsman,* XXI, November, 1911, 121; Howe, *The City,* pp. 170–173, 178–183; *Wisconsin,* pp. 51–62, 153–156, 189–190; Royce, *Race Questions,* pp. 86–87 (1902), 135, 139, 142, 145, 154, 164–165 (1899); Giddings, *Democracy,* pp. 213 (1896), 253–255 (1897), 308 (1899); *Descriptive Sociology,* p. 521; *Elements,* pp. 110–111, 226, 314–321, 328–329; Franklin H. Giddings, "Popular Government the Issue," *Van Norden Magazine,* November, 1907, 27–32; Follett, *New State,* pp. 174–178, 245–247; *Creative Experience,* pp. 3–9, 19, 26–27, 30, 213–214; Dewey, *New Republic,* XXX, 286–288; XLV, 52–54; Cooley, *Social Organization,* pp. 125–128, 131–142.

18. Walter Lippmann, *Public Opinion,* New York, 1922, p. 396; Dewey, *New Republic,* XXX, 286–288; XLV, 52–54; Follett, *Creative Experience,* pp. 3–9, 27–29; Franklin H. Giddings, "Social Control in a Democracy," *Publications of the American Sociological Society,* XII, 1917, 201–206; *Scientific Study,* pp. 145, 154, 171.

19. Cooley, *Social Organization,* p. 147.

20. Cf. Lippmann, *Public Opinion,* pp. 362, 375, 396.

21. Cooley, *Social Organization,* p. 54.

22. On the difference between the classical public, which was Cooley's model, and the mass, see C. Wright Mills, "Mass Society and Liberal Education," *Power, Politics and People: The Collected Essays of C. Wright Mills,* ed. with an Introduction by Louis Horowitz, New York, 1963, p. 355 (1954). Hofstadter emphasizes the connection between direct democracy and the town meeting. Hofstadter, *Age,* pp. 263–264.

23. White, *Post,* CLXXVII, 1–2; *Old Order,* pp. 133–134, 137; William Allen White, *Forty Years on Main Street,* compiled by Russell H. Fitzgibbon from the columns of the Emporia *Gazette,* New York, 1937, pp. 306–307 (1906).

24. Howe, *The City,* pp. 250–252, 276–279; *Land,* pp. 174–175; *Confessions,* pp. 188–189.

25. On this, see Walter I. Trattner, "Progressivism and World War I: A Re-appraisal," *Mid-America,* XLIV, July, 1962, 131–145; Haber, *Efficiency and Uplift,* pp. 117–131; Allen F. Davis, "Welfare, Reform and World War I," *American Quarterly,* XIX, Fall, 1967, 516–533.

26. Park, *Society,* p. 146 (1918).

27. Follett, *New State,* p. 257. See also pp. 246–248. Other observations of this phenomenon came from Howe, *Land,* p. 14; *Denmark: the Coöperative Way,* xi–xii; Dewey, *Characters,* II, 551–560 (1918), 745–759 (1918); White, *Gazette,* May 24, 1917; July 26, 1917; Giddings, *Responsible State,* pp. 76–77. In addition to approving of the communal spirit of wartime, they agreed with William James on the need to find a moral equivalent of war. Addams, *Newer Ideals,* pp. 24, 217, 219, 236–237; Dewey, *Human Nature,* pp. 112–115; Royce, *Loyalty,* p. 268; Follett, *New State,* p. 195; Cooley, *Social Process,* pp. 147–148. Addams and Dewey cited James on this.

28. Follett, *New State,* p. 161.

29. *Ibid.,* p. 194.

30. *Ibid.,* pp. 246–248, 326–330.

31. *Ibid.,* p. 160.

32. Frederic C. Howe, *Socialized Germany,* New York, 1915, p. 335. See also *Wisconsin,* vii; John Dewey, *German Philosophy and Politics,* New York, 1915, pp. 28–30, 34, 128; *Characters,* II, 552 (1918); Giddings, *Western Hemisphere,* pp. 35–39; Royce, *Hope,* pp. 4–12, 61; Cooley, Journal, 1914.

33. Park, *Society,* p. 146 (1918).

34. *Ibid.,* n., p. 151 (1918).

35. Dewey, *Characters,* II, 557 (1918). See also 746–753 (1918); Cooley, *Social Process,* pp. 241–254.

36. White, *Gazette,* April 26, 1917; letter to Mark Sullivan, January 28, 1918, in Johnson, ed., *Letters,* p. 185; Johnson, *White's America,* p. 274.

37. Giddings, *Responsible State,* p. 106.

38. Giddings, *Scientific Study,* pp. 166–167; *Civilization,* p. 334.

39. Howe, *Land,* p. 9. See pp. 10–11, 19, 75; Frederic C. Howe, *Why War,* New York, 1916, xi, pp. 311, 313, 315, 317; *Confessions,* pp. 266–277.

40. Howe, *Land,* p. 11. See pp. 9, 14, 23, 40–41, 174–175.

41. *Ibid.,* p. 24. See pp. 25, 38, 54, 70.

42. Follett, *New State,* pp. 116–121, 260–270; *Creative Experience,* xix.

43. Follett, *New State*, p. 117. See pp. 327–330.

44. *Ibid.*, pp. 303–304. Italics Follett's. See pp. 262–267, 322, 330.

45. Dewey, *Characters*, II, 558–559 (1918).

46. Royce, *Hope*, p. 60. See also pp. 59–61; *War*, iii, iv, pp. 61–63, 72–78. Royce applied the triadic notion of interpretation to insurance. The three elements were the adventurer, the insurer, and the beneficiary. In the case of war, the triadic relationship existed between the aggressor (A), and the trustees of the international insurance fund (B), and the nations which were beneficiaries (C).

47. Royce, *War*, p. 80. Italics omitted.

48. Howe, *The City*, pp. 178–183; Park, in *The City*, pp. 33–37; White, *Old Order*, pp. 110–113; Follett, *New State*, pp. 174–175. See E. E. Schattschneider, *Party Government*, New York, 1942, pp. 309–343, on the tendency of these innovations to centralize power. The rise of functional over local organization of politics has been studied by Lubove, *Professional Altruist*, pp. 157–182; Samuel P. Hays, "The Politics of Reform in Municipal Government in the Progressive Era," *Pacific Northwest Quarterly*, LV, October, 1964, 157–169; "The Social Analysis of American Political History," *Political Science Quarterly*, LXXX, September, 1965, 373–394.

49. Park, in *The City*, p. 33.

50. The term bureaucracy was used by Addams, *Twenty Years*, p. 335; by Cooley, *Social Organization*, p. 342; *Social Process*, p. 148; by Howe, *Privilege*, p. 256; *Denmark: The Coöperative Way*, xiv; by Follett, *New State*, p. 330; by Dewey, *Characters*, II, 553 (1918).

51. Park, *Society*, p. 147 (1918). See also Park, in *The City*, pp. 13–14, 23–24.

52. Park, *Science of Sociology*, p. 329. See pp. 287, 438–439, 488–490; *The City*, pp. 106–107, 119; *Society*, pp. 147–148.

53. Park, *Old World*, p. 262.

54. *Ibid.*, pp. 261–262; *Science of Sociology*, p. 287.

55. Royce, *Race Questions*, p. 86 (1902).

56. Royce, *Race Questions*, pp. 75–79, 87, 98 (1902); *Loyalty*, pp. 80–83; *Christianity*, II, 8; Cooley, *Social Organization*, pp. 54, 320, 342.

57. Howe, *Germany*, pp. 1–2; *Denmark: The Coöperative Way*, xiv; Dewey, *Characters*, II, 551–560 (1918), 745–759 (1918); Follett, *New State*, pp. 326–330; Cooley, *Social Organization*, p. 408; *Social Process*, p. 148 (1918).

58. Cooley, *Social Organization*, p. 409. See Journal, 1890.

59. Cooley, *Social Organization*, p. 404. See also pp. 405–409.

60. Follett, *New State,* p. 202. See pp. 73, 302.

61. *Ibid.,* p. 255.

62. *Ibid.,* pp. 73–74.

63. *Ibid.,* pp. 326–327.

64. Howe, *Denmark: The Coöperative Way,* xiv. Howe served under Franklin Roosevelt in the AAA, but his political views were to the left of the New Deal. Otis L. Graham, Jr., *An Encore for Reform: The Old Progressives and the New Deal,* New York, 1967, pp. 106, 133.

65. Howe, *Privilege,* p. 256. See also pp. 255, 257, 259; *Germany,* p. 1; *Confessions,* pp. 188–189; Frederic C. Howe, "A Political Utopia," *The Nation,* CXXVII, August 22, 1928, 178–179. Howe argued that both he and Henry George were for small government. Although many of George's contemporaries thought that he stood for state ownership of land, he in fact wanted society to be just the rent collector. On this see Charles Albro Barker, *Henry George,* New York, 1955, pp. 297–298 and Steven B. Cord, *Henry George: Dreamer or Realist,* Philadelphia, 1965, pp. 61–62, 181–183, 221.

66. Howe, *Denmark: The Coöperative Way,* p. 229. See pp. 192–195; *Privilege,* p. 263.

67. Howe, *Denmark: The Coöperative Way,* xiv.

68. See chapter I, p. 17.

69. Howe, *The City,* p. 17.

70. *Ibid.,* pp. 17–19; *British City,* pp. 349–351.

71. Howe, *The City,* p. 303. See pp. 168–169.

72. *Ibid.,* pp. 170, 302.

73. *Ibid.,* p. 164. See *British City,* p. 360, for the same idea. The encroachment of the state governments on municipal affairs is described by Austin F. MacDonald, *American City Government and Administration,* New York, 1947, pp. 78–79.

74. Howe, *The City,* pp. 166, 292–293, 303, 312.

75. William Allen White, *A Certain Rich Man,* New York, 1909; *Masks in a Pageant,* New York, 1928, p. 284; *Old Order,* pp. 66, 232; Royce, *Race Questions,* pp. 104–108 (1899); *Loyalty,* pp. 233, 239, 243, 245–246; Dewey, *Proceedings of the NEA,* 1902, p. 375; *Ethics,* p. 471; *Characters,* II, 541 (1920); *Public,* pp. 126–127, 211–213; Park, in *The City,* pp. 1–46, 99–122.

76. White, *Gazette,* Feb. 1, 1912. See also *American Magazine,* LXIII, 263; *Old Order,* pp. 99–101. His definition of a country town included those from 3,000 to those of 100,000. White, *Autobiography,* p. 205; *Harper's,* CXXXII, 887. White was interested in differentiating

the town and the small city, which he thought essentially alike, from the country on the one side and the big city on the other. Strauss, *Images of the City,* pp. 190–192.

77. White, *American Magazine,* LXIII, 263–264; *Old Order,* pp. 99–101; *Gazette,* Feb. 1, 1912; June 20, 1912; William Allen White, "The Challenge to the Middle Class," *Atlantic Monthly,* CLX, August, 1937, 198–199; *West,* pp. 22, 28–33, 52, 57–58, 61, 81–86.

78. White, *Harper's,* CXXXII, 887; *West,* pp. 81–82.

79. White, *Gazette,* Dec. 15, 1896; Jan. 20, 1897; Oct. 31, 1901; Nov. 22, 1902; Nov. 22, 1906; Sept. 9, 1909; Dec. 4, 1924.

80. White, *Heart of a Fool,* p. 69.

81. White, *Old Order,* pp. 3, 7, 71–81, 144–146; *Gazette,* Sept. 12, 1912; Sept. 19, 1912; Sept. 26, 1912; Oct. 10, 1912.

82. White, *West,* p. 33.

83. Park, in *The City,* p. 122. Stein emphasizes the role of functional organization in Park's thought; White and White emphasize his attachment to primary group organization. Cf. Stein, *Eclipse,* pp. 15–27, and White and White, *Intellectual versus City,* p. 156–165.

84. Park, in *The City,* p. 37. See also pp. 2, 8, 12, 23–24, 29, 33–38.

85. *Ibid.,* p. 117

86. Park, *Science of Sociology,* p. 830. See pp. 831–837; *Society,* pp. 94 (1923), 283–284 (1931). A similar attitude was held by White and Dewey. William Allen White, *The Editor and His People: Editorials by William Allen White.* Selected from the Emporia *Gazette* by Helen O. Mahin, New York, 1924, p. 307 (1901); *Forty Years,* pp. 182–183 (1926); Dewey, *Characters,* II, 776–781 (1922). For the effect of the war on ideas about public opinion, see Walter Lippmann, *Liberty and the News,* New York, 1920, pp. 10–37.

87. Park, in *The City,* p. 122.

88. *Ibid.,* pp. 119–122; Park, *Old World,* pp. 126–129, 132, 204, 211.

89. Park, *Old World,* pp. 294–295.

90. *Ibid.,* pp. 41, 261–262, 296–308; Park, in *The City,* pp. 1–46, 99–112.

91. "Park, Robert Ezra," *Who Was Who in America: A Companion Biographical Reference Work to Who's Who in America,* II, 1950, 412; Clarke, *The Little Democracy,* p. 17.

92. Park, in *The City,* pp. 33–37, 117–119; *Society,* p. 149 (1918).

93. Harvey Warren Zorbaugh, *The Gold Coast and the Slum: A Sociological Study of Chicago's Near North Side,* with an Introduction by Robert Park, Chicago, 1929, pp. 202–216, 267.

94. Park, *Human Communities,* p. 90 (1929). This is a reprinting of the Introduction to Zorbaugh.

95. Dewey, *Public,* pp. 126–127.

96. *Ibid.,* p. 110.

97. *Ibid.,* p. 126.

98. Dewey, *School and Society; Proceedings of the NEA,* 1902, pp. 373–383.

99. Dewey, *Public,* p. 218. See pp. 147, 174, 184, 211–213.

100. *Ibid.,* pp. 218–219.

101. *Ibid.,* p. 214. See pp. 148, 212–215. This aspect of Dewey's thought is explored by Floyd Henry Allport, *Institutional Behavior: Essays toward a Re-Interpreting of Contemporary Social Organization,* Chapel Hill, N.C., 1933, pp. 86–105. Cf. Follett, *New State,* pp. 195–203, 256–257, 320–321.

102. Dewey, *Public,* p. 213.

103. *Ibid.,* p. 214.

104. Dewey, *Individualism,* p. 119.

105. Royce, *Loyalty,* p. 242. His discussion of provincialism occurred in *Race Questions* (1902), *Loyalty* (1908) and in *Putnam's* (1909). His later views on communities of interpretation were analyzed in *Hope* (1916).

106. Royce, *Christianity,* II, 82–92.

107. Royce, *Race Questions,* pp. 97–98 (1902).

108. Royce, *Putnam's,* VII, 234. See *Race Questions,* 51–61 (1902). Other obstacles to a healthy provincialism were mobility and the presence of large numbers of immigrants. Royce, *Race Questions,* pp. 68–69 (1902); *Putnam's,* VII, 239.

109. Royce, *Race Questions,* p. 75 (1902).

110. *Ibid.,* pp. 75–77, 85–88 (1902).

111. *Ibid.,* pp. 115–130 (1899) ; *Loyalty,* pp. 132, 134, 216–220, 229–230.

112. Royce, *Race Questions,* p. 118 (1899).

113. Royce, *Loyalty,* p. 248.

114. *Ibid.,* p. 245. Italics Royce's.

Bibliography

Aaron, Daniel. *Men of Good Hope: A Story of American Progressives.* New York, 1951.

Abbott, Lyman. *The Evolution of Christianity.* Boston, 1892.

Adams, Henry. *The Education of Henry Adams.* New York, 1931.

Adams, Herbert B. "The Germanic Origin of New England Towns." *Johns Hopkins University Studies in Historical and Political Science.* Baltimore, 1883, Vol. I, 5–38.

Addams, Jane, "Child Labor and Pauperism." *Charities,* XI, 300–304.

―――. "The College Woman and Christianity." *The Independent,* LIII, August, 1901, 1852–1855.

―――. *Democracy and Social Ethics.* New York, 1902.

―――. *The Excellent Becomes Permanent.* New York, 1932.

―――. "A Function of the Social Settlement." *Annals of the American Academy of Political and Social Science,* XIII, May, 1899, 323–355.

―――. "The Humanitarian Value of Civil Service." *The Survey,* XXVIII, April 6, 1912, 14–16.

―――. "The Humanizing Tendency of Industrial Education." *The Chautauquan,* XXXIX, May, 1904, 266–272.

―――. "Introduction." *Religion in Social Action.* By Graham Taylor. New York, 1913.

―――. "A Modern Lear." *The Survey,* XXIX, November 2, 1912, 131–137.

―――. "My Experiences as a Progressive Candidate." *McClures,* XL, November, 1912, 12–14.

―――. *Newer Ideals of Peace.* New York, 1907.

―――. "Objective Value of a Social Settlement." *Philanthropy and Social Progress.* Ed. Henry C. Adams. New York, 1893.

―――. *Peace and Bread in Time of War.* New York, 1922.

―――. "The Present Crisis in Trade-Union Morals." *North American Review,* CLXXIX, August, 1904, 178–193.

_____. "Problems of Municipal Administration." *The American Journal of Sociology*, X, January, 1905, 425–444.

_____. "The Reaction of Modern Life upon Religious Thought." *Religious Education*, IV, April, 1909, 23–29.

_____. "Religious Education and Contemporary Social Conditions." *Religious Education*, VI, June, 1911, 145–152.

_____. *The Second Twenty Years at Hull-House: September 1909 to September 1929.* New York, 1930.

_____. "The Settlement as a Factor in the Labor Movement," *Hull-House Maps and Papers, by Residents of Hull-House, A Social Settlement, a Presentation of Nationalities and Wages in a Congested District of Chicago together with Comments and Essays on Problems Growing Out of the Social Conditions.* New York, 1895.

_____. *The Social Thought of Jane Addams.* Ed. with an Introduction by Christopher Lasch. Indianapolis, 1965.

_____. *The Spirit of Youth and the City Streets.* New York, 1909.

_____. "The Subjective Necessity for Social Settlements." *Philanthropy and Social Progress.* Ed. Henry C. Adams. New York, 1893.

_____. "Toast to John Dewey." *The Survey*, LXIII, November 15, 1929, 203–204.

_____. "Trade Unions and Public Duty." *The American Journal of Sociology*, IV, January, 1898, 448–462.

_____. *Twenty Years at Hull-House.* New York, 1910.

_____. "Why the Ward Boss Rules." *The Outlook*, LVIII, April 2, 1898, 879–882.

Ahlstrom, Sydney E. "Theology in America: A Historical Survey," in *Religion in American Life.* Eds. James Ward Smith and A. Leland Jamison. Princeton, N.J., 1961, Vol. I.

Allport, Floyd Henry. *Institutional Behavior: Essays toward a Re-Interpreting of Contemporary Social Organization.* Chapel Hill, N.C., 1933.

Allport, Gordon W. "Dewey's Individual and Social Psychology." *The Philosophy of John Dewey.* Ed. Paul Arthur Schilpp. Evanston, Ill., 1939.

Angell, Robert C. "The Sociology of Human Conflict," in *The Nature of Human Conflict.* Ed. Elton B. McNeil. Englewood Cliffs, N.J., 1965.

Arendt, Hannah. *The Human Condition.* Chicago, 1958.

Arensberg, Conrad. "American Communities." *American Anthropologist*, LVII, 1955, 1143–1162.

Arnold, Matthew. *Culture and Anarchy: An Essay in Political and Social Criticism.* New York, 1883.

――――. *Discourses in America.* London, 1889.

Atherton, Lewis. *Main Street on the Middle Border.* Bloomington, Ind., 1954.

Babbitt, Irving. *Literature and the American College.* Boston, 1908.

Baker, Melvin C. *Foundations of John Dewey's Educational Theory.* New York, 1955.

Baldwin, James Mark. *Social and Ethical Interpretations in Mental Development.* New York, 1902.

Baritz, Loren. *The Servants of Power: A History of the Use of Social Science in American Industry.* Middletown, Conn., 1960.

Barker, Charles Albro. *Henry George.* New York, 1955.

Barnes, Harry Elmer, and Becker, Howard. *Social Thought from Lore to Science.* Boston, 1938.

Bell, Daniel. "The Debate on Alienation." *Revisionism: Essays on the History of Marxist Ideas.* Ed. Leopold Labedz. New York, 1962.

――――. *The End of Ideology.* Glencoe, Ill., 1960.

――――. *The Reforming of General Education: The Columbia College Experience in Its National Setting.* New York, 1966.

Bellamy, Edward. *Looking Backward: 2000–1887.* Boston, 1917.

Benson, Lee. "The Historical Background of Turner's Frontier Essay." *Agricultural History,* XXV, April, 1951, 59–82.

Blau, Joseph L. *Men and Movements in American Philosophy.* New York. 1952.

Bledstein, Burton. "Cultivation and Custom: The Idea of Liberal Culture in Post Civil War America." Unpublished Ph.D. dissertation, Princeton University, 1967.

Blewett, John, S.J. "Democracy as Religion: Unity in Human Relations." *John Dewey: His Thought and Influence.* Ed. John Blewett, S.J. New York, 1960.

Boas, Franz. "The History of Anthropology." *Congress of Arts and Science: Universal Exposition, St. Louis, 1904.* Ed. Howard J. Rogers. Boston, 1905, Vol. V.

Boorstin, Daniel J. *The Image or What Happened to the American Dream.* New York, 1962.

Boring, Edwin G. "The Influence of Evolutionary Theory upon American Psychological Thought." *Evolutionary Thought in America.* Ed. Stow Persons. New Haven, Conn., 1950.

Bowers, David F. "Hegel, Darwin and the American Tradition."

Foreign Influences in American Life: Essays and Critical Bibliographies. Ed. David F. Bowers. Princeton, N.J., 1944.

Bramson, Leon. *The Political Context of Sociology.* Princeton, N.J., 1961.

Brown, Stuart Gerry, ed. *The Religious Philosophy of Josiah Royce.* Syracuse, N.Y., 1952.

————, ed. *The Social Philosophy of Josiah Royce.* Syracuse, N.Y., 1950.

Brown, William Adams. "The Problem of Christianity." Papers in Honor of Josiah Royce on his Sixtieth Birthday. Ed. J. E. Creighton. *The Philosophical Review,* XXV, 1916, 81–86.

Bryson, Gladys. *Man and Society: The Scottish Inquiry of the Eighteenth Century.* Princeton, N.J., 1945.

————. "Sociology Considered as Moral Philosophy." *The Sociological Review,* XXIV, January, 1932, 26–36.

Buckham, John Wright. "The Contribution of Professor Royce to Christian Thought." *The Harvard Theological Review,* VIII, April, 1915, 219–237.

Buranelli, Vincent. *Josiah Royce.* New York, 1964.

Burgess, Ernest W. "In Memoriam: Robert E. Park, 1864–1944." *The American Journal of Sociology,* XLIX, March, 1944, 478.

Butts, R. Freeman. *The College Charts Its Course.* New York, 1939.

Cabot, Richard C. "Mary Parker Follett, An Appreciation." *Radcliffe Quarterly,* April, 1934, pp. 80–82.

Catlin, Gordon E. "The Meaning of Community." *Community.* Ed. Carl J. Friedrich. New York, 1959.

Chadbourne, Richard McClain. "Two Organizers of Divinity: Ernest Renan and John Dewey." *Thought: Fordham University Quarterly,* XXIV, September, 1949, 430–448.

Chapman, Edmund H. *Cleveland: Village to Metropolis: A Case Study of Problems of Urban Development in Nineteenth-Century America.* Cleveland, 1964.

Charles Horton Cooley Papers. Michigan Historical Collections, The University of Michigan.

Chinoy, Ely. *Sociological Perspective: Basic Concepts and Their Application.* Garden City, N.Y., 1954.

Clark, John B. *The Philosophy of Wealth: Economic Principles Newly Formulated.* Boston, 1886.

Clarke, Ida Clyde. *The Little Democracy,* New York, 1918.

Clendenning, John, ed. *The Letters of Josiah Royce.* Chicago, 1970.

Coates, A. W. "American Scholarship Comes of Age." *Journal of the History of Ideas*, XXII, July-September, 1961, 404–417.

Compendium of the Tenth Census, June 1, 1880. Washington, D.C., 1883, Vol. I.

Comte, Auguste. *The Positive Philosophy of Auguste Comte*. 3 vols. Trans. Harriet Martineau. London, 1896.

Conway, Jill. "Jane Addams: An American Heroine." *Dædalus*, XCIII, Spring, 1964, 761–780.

Cooley, Charles Horton. *Human Nature and the Social Order*. New York, 1902.

———. *Human Nature and the Social Order*. 2nd ed. revised. New York, 1922.

———. *Life and the Student*. New York, 1927.

———. "A Primary Culture for Democracy." *Publications of the American Sociological Society*, XIII, Chicago, 1918, 1–10.

———. "The Process of Social Change." *Political Science Quarterly*, XII, March, 1897, 63–81.

———. *Social Organization: A Study of the Larger Mind*. Introduction by Philip Rief. New York, 1962.

———. *Social Process*. New York, 1922.

———. *Sociological Theory and Social Research*. New York, 1930.

Cord, Steven B. *Henry George: Dreamer or Realist*. Philadelphia, 1965.

Coser, Lewis A. *The Functions of Social Conflict*. Glencoe, Ill., 1956.

Cotton, J. Harry. *Royce on the Human Self*. Cambridge, Mass., 1954.

Cremin, Lawrence A. *The Transformation of the School: Progressivism in American Education 1876–1957*. New York, 1962.

Crick, Bernard. *The American Science of Politics: Its Origins and Conditions*. Berkeley, Cal., 1959.

Croly, Herbert. *Progressive Democracy*. New York, 1914.

———. *The Promise of American Life*. New York, 1909.

Curti, Merle. "Jane Addams on Human Nature." *Journal of the History of Ideas*, XXII, April-June, 1961, 240–253.

———. *The Making of an American Community: A Case Study of Democracy in a Frontier County*. Stanford, Cal., 1959.

Dahrendorf, Ralf. *Class and Class Conflict in Industrial Society*. Stanford, Cal., 1959.

———. "Out of Utopia: Toward a Reorientation of Sociological Analysis." *The American Journal of Sociology*, LXIV, September, 1958, 115–127.

Davis, Allen F. "Welfare, Reform and World War I." *American Quarterly,* XIX, Fall, 1967, 516–533.

Degler, Carl. "The Sociologist as Historian." *American Quarterly,* XV, Winter, 1963, 483–497.

Dewey, Jane M., ed. "Biography of John Dewey," in *The Philosophy of John Dewey.* Ed. Paul Arthur Schilpp. Evanston, Ill., 1939.

Dewey, John. "Are the Schools Doing What People Want Them to Do?" *Educational Review,* XXI, May, 1901, 459–474.

————. *Characters and Events: Popular Essays in Social and Political Philosophy.* Ed. Joseph Ratner. 2 vols. New York, 1929.

————. "Christianity and Democracy." *Religious Thought at the University of Michigan: Being Addresses Delivered at the Sunday Morning Services of the Students' Christian Association.* Ann Arbor, Mich., 1893.

————. *A Common Faith.* New Haven, Conn., 1934.

————. *Democracy and Education: An Introduction to the Philosophy of Education.* New York, 1916.

————. *Education Today.* Ed. with a Foreword by Joseph Ratner. New York, 1940.

————. *The Educational Situation.* Chicago, 1902.

————. "Ethics and Physical Science." *Andover Review,* VII, June, 1887, 573–591.

————. *The Ethics of Democracy.* Ann Arbor, Mich., 1888.

————. *Experience and Education.* New York, 1938.

————. *Experience and Nature.* New York, 1929.

————. *Freedom and Culture.* New York, 1939.

————. *German Philosophy and Politics.* New York, 1915.

————. "Green's Theory of the Moral Motive." *Philosophical Review,* I, November, 1892, 593–612.

————. *Human Nature and Conduct.* New York, 1922.

————. *Individualism Old and New.* New York, 1930.

————. "The Influence of Darwinism on Philosophy." *American Thought: Civil War to World War I.* Ed. with an Introduction by Perry Miller. New York, 1954.

————. *Intelligence in the Modern World: John Dewey's Philosophy.* Ed. with an Introduction by Joseph Ratner. New York, 1939.

————. *John Dewey on Education: Selected Writings.* Ed. Reginald D. Archambault. New York, 1964.

————. *Lectures in the Philosophy of Education: 1899.* Ed. with an Introduction by Reginald D. Archambault. New York, 1966.

_____. *Liberalism and Social Action.* New York, 1935.

_____. "The Need for Social Psychology." *Psychological Review,* XXIV, July, 1917, 266–277.

_____. *On Experience, Nature, and Freedom: Representative Selections.* Ed. Richard J. Bernstein. New York, 1960.

_____. *Outlines of a Critical Theory of Ethics.* Ann Arbor, Mich., 1891.

_____. "Practical Democracy." Review of *The Phantom Public,* by Walter Lippmann. *The New Republic,* XLV, December 2, 1925, 52–54.

_____. "Psychology and Social Practice." *John Dewey: Philosophy, Psychology and Social Practice.* Ed. Joseph Ratner, New York, 1963.

_____. *The Public and Its Problems.* New York, 1927.

_____. "Public Opinion." Review of *Public Opinion,* by Walter Lippmann. *The New Republic,* XXX, May 3, 1922, 286–288.

_____. "Reconstruction." *The Monthly Bulletin* of the Students' Christian Association of the University of Michigan, XV, June, 1894, 149–156.

_____. *Reconstruction in Philosophy.* Boston, 1957.

_____. "The Relation of Philosophy to Theology," *The Monthly Bulletin* of the Students' Christian Association of the University of Michigan, XIV, January, 1893, 67–68.

_____. *The School and Society.* Chicago, 1899.

_____. "The School as Social Center." *Proceedings of the National Education Association.* 1902, 373–383.

_____. "Some Stages of Logical Thought." *Philosophical Review,* IX, September 1900, 465–489.

_____. "The St. Louis Congress of the Arts and Sciences." *Science,* XVIII, August 28, 1903, 275–278.

_____. "The Subject-Matter of Metaphysical Inquiry." *Journal of Philosophy,* XII, June 24, 1915, 337–345.

_____. *The Way Out of Educational Confusion.* Cambridge, Mass., 1931.

Dewey, John and Dewey, Evelyn. *Schools of Tomorrow.* New York, 1915.

Dewey, John and Tufts, James H. *Ethics.* New York, 1908.

Dewey, Richard. "Charles Horton Cooley: Pioneer in Psychosociology." *An Introduction to the History of Sociology.* Ed. Harry Elmer Barnes. Chicago, 1948.

Dimock, Marshall E. *Administrative Vitality: The Conflict with Bureaucracy.* New York, 1959.

Donohue, John W., S. J. "Dewey and the Problem of Technology." *John Dewey: His Thought and Influence.* Ed. John Blewett, S.J. New York, 1960.

Durkheim, Emile. *The Division of Labor in Society.* Trans. George Simpson. Glencoe, Ill., 1960.

_____. *Education and Sociology.* Trans. with an Introduction by Sherwood D. Fox. Glencoe, Ill., 1951.

_____. *Moral Education.* Trans. by Everett K. Wilson and Herman Schhurer. Ed. with an Introduction by Everett K. Wilson. Glencoe, Ill., 1961.

_____. *Suicide: A Study in Sociology.* Trans. John A. Spaulding and George Simpson. Ed. with an Introduction by George Simpson. Glencoe, Ill., 1951.

Dykhuizen, George. "John Dewey: the Chicago Years." *Journal of the History of Philosophy,* XXV, October, 1964, 227–237.

_____. "John Dewey at Johns Hopkins (1882–1884)." *Journal of the History of Ideas,* XXII, January–March, 1961, 103–116.

_____. "John Dewey: The Vermont Years." *Journal of the History of Ideas,* XX, October-December, 1959, 515–544.

Eliot, Charles William. *Educational Reform. Essays and Addresses.* New York, 1901.

_____. *The Man and his Beliefs.* Ed. William Allan Neilson. 2 vols. New York, 1926.

Elkins, Stanley, and McKitrick, Eric. "A Meaning for Turner's Frontier Thesis: Part I: Democracy in the Old Northwest." *Political Science Quarterly,* LXIX, September, 1954, 321–353.

_____. "A Meaning for Turner's Frontier Thesis: Part II: The Southwest Frontier and New England." *Political Science Quarterly,* LXIX, December, 1954, 565–602.

Ely, Richart T. *An Introduction to Political Economy.* New York, 1889.

_____. *The Past and Present of Political Economy.* Baltimore, 1884.

_____. *The Social Law of Service.* New York, 1896.

_____. *Studies in the Evolution of Industrial Society.* New York, 1903.

Emporia *Gazette.* 1895–1920.

Faris, Ellsworth. "The Primary Group: Essence and Accident." *The American Journal of Sociology,* XXXVIII, July, 1932, 41–50.

Farrell, John C. *Beloved Lady: A History of Jane Addams' Ideas on Reform and Peace.* Baltimore, 1967.

Faulkner, Harold U. *The Decline of Laissez Faire, 1897–1917.* New York, 1951.

Feuer, Lewis S. "H.A.P. Torrey and John Dewey: Teacher and Pupil." *American Quarterly,* X, Spring, 1958, 34–54.

————. "John Dewey and the Back to the People Movement in American Thought." *Journal of the History of Ideas,* XX, October-December, 1959, 545–568.

Filler, Louis. *Crusaders for American Liberalism.* New York, 1939.

Follett, Mary Parker. *Creative Experience.* New York, 1924.

————. "Community is a Process." *Philosophical Review,* XXVIII, November, 1919, 576–588.

————. *Dynamic Administration: The Collected Papers of Mary Parker Follett.* Ed. with an Introduction by Henry C. Metcalf and L. Urwick. New York, 1940.

————. "Evening Centers—Aims and Duties Therein." A Paper Given to Managers and Leaders of the Evening Centers of the Boston Public School System, printed, January, 1913.

————. *The New State.* New York, 1918.

————. *The Speaker of the House of Representatives.* New York, 1896.

"Follett, Mary Parker." *Who's Who in America.* Vol. XVIII, 1934, 877.

Forcey, Charles. *The Crossroads of Liberalism: Croly, Weyl, Lippmann, and the Progressive Era: 1900–1925.* New York, 1961.

Ford, Franklin. "Draft of Action." Ann Arbor, Mich. Privately printed, 1892.

Frankel, Charles. "John Dewey's Legacy." *The American Scholar,* XXIX, Summer, 1960, 313–331.

Franklin H. Giddings Papers. Columbia University.

French, Laura M. *History of Emporia and Lyon County.* Emporia, Kans., 1929.

Friedrich, Carl J. "The Concept of Community in the History of Political and Legal Philosophy." *Community.* Ed. Carl J. Friedrich. New York, 1959.

Fuss, Peter. *The Moral Philosophy of Josiah Royce.* Cambridge, Mass., 1965.

Giddings, Franklin H. "The American Idea." *Harper's Weekly,* XLVIII, November 5, 1904, 1702, 1713.

————. "The American People." *International Quarterly,* VII, June, 1903, 281–299.

————. "The Bolsheviki Must Go." *Independent,* XCVII, January 18, 1919, 88.

————. "Can the Churches Be Saved?" *Independent,* CVI, August 20, 1921, 67, 87–89.

————. "Can Education Humanize Civilization?" *School and Society,* XXIV, July 10, 1926, 25–31.

————. *Civilization and Society: An Account of the Development and Behavior of Human Society.* Ed. Howard W. Odum. New York, 1932.

————. "The Concepts and Methods of Sociology." *Congress of Arts and Science: Universal Exposition, St. Louis, 1904.* Ed. Howard J. Rogers. Boston, 1905, Vol. V.

————. *Democracy and Empire: With Studies of Their Psychological, Economic, and Moral Foundations.* New York, 1900.

————. *The Elements of Sociology.* London, 1898.

————. "Folly at Albany." *Independent,* CI, January 24, 1920, 138, 159.

————. "The Greatest Reformative Period in the History of the World." *Munsey's Magazine,* XXXVIII, November, 1907, 171–177.

————. "The Greatness of Herbert Spencer." *Independent,* LV, December 17, 1903, 2959–2962.

————. "Intellectual Consequences of the War." *Transactions of the Royal Canadian Institute,* XII, May, 1919, 103–116.

————. "Internal Improvements." *The Chautauquan,* IX, May, 1889, 460–462.

————. *The Mighty Medicine: Superstition and Its Antidote: A New Liberal Education.* New York, 1929.

————. "Mr. Bryan and Our Complex Social Order." *The Century,* LXXIII, November, 1906, 154–157.

————. "One Big Union Idea." *Independent,* CII, May 1, 1920, 165.

————. *Outline of Lectures on Political Economy Delivered in the Bryn Mawr College.* Philadelphia, 1891.

————. "Popular Government the Issue." *Van Norden Magazine,* November, 1907, 27–32.

————. *The Principles of Sociology: An Analysis of the Phenomena of Association and Social Organization.* New York, 1896.

————. "Profit Sharing." *Seventeenth Annual Report of the Massachusetts Bureau of Statistics.* Boston, March, 1886.

————. "The Province of Sociology." *Annals of the American Academy of Political and Social Science,* I, July, 1890, 66–77.

_____. *Readings in Descriptive and Historical Sociology.* New York, 1906.

_____. "The Red Tape Turnover." *Independent,* CVI, July 9, 1921, 4.

_____. *The Responsible State: a Reëxamination of Fundamental Political Doctrines in the Light of World War and the Menace of Anarchism.* Boston, 1918.

_____. "The Resurgent Middle Class." *The New York Times,* December 31, 1922.

_____. *The Scientific Study of Human Society.* Chapel Hill, N.C., 1924.

_____. "Social Control in a Democracy." *Publications of the American Sociological Society,* XII, 1917, 201–206.

_____. "The Sociological Character of Political Economy." *Proceedings of the American Economic Association,* III, March, 1888, 29–47.

_____. "Sociology and the Abstract Sciences: The Origin of the Social Feelings." *Annals of the American Academy of Political and Social Science,* V, March, 1895, 746–753.

_____. *Studies in the Theory of Human Society.* New York, 1922.

_____. *The Theory of Sociology.* Philadelphia, 1894.

_____. "Unemployment: The Views of a Sociologist." *Independent,* CVII, October 8, 1921, 23–24.

_____. "Utility, Economics and Sociology." *Annals of the American Academy of Political and Social Science,* V, November, 1894, 398–404.

_____. *The Western Hemisphere in the World of Tomorrow.* New York, 1915.

_____. "What the Economic Crisis Calls For." *Independent,* XCIX, 216–217.

_____. "What the War Was Worth." *Independent,* XCIX, July 5, 1919, 16–17.

_____. "World Tendencies and China." *Chinese Students' Monthly,* XVIII, January, 1923, 8–10.

Giedion, Sigfried. *Mechanization Takes Command: A Contribution to Anonymous History.* New York, 1948.

Gillin, John L. "Franklin Henry Giddings." *American Masters of Social Science.* Ed. Howard W. Odum. New York, 1927.

Ginger, Ray. *Atgeld's America: The Lincoln Ideal versus Changing Realities.* New York, 1958.

Glaab, Charles N., and Brown, A. Theodore. *A History of Urban America.* New York, 1967.

Graham, Otis L., Jr. *An Encore for Reform: The Old Progressives and the New Deal.* New York, 1967.

Green, Constance McLaughlin. *American Cities in the Growth of the Nation.* New York, 1965.

Greer, Scott. "Individual Participation in Mass Society." *Approaches to the Study of Politics.* Ed. Roland Young. Evanston, Ill., 1958.

Grodzins, Morton. *The Loyal and the Disloyal: Social Boundaries of Patriotism and Treason.* Chicago, 1956.

Haber, Samuel. *Efficiency and Uplift: Scientific Management in the Progressive Era: 1890–1920.* Chicago, 1964.

Hacker, Andrew. "Sociology and Ideology." *The Social Theories of Talcott Parsons.* Ed. Max Black. Englewood Cliffs, N.J., 1961.

Hall, Granville Stanley. "The Unity of Mental Science." *Congress of Arts and Science: Universal Exposition, St. Louis, 1904.* Ed. Howard J. Rogers. Boston, 1905, Vol. V.

Hankins, F. H. "Franklin Henry Giddings, 1855–1931: Some Aspects of His Sociological Theory." *The American Journal of Sociology,* XXXVII, November, 1931, 349–367.

Harmon, Frances. *The Social Philosophy of the St. Louis Hegelians.* New York, 1943.

Hartley, Eugene L., and Hartley, Ruth E. *Fundamentals of Social Psychology.* New York, 1952.

Hartz, Louis. *The Liberal Tradition in America.* New York, 1955.

The Harvard University Catalogue: 1889–1890. Cambridge, Mass., 1889.

Hawkins, Richard Laurin. *Positivism in the United States: 1853–1861.* Cambridge, Mass., 1938.

Hays, Samuel P. "The Politics of Reform in Municipal Government in the Progressive Era." *Pacific Northwest Quarterly,* LV, October, 1964, 157–169.

_____. "The Social Analysis of American Political History." *Political Science Quarterly,* LXXX, September, 1965, 373–394.

Hegel, G. W. F. *Lectures on the Philosophy of Religion.* Ed. E. B. Speirs. London, 1895, Vol. II.

_____. *The Philosophy of Hegel.* Ed. with an Introduction by Carl J. Friedrich. New York, 1953.

Herbst, Jurgen. *The German Historical School in American Scholarship: A Study in the Transfer of Culture.* Ithaca, N.Y., 1965.

Herron, Ima Honaker. *The Small Town in American Literature.* Durham, N.C., 1939.

Hesseltine, William B. "Four American Traditions." *The Journal of Southern History,* XXVII, February, 1961, 3–32.

Higham, John. "The Schism in American Scholarship." *The American Historical Review,* LXXII, October, 1966, 1–21.

Hinkle, Roscoe C., Jr. "Durkheim in American Sociology." *Emile Durkheim: 1858–1917: A Collection of Essays with Translations and a Bibliography.* Ed. Kurt H. Wolff. Columbus, Ohio, 1960.

Hinkle, Roscoe C., and Hinkle, Gisela J. *The Development of Modern Sociology: Its Nature and Growth in the United States.* Garden City, N.Y., 1954.

Hobson, J. A. *John Ruskin: Social Reformer.* London, 1898.

_____. *Veblen.* London. 1936.

Hofstadter, Richard. *The Age of Reform: From Bryan to F.D.R.* New York, 1955.

_____. *Social Darwinism in American Thought.* Boston, 1955.

Hofstadter, Richard, and Metzger, Walter. *The Development of Academic Freedom in the United States.* New York, 1955.

Hofstadter, Richard, and Smith, Wilson, eds. *American Higher Education: A Documentary History.* Chicago, 1961, 2 vols.

Holby, H. H. Letter. Quincy Historical Society. Quincy, Mass., April 5, 1965.

Hook, Sidney. *From Hegel to Marx: Studies in the Intellectual Development of Karl Marx.* New York, 1950.

Hopkins, Charles Howard. *The Rise of the Social Gospel in American Protestantism: 1865–1915.* New Haven, Conn., 1940.

Houghton, Walter E. *The Victorian Frame of Mind: 1830–1837.* New Haven, Conn., 1957.

Howe, Frederic C. *The British City: The Beginnings of Democracy.* New York, 1907.

_____. *The City: The Hope of Democracy.* New York, 1905.

_____. *The Confessions of a Reformer.* New York, 1925.

_____. *Denmark: A Cooperative Commonwealth.* New York, 1921.

_____. *Denmark: The Coöperative Way.* New York, 1936.

_____. *European Cities at Work.* New York, 1913.

_____. *The Land and the Soldier.* New York, 1919.

_____. *The Modern City and Its Problems.* New York, 1915.

_____. "A Political Utopia," *The Nation,* CXXVII, August 22, 1928, 178–179.

———. *Privilege and Democracy in America.* New York, 1910.

———. *Socialized Germany.* New York, 1915.

———. "Where Are the Pre-War Radicals?" *The Survey,* LVI, April, 1926, 33–51.

———. *Why War.* New York, 1916.

———. *Wisconsin: An Experiment in Democracy.* New York, 1912.

Howison, George. *The Limits of Evolution and Other Essays.* New York, 1901.

———. "Philosophy: Its Fundamental Conceptions and Its Methods." *Congress of Arts and Science: Universal Exposition, St. Louis, 1904.* Ed. Howard J. Rogers. Boston, 1905, Vol. I.

Hudson, Winthrop S. *The Great Tradition of the American Churches,* New York, 1953.

Huthmacher, J. Joseph. *Massachusetts People and Politics: 1919–1933.* Cambridge, Mass., 1959.

Innis, Harold A. *The Bias of Communication.* Introduction by Marshall McLuhan. Toronto, 1951.

James, William. *A Pluralistic Universe.* London, 1920.

Jandy, Edward C. *Charles Horton Cooley: His Life and His Social Theory.* New York, 1942.

Jane Addams Papers. Swarthmore Peace Collection. Swarthmore College.

John B. Clark Papers. Columbia University.

Johnson, Paul E. "Josiah Royce: Theist or Pantheist?" *Harvard Theological Review,* XXI, July, 1928, 197–205.

Johnson, Walter, ed. *Selected Letters of William Allen White: 1899–1943.* New York, 1947.

Johnson, Walter. *William Allen White's America.* New York, 1947.

Jones, W. T. *The Romantic Syndrome: Toward a New Method in Cultural Anthropology and the History of Ideas.* The Hague, 1961.

Kamenka, Eugene. *The Ethical Foundations of Marxism.* London, 1962.

Kariel, Henry S. *The Decline of American Pluralism.* Stanford, Cal., 1961.

———. *In Search of Authority: Twentieth-Century Political Thought.* Glencoe, Ill., 1964.

———. "The New Order of Mary Parker Follett." *Western Political Quarterly,* VIII, September, 1955, 425–440.

Karpf, Fay Berger. *American Social Psychology.* New York, 1932.

Kimball, Solon T., and McClellan, James E. *Education and the New America*. New York, 1962.

Kolko, Gabriel. *The Triumph of Conservatism: A Reinterpretation of American History: 1900–1916*. New York, 1963.

Larsen, Otto N. "Social Effects of Mass Communications." *Handbook of Modern Sociology*. Ed. Robert E. L. Faris. Chicago, 1964.

Lasch, Christopher. *The New Radicalism in America: 1889–1963: The Intellectual as a Social Type*. New York, 1965.

Levi, Albert William. *Philosophy and the Modern World*. Bloomington, Ind., 1959.

Levine, Daniel. "Jane Addams: Romantic Radical, 1889–1912." *Mid-America*, XLIV, October, 1962, 195–210.

_____. *Varieties of Reform Thought*. Madison, Wisc., 1964.

Linn, James Weber. *Jane Addams: A Biography*. New York, 1935.

Lippmann, Walter. *Drift and Mastery*. New York, 1914.

_____. *Liberty and the News*. New York, 1920.

_____. *Public Opinion*. New York, 1922.

Lubove, Roy. *The Professional Altruist: The Emergence of Social Work As a Career: 1880–1930*. Cambridge, Mass., 1965.

MacDonald, Austin F. *American City Government and Administration*. New York, 1947.

MacIver, Robert M. *Community*. London, 1920.

Maine, Sir Henry Sumner. *Ancient Law: Its Connection with the Early History of Society, and Its Relation to Modern Ideas*. New York, 1884.

Mann, Arthur. "British Social Thought and American Reformers of the Progressive Era." *The Mississippi Valley Historical Review*, XLII, March, 1956, 672–692.

_____. *Yankee Reformers in the Urban Age*. Cambridge, Mass.,

Margulies, Herbert F. "Recent Opinion on the Decline of the Progressive Movement." *Mid-America*, XLV, October, 1963, 250–268.

Martindale, Don. *The Nature and Types of Sociological Theory*. Boston, 1960.

Marx, Karl, and Engels, Friedrich. *Basic Writings on Politics and Philosophy*. Ed. Lewis S. Feuer. New York, 1959.

May, Henry F. *The End of American Innocence: A Study of the First Years of Our Own Time: 1912–1917*. Chicago, 1959.

_____. *Protestant Churches and Industrial America*. New York, 1949.

Mayo, Elton. *The Human Problems of an Industrial Civilization.* New York, 1933.

McCaul, Robert L. "Dewey's Chicago." *The School Review,* LXVII, Summer, 1959, 258–280.

McCluskey, Neil Gerard. *Public Schools and Moral Education: The Influence of Horace Mann, William Torrey Harris, and John Dewey.* New York, 1958.

McKay, Paul L. "The Religious Aspect of the Philosophy of Josiah Royce." Unpublished Ph.D. dissertation, New York University, 1944.

McKelvey, Blake. *The Urbanization of America: 1860–1915.* New Brunswick, N.J., 1963.

McLuhan, Marshall. *The Gutenberg Galaxy: The Making of Typographic Man.* Toronto, 1962.

————. *Understanding Media: The Extensions of Man.* New York, 1964.

McVikar, John. *Outlines of Political Economy.* New York, 1825.

Mead, George Herbert. "Cooley's Contribution to Social Thought." *The American Journal of Sociology,* XXXV, March, 1930, 693–706.

————. *Mind, Self and Society: From the Standpoint of a Social Behaviorist.* Ed. with an Introduction by Charles W. Morris. Chicago, 1934.

————. "The Philosophies of Royce, James, and Dewey in Their American Setting." *The Development of American Philosophy: A Book of Readings.* Ed. Walter G. Muelder and Laurence Sears. Boston, 1940.

Miller, Perry. *The Life of the Mind in America: From the Revolution to the Civil War.* New York, 1965.

Mills, C. Wright. "Mass Society and Liberal Education." *Power, Politics and People: The Collected Essays of C. Wright Mills.* Ed. with an Introduction by Louis Horowitz. New York, 1963.

————. "The Professional Ideology of Social Pathologists." *The American Journal of Sociology,* XLIX, September, 1943, 165–180.

————. *Sociology and Pragmatism: The Higher Learning in America.* Ed. Louis Horowitz. New York, 1964.

————. *White Collar: The American Middle Classes.* New York, 1951.

Mogey, John. "Follett, Mary Parker." *International Encyclopedia of the Social Sciences.* 1968. Vol. IV.

Mott, Frank Luther. *American Journalism: A History of Newspapers in the United States through 260 Years: 1690 to 1950.* New York, 1950.

Mowry, George E. *The California Progressives.* Berkeley, Cal., 1951.

_____. *The Era of Theodore Roosevelt and the Birth of Modern America: 1900–1912.* New York, 1958.

Mumford, Lewis. *The Golden Day.* New York, 1926.

Münsterberg, Hugo. "The Scientific Plan of the Congress." *Congress of Arts and Science: Universal Exposition, St. Louis, 1904.* Ed. Howard J. Rogers. Boston, 1905, Vol. I.

Neyer, Joseph. "Individualism and Socialism in Durkheim." *Emile Durkheim: 1858–1917: A Collection of Essays with Translations and a Bibliography.* Ed. Kurt H. Wolff. Columbus, Ohio, 1960.

Niebuhr, H. Richard. *The Kingdom of God in America.* New York, 1937.

Nicholson, Meredith. *The Hoosiers.* New York, 1916.

_____. *The Man in the Street: Papers on American Topics.* New York, 1921.

_____. *The Provincial American and Other Papers.* Boston, 1912.

_____. *The Valley of Democracy.* New York, 1918.

Nisbet, Robert A. "The French Revolution and the Rise of Sociology." *The American Journal of Sociology,* XLIX, September, 1943, 156–164.

_____. *The Quest for Community: A Study in the Ethics of Order and Freedom.* New York, 1953.

Noble, David W. *The Paradox of Progressive Thought.* Minneapolis, Minn., 1958.

Nye, Russell B. *Midwestern Progressive Politics: A Historical Study of Its Origins and Development: 1870–1950.* East Lansing, Mich., 1951.

Ogburn, William F. *Social Change with Respect to Culture and Original Nature.* New York, 1922.

Page, Charles Hunt. *Class and American Sociology: From Ward to Ross.* New York, 1940.

Park, Robert E. "The City: Suggestions for the Investigation of Human Behavior in the Urban Environment." *The City.* By R. E. Park, E. W. Burgess, and R. D. McKenzie. Chicago, 1925.

_____. "Community Organization and Juvenile Delinquency." *The City.* By R. E. Park, E. W. Burgess, and R. D. McKenzie. Chicago, 1925.

_____. "Community Organization and the Romantic Temper." *The City.* By R. E. Park, E. W. Burgess, and R. D. McKenzie. Chicago, 1925.

_____. *Human Communities: The City and Human Ecology.* Ed. Everett Cherrington Hughes, *et al.* Glencoe, Ill., 1952.

_____. *Masse und Publikum: eine methodologische und soziologische Untersuchung.* Bern, 1904.

_____. *The Principles of Human Behavior*. Chicago, 1915.

_____. *Race and Culture*. Ed. Everett Cherrington Hughes, *et al.* Glencoe, Ill., 1950.

_____. *Society: Collective Behavior, News and Opinion, Sociology and Modern Society*. Ed. Everett Cherrington Hughes, *et al.* Glencoe, Ill., 1955.

Park, Robert E., and Burgess, Ernest W. *Introduction to the Science of Sociology*. Chicago, 1921.

Park, Robert E., and Miller, Herbert A. *Old World Traits Transplanted*. New York, 1921.

"Park, Robert Ezra." *National Cyclopedia of American Biography*. XXXVII. 1951.

"Park, Robert Ezra." *Who Was Who in America: A Companion Biographical Reference Work to Who's Who in America*. Vol. II. 1950.

Parrington, Vernon Louis, Jr. *American Dreams: A Study of American Utopias*. New York, 1964.

Parsons, Talcott. "Cooley and the Problem of Internalization." *Cooley and Sociological Analysis*. Ed. Albert J. Reiss, Jr. with an Introduction by Robert Cooley Angell. Ann Arbor, Mich., 1968.

_____. *The Structure of Social Action*. Glencoe, Ill., 1949.

Patten, Simon. "Present Problems in the Economic Interpretation of History." *Congress of Arts and Science: Universal Exposition, St. Louis, 1904*. Ed. Howard J. Rogers. Boston, 1905, Vol. II.

Peirce, Charles Sanders. *Collected Papers of Charles Sanders Peirce*. Eds. Charles Hartshorne and Paul Weiss. Cambridge, Mass., VI, 1935.

Perry, Bliss. *The American Mind*. Boston, 1912.

Perry, Ralph B. *The Thought and Character of William James*. 2 vols. Boston, 1935.

Persons, Frederick T. "Follett, Mary Parker." *Dictionary of American Biography*. 1944, Vol. XXI, Supplement One.

Persons, Stow. *American Minds: A History of Ideas*. New York, 1958.

Pierce, Bessie Louise. *A History of Chicago*. Vol. III. Chicago, 1957.

Pottishman, Nancy Portia. "Jane Addams and Education." Unpublished Master's thesis, Columbia University, 1961.

Raleigh, John Henry. *Matthew Arnold and American Culture*. Berkeley, Cal., 1957.

Randall, John Herman, Jr. "The Religion of Shared Experience." *The Philosopher of the Common Man: Essays in Honor of John Dewey to Celebrate His Eightieth Birthday*. Foreword by Sidney Ratner. New York, 1940.

Rasmussen, C. A. *A History of the City of Red Wing, Minnesota.* Privately printed, 1933.

"Red Wing." *Collier's Encyclopedia.* Vol. XIX, 1965.

Rich, Everett. *William Allen White: The Man from Emporia.* New York, 1941.

Richter, Melvin. "Durkheim's Politics and Political Theory." *Emile Durkheim: 1858–1917: A Collection of Essays with a Bibliography.* Ed. Kurt H. Wolff. Columbus, Ohio, 1960.

Robinson, James H. "The Conception and Methods of History." *Congress of Arts and Science: Universal Exposition, St. Louis, 1904.* Ed. Howard J. Rogers. Boston, 1905, Vol. II.

Roelofs, H. Mark. *The Tension of Citizenship: Private Man and Public Duty.* New York, 1957.

Roper, Marion Wesley. "The City and the Primary Group." *Contributions to Urban Sociology.* Ed. Ernest W. Burgess and Donald J. Bogue. Chicago, 1964.

Ross, Edward Alsworth. *Social Control.* New York, 1901.

Royce, Josiah. *California: From the Conquest in 1846 to the Second Vigilance Committee in San Francisco: A Study in American Character.* New York, 1948.

_____. *Fugitive Essays.* Ed. J. Loewenberg. Cambridge, Mass., 1920.

_____. *The Hope of the Great Community.* New York, 1916.

_____. "Introduction." *The Foundations of Science.* By Henri Poincaré. New York, 1913.

_____. "Joseph Le Conte." *International Monthly,* IV, July–December, 324–334.

_____. *The Philosophy of Loyalty.* New York, 1908.

_____. "Present Ideals of University Life." *Scribner's Magazine,* X, July, 1891, 376–388.

_____. *The Problem of Christianity.* 2 vols. New York, 1913.

_____. "Provincialism." *Putnam's Magazine,* VII, November, 1908, 232–240.

_____. *Race Questions, Provincialism and other American Problems.* New York, 1908.

_____. *The Religious Aspect of Philosophy,* Boston, 1885.

_____. "The Sciences of the Ideal." *Congress of Arts and Science: Universal Exposition, St. Louis, 1904.* Ed. Howard J. Rogers. Boston, 1905, Vol. I.

_____. *The Sources of Religious Insight.* New York, 1912.

————. *The Spirit of Modern Philosophy*. Boston, 1892.

————. *War and Insurance*. New York, 1914.

————. *The World and the Individual*. 2 Series. New York, 1959.

Royce, Josiah, *et al. The Conception of God: A Philosophical Discussion Concerning the Nature of the Divine Idea as a Demonstrable Reality*. New York, 1897.

Royce, Sarah. *A Frontier Lady: Recollections of the Gold Rush and Early California*. Ed. Ralph Henry Gabriel. New Haven, Conn., 1932.

Ruskin, John. *The Complete Works of John Ruskin*. Vol. XIII. New York, 1894.

Santillana, Giorgio de. "Positivism and the Technocratic Ideal in the Nineteenth Century." *Studies in the History of Science and Learning in Homage to George Sarton on the Occasion of his Sixtieth Birthday*. Ed. M. F. Ashley Montagu, New York, 1947.

Savage, Willinda. "The Evolution of John Dewey's Social Philosophy at the University of Michigan." Unpublished Ph.D. dissertation, University of Michigan, 1950.

Schäffle, Albert. *Bau und Leben des Socialen Körpers*. 2 vols. Tübingen, 1896.

Schattschneider, E. E. *Party Government*. New York, 1942.

Schneider, Herbert W. "Community, Communications, and Communion." *Community*. Ed. Carl J. Friedrich. New York, 1959.

————. *Religion in 20th Century America*. Cambridge, Mass., 1952.

Seagle, William. "Thomas McIntyre Cooley." *Encyclopedia of the Social Sciences*. 1931, Vol. IV.

Shaw, Albert. "Local Government in Illinois." *Johns Hopkins University Studies in Historical and Political Science*. Baltimore, 1883, Vol. III.

Shils, Edwards. "The Contemplation of Society in America." *Paths of American Thought*. Eds. Arthur M. Schlesinger, Jr., and Morton White. Boston, 1963.

————. *The Present State of American Sociology*. Glencoe, Ill., 1948.

Simmel, Georg. *The Sociology of Georg Simmel*. Trans. Kurt H. Wolff. Glencoe, Ill., 1950.

Simon, W. M. *European Positivism in the Nineteenth Century: An Essay in Intellectual History*. Ithaca, N.Y., 1963.

Singer, Milton. "The Concept of Culture." *International Encyclopedia of the Social Sciences*, 1968, III.

Small, Albion. *General Sociology: An Exposition of the Main Development in Sociological Theory from Spencer to Ratzenhofer.* Chicago, 1905.

————. "Points of Agreement among Sociologists." *Proceedings of the American Sociological Society,* I, 1907, 55–77.

Small, Albion W., and Vincent, George E. *An Introduction to the Study of Society.* New York, 1894.

Smith, Gerald Birney. *Social Idealism and the Changing Theology: A Study of the Ethical Aspects of Christian Doctrine.* New York, 1913.

Smith, John E. *Royce's Social Infinite: The Community of Interpretation.* New York, 1950.

Smith, Page. *As a City upon a Hill: The Town in American History.* New York, 1966.

Smith, T. V. *Beyond Conscience.* New York, 1934.

Sorokin, Pitirim. *Contemporary Sociological Theory.* New York, 1928.

Spencer, Herbert. *The Principles of Sociology.* 2. vols. Westminster edition. New York, 1896.

Spengler, Joseph J. "Evolutionism in American Economics: 1800–1946." *Evolutionary Thought in America.* Ed. Stow Persons. New Haven, Conn., 1950.

Sprague, Wayne. "The Community and the Individual in the Later Philosophy of Josiah Royce." Unpublished Ph.D. dissertation, Boston University, 1953.

Stearns, Harold. *America and the Young Intellectuals.* New York, 1921.

Stein, Maurice R. *The Eclipse of Community: An Interpretation of American Studies.* Princeton, N.J., 1960.

Steiner, Jesse Frederick. "Community Centers." *Encyclopedia of the Social Sciences.* 1931, Vol. IV.

Strauss, Anselm L. *Images of the American City.* New York, 1961.

Strong, Josiah. *The New Era or the Coming Kingdom.* New York, 1893.

Sumner, William Graham, and Keller, Albert Galloway. *The Science of Society.* 4 vols. New Haven, Conn., 1927.

Swift, Morrison I. *A League of Justice or Is It Right to Rob Robbers?* Boston, 1893.

Tarde, Gabriel. *The Laws of Imitation.* Trans. Elsie Clews Parsons with an Introduction by Franklin H. Giddings. New York, 1903.

————. *L'Opinion et la Foule.* Paris, 1901.

Taylor, Frederick W. *The Principles of Scientific Management.* New York, 1911.

Taylor, George Rogers. *The Transportation Revolution: 1815–1860.* New York, 1951.

Tenney, Alvan A. "Franklin Henry Giddings: 1855–1931." *Columbia University Quarterly.* XXIII, September, 1931, 319–324.

Thernstrom, Stephan. *Poverty and Progress: Social Mobility in a Nineteenth Century City.* Cambridge, Mass., 1964.

Thiseth, C. J. Letter. Goodhue County Historical Society. Red Wing, Minn., February 19, 1965.

Thomas, Chauncy. *The Crystal Button.* Boston, 1891.

Tocqueville, Alexis de. *Democracy in America.* 2 vols. New York, 1954.

Tönnies, Ferdinand. *Fundamental Concepts of Sociology.* Trans. and ed. Charles P. Loomis. New York, 1940.

Trattner, Walter I. "Progressivism and World War I: a Reappraisal." *Mid-America,* XLIV, July, 1962, 131–145.

Turner, Frederick Jackson. "Problems in American History." *Congress of Arts and Science: Universal Exposition, St. Louis, 1904.* Ed. Howard J. Rogers. Boston, 1905, Vol. II.

Urwick, L. F. Letter, 83 Kenneth St., Longueville, N.S.W., Australia, December 31, 1969.

U.S. Bureau of the Census. *Historical Statistics of the United States: Colonial Times to 1957.* Washington, D.C., 1960.

————. *Twelfth Census of the United States taken in the year 1900.* Washington, D.C., 1901, Vol. I.

Vahanian, Gabriel. *The Death of God: The Culture of Our Post-Christian Era.* New York, 1957.

Veblen, Thorstein. *Essays in Our Changing Order.* Ed. Leon Ardzrooni. New York, 1934.

————. *The Instinct of Workmanship and the Industrial Arts.* New York, 1914.

————. *The Portable Veblen.* Ed. with an Introduction by Max Lerner. New York, 1948.

Veysey, Laurence R. *The Emergence of the American University.* Chicago, 1965.

Wade, Richard C. *The Urban Frontier: Pioneer Life in Early Pittsburgh, Cincinnati, Lexington, Louisville, and St. Louis.* Chicago, 1964.

Waldo, Dwight. *The Administrative State: A Study of the Political Theory of American Public Administration.* New York, 1948.

Wallas, Graham. *The Great Society: A Psychological Analysis.* New York, 1914.

Ward, E. J., ed. *The Social Center,* New York, 1914.

Ward, Lester Frank. "The Evolution of Social Structures." *Congress of Arts and Science: Universal Exposition, St. Louis, 1904.* Ed. Howard J. Rogers. Boston, 1905, Vol. V.

————. *Psychic Factors in Civilization.* Boston, 1893.

Warner, Landon. "Howe, Frederic Clemson." *Dictionary of American Biography.* 1958. Vol. XXII, Supplement Two.

Warner, Sam Bass, Jr. "If All the World Were Philadelphia: A Scaffolding for Urban History, 1774–1930." *American Historical Review,* LXXIV, October, 1968, 26–43.

————. *Streetcar Suburbs: The Process of Growth in Boston, 1870–1900.* Cambridge, Mass., 1962.

Wayland, Francis. *Elements of Political Economy.* New York, 1937.

Weaver, Earl James. "John Dewey: A Spokesman for Progressive Liberalism." Unpublished Ph.D. dissertation, Brown University, 1963.

Weber, Max. *From Max Weber: Essays in Sociology.* Trans., ed. with an Introduction by H. H. Gerth and C. Wright Mills. New York, 1958.

Weeks, O. Douglas. "Some Political Ideas of Thomas McIntyre Cooley." *The Southwestern Political and Social Quarterly,* VI, June, 1925, 30–39.

Weimer, David R. *The City as Metaphor.* New York, 1966.

Wells, David A. *Recent Economic Changes and Their Effect on the Production and Distribution of Wealth and the Wellbeing of Society.* New York, 1889.

West, Andrew Fleming. *American Liberal Education.* New York, 1907.

"Where Are the Pre-War Radicals? A Symposium." *The Survey,* LV, February 1, 1926, 556–566.

White, Morton. *The Origins of Dewey's Instrumentalism.* New York, 1943.

————. *Social Thought in America: The Revolt Against Formalism.* Boston, 1957.

White, Morton, and White, Lucia. *The Intellectual versus the City: From Thomas Jefferson to Frank Lloyd Wright.* Cambridge, Mass., 1962.

White, William Allen. *The Autobiography of William Allen White.* New York, 1946.

————. *Calvin Coolidge: The Man Who Is President.* New York, 1925.

————. *A Certain Rich Man.* New York, 1909.

————. "The Challenge to the Middle Class." *Atlantic Monthly,* CLX, August, 1937, 196–201.

————. *The Changing West.* New York, 1939.

————. "The Country Newspaper." *Harper's Magazine,* CXXXII, May, 1916, 887–891.

————. "A Democratic View of Education." *Craftsman,* XXI, November, 1911, 119–130.

————. *The Editor and His People: Editorials by William Allen White.* Selected from the Emporia *Gazette* by Helen O. Mahin. New York, 1924.

————. "Emporia and New York." *American Magazine,* LXIII, January, 1907, 258–264.

————. "Fifty Years of Kansas." *World's Work,* VIII, June, 1904, 4870–4872.

————. *Forty Years on Main Street.* Compiled by Russell H. Fitzgibbon from the columns of the Emporia *Gazette.* New York, 1937.

————. "The Glory of the States: Kansas." *American Magazine,* LXXXI, January, 1916, 41, 165.

————. *In the Heart of a Fool.* New York, 1918.

————. "Kansas: A Puritan Survival." *These United States: A Symposium.* Ed. Ernest Gruening. New York, 1923.

————. *Masks in a Pageant.* New York, 1928.

————. *The Old Order Changeth.* New York, 1910.

————. "The Partnership of Society." *American Magazine,* LXII, October, 1906, 576–585.

————. "The Reorganization of the Republican Party." *Saturday Evening Post,* CLXXVII, December 3, 1904, 1–2.

————. *Some Cycles of Cathay.* Chapel Hill, N.C., 1925.

————. "What's the Matter with America?" *Colliers,* XXXVIII, October 20, 1906, 18–19, 28.

————. *Woodrow Wilson: The Man, His Times and His Task.* Boston, 1924.

Wiebe, Robert H. *The Search for Order: 1877–1920.* New York, 1967.

Wiener, Philip Paul. *Evolution and the Founders of Pragmatism.* Cambridge, Mass., 1949.

William Allen White Papers. The Library of Congress, Washington, D.C.

Williams, Daniel Day. *The Andover Liberals*. New York, 1941.

Williams, Raymond. *Culture and Society: 1780–1950*. New York, 1960.

Williams, Robin M., Jr. *American Society: A Sociological Interpretation*. New York, 1960.

Wilson, R. Jackson. *In Quest of Community: Social Philosophy in the United States, 1860–1920*. New York, 1968.

Wilson, Woodrow. "The Variety and Unity of History." *Congress of Arts and Science: Universal Exposition, St. Louis, 1904*. Ed. Howard J. Rogers. Boston, 1905, Vol. II.

Wirth, Arthur G. *John Dewey as Educator: His Design for Work in Education (1894–1904)*. New York, 1966.

Wirth, Louis. "Urbanism as a Way of Life." *The American Journal of Sociology*, XLIV, July, 1938, 1-24.

Wood, Arthur Evans, "Charles Horton Cooley: An Appreciation." *The American Journal of Sociology*, XXXV, March, 1930, 707–717.

Wood, Robert C. *Suburbia: Its People and Their Politics*. Boston, 1959.

Zorbaugh, Harvey Warren. *The Gold Coast and the Slum: A Sociological Study of Chicago's Near North Side*. Introduction by Robert Park. Chicago, 1929.

Index

This book was set in Baskerville Linotype and printed by offset on P & S Old Forge manufactured by P. H. Glatfelter Co., Spring Grove, Pa. Composed, printed and bound by Quinn & Boden Company, Inc., Rahway, N. J.